Why Am I Like This?
Illuminating the Traumatized Self

Natalia Rachel

PENGUIN BOOKS

An imprint of Penguin Random House

PENGUIN BOOKS

USA | Canada | UK | Ireland | Australia
New Zealand | India | South Africa | China | Southeast Asia

Penguin Books is part of the Penguin Random House group of companies
whose addresses can be found at global.penguinrandomhouse.com

Published by Penguin Random House SEA Pvt. Ltd
9, Changi South Street 3, Level 08-01,
Singapore 486361

First published in Penguin Books by Penguin Random House SEA 2022
Copyright © Natalia Rachel 2022

10 9 8 7 6 5 4 3 2 1

The views and opinions expressed in this book are the author's own and the
facts are as reported by her which have been verified to the extent possible,
and the publishers are not in any way liable for the same.

ISBN 9789815017908

Typeset in Garamond by MAP Systems, Bengaluru, India

www.penguin.sg

To those who have walked by my side,
For moments or years.

To those who loved me in my imperfection,
Sat with me in my pain,
Whispered messages of hope,
Or held my aching body.

To the ones who cradled my babies when I could not.

And to those who taught me through their wisdom or ignorance;
Their kindness or cruelty.

You are the net of my transformation.

Thank you.

Contents

Introduction

'Why am I like this?'

I've been seeking the answer to this questions since I was seven years old.

And if you're here reading this book, I assume you've asked it of yourself . . . at least once, if not hundreds of times.

Such are the questions we ask ourselves when the world we live in doesn't make sense. When the way we feel in our relationships doesn't make sense. When we don't make sense. When we feel oppressed and far away from our true self and the life we crave, but we don't understand why.

Within these pages, I've answered the question as clearly and nuancedly as I can. The thing about healing from trauma and shifting from oppression to empowerment is that it is an incredibly textured and non-linear journey. There is no such thing as a one-size-fits-all approach. And it is never-ending . . . it is not a process to complete but a way of life to choose and return to, again and again.

My perspective traverses the experience of a deeply traumatized child, a mentally ill young woman, a sexual abuse survivor, and a woman who became incredibly sick and incapacitated. It also draws on my own epic quest to heal, thrive and put the pieces of my shattered body and broken heart back together again, and create a life full of peace and power. Lastly, it includes my professional experience as a practitioner, clinic director and educator, working with trauma survivors to ignite their own paths to healing and embodiment.

Existence is contextual. So our journey to heal from trauma and oppression must be considered as part of the context of the world we live in—which I believe is a traumatized one. Although, I hope and sense that we are on the way to incredible collective change.

I hope that my experiences—the concepts, stories, questions and somatic healing practices I share—ignite your curiosity, self-inquiry and desire to heal. That my words are felt in your heart, and within the palpable life force that flows through your deserving body.

Some of what I share, you may already know; some of it may illuminate new pathways to healing. You may disagree with some things . . . and some of my beliefs may even trigger you. I invite you to welcome your response in its entirety as the gateway to your own unique and splendid process.

Here's what to expect as you read:

Each part of the book has been developed to unlock new layers of awareness to understand the traumatized self and piece together answers to the core question, 'Why am I like this?' Each part offers a conceptual learning, a piece of my personal story through which I lived and learned the concept, as well as some self-inquiry questions and a somatic healing practice to support your own healing process. Some of the practices also offer Trauma-informed Notes to help you feel safe with and contain your experiences. You can go as deeply into this work as it feels right for you. For an embodied journey, you may like to keep a diary and a yoga mat handy so you can process as you read. However, the questions and practices are there for you to return to at any point in your journey. Your healing journey is your own, so you can go at the pace that feels right for you and welcome the spirals in and out of the process.

In part one, we explore 'the existential shift' that occurs when we experience trauma or oppression. Understanding how our fundamental experience of aliveness may be completely altered by trauma is the point of departure for the entire book and for profound healing. In part two, we explore the 'prologue to self' to understand the person we are through the lens of the nervous system, somatics, the subconscious mind and attachment theory. Understanding ourselves as a very complex series of patterns empowers us to start rewriting the code that creates us. In part three, we explore 'the fragmented self' and begin to untangle and welcome our complexity, our trauma responses and our very real adaptations to the modern world. It is through healing the fragmented self that we may re-animate and come alive in our entirety. In part four, we explore 'the unified emotions of trauma', to understand all that we have suppressed and all that we have projected or let leak into the world around us. I believe that emotions are the central theme for all processing and being able to understand how our suppressed emotions decontextualize within and around us, pivots the way we engage both with our own healing work and the world around us. In part five, we simply breathe in the beauty of 'the point of freedom'—the place when our core healing work is done and we become conscious creators of our lives. In part six, we explore 'embodiment and the laws of peace and power'. It is in this final part of the book that I share what I believe are the fundamental laws we need to learn and live by, in order to attain a true state of inner peace and relational harmony. These are the ingredients for well-being and adopting healing as a way of life.

I have lived through, believe in, and embody every single thing I have written. Your healing journey asks you to live your own story and define and embody your own beliefs. It is in our individual and shared healing that we can co-create a kinder world.

It all starts with the question, 'Why am I like this?'

Illumination has been the gift that has allowed me to heal. I share mine with you; in freedom and in love.

All the works referred to and referenced have been condensed, simplified and expressed through my own unique lens. I encourage you to seek out the original authors and teachers for their intended message, in full.

Support your healing journey with free additional resources online.

https://www.nataliarachel.com/why-am-i-like-this-resources

Part I

The Existential Shift

When threat and exclusion are at our core, the world and everything in it is a source of danger . . . and we are alone.

1

The Existential Nature of Trauma

When we survive trauma or any kind of oppression, the way we experience the world is altered. Our experience of being human and relating to other humans is fundamentally different to those who grew up with the basic human rights to:

a) safety,
b) belonging,
c) expression and sharing.

When these three things are taken away from us, or are used as shiny bright tools for manipulation, we lose touch with our innate human nature.

Being human becomes secondary to survival. Peace becomes an abstract concept and authenticity remains unknown. Threat becomes our baseline. Vulnerability is impossible.

In order to survive, we have to protect ourselves so fiercely that we end up living alone inside the castle of our own survival and coping mechanisms. We often have no idea that we are living in a fortress of our own making. It's the only reality we know. When survival and aloneness become the seed of our existential experience at an early stage, we are screwed from the start because expression and sharing become impossible.

Expression and sharing are cut from the same cloth. Expression is the essence of our life force, and sharing is expression within connection. Sharing is the fabric of humanity. When expression and sharing are not possible, our intended self ceases to exist. Our world as is intended, ceases to exist. Without these agents, we are aliens in human bodies, speaking to each other in different languages, in some strange reality, that doesn't feel quite like its meant to.

And that's exactly how many of us with unresolved trauma feel . . . foreign, misunderstood and displaced. And we are powerless to change it. Until we begin to heal.

The Healing Paradox

Healing asks us to find a way back to our true nature. To reclaim our sense of peace and power. To purify the sense of threat from inside us and remedy our aloneness. The goal is to find a way back to safety and belonging where we are truly welcome. To create a reality where we no longer have to tie ourselves in knots to feel a semblance of safety and the pretense of belonging (aka inclusion).

Whether intentional or not, most of us are trying to heal in every moment. We are trying to create feelings of safety and belonging . . . in the best way we know how.

Unfortunately, when healing remains an unconscious attempt, the process is often hijacked by our survival responses, and instead of healing, we travel further and further into our trauma or oppression.

The trauma we cannot see will consume us. The moment we see it clearly; we can forge a path to healing and restoration.

The way back to safety and belonging is through expression and sharing. But sharing and expression are not possible in the face of threat. And herein lies the healing paradox that keeps us stuck.

How do we heal when we are terrified to start unpacking the truth of our trauma?

How do we heal when we are living in an alternate reality?
How do we heal when we feel powerless to create change?

Origins of trauma

When we exist in a family, a community, or in fact a world that is dangerous, disconnected and where expression incites harm, we can do nothing more than survive. Our beautiful brains have an in-built emergency switch. When we sense threat, it is time to activate our internal physiological and psychological army. Mission Survival. Essentially, we are primed to alter our way of experiencing, expressing and relating in order to make it to the other side of danger. We will do anything within our power to access a semblance of safety. A shred of peace. The mission is a solitary one. As the saying goes, 'every man for himself'.[1]

Trauma is when a past experience of threat is over, but continues living and breathing in us now. The danger has passed but our survival responses have remained.

When the threat is acute or chronic, we end up staying in this altered state. It becomes our new normal. We unconsciously and neuro-physiologically come to see the world as inherently dangerous. The entire personality we thus create is a reaction to threat. The body we develop is a reaction to threat. The relationships we engage in are a reaction to threat.

Although we have an innate and unconscious impulse to heal, it is thwarted by our survival self. Any attempts are either shut down or disfigured through the filter of our trauma, and eventually trauma starts spilling out into the world.

Trauma ignites through harmful relationships. Trauma spreads like wildfire. It runs in cycles, so we are stuck in it . . . until we learn how to break the cycle.

---

[1] Geoffrey Chaucer, 'The Knight's Tale: One', *The Canterbury Tales* (1392).

Personal Share

I experienced this existential shift at a very young age. My earliest memories of knowing something was wrong are from when I was age seven. But I kept quietening the part of me that knew, because there was nothing I could do about it. I was powerless in the world. I remember feeling the pounding of my heartbeat when I heard my father's footsteps become heavier, or the angry frown that appeared on his face. I remember my body feeling tensed and taut before a beating, bracing myself for the pain. And I remember feeling like a mix of jelly and a dead animal later, when I cried in my bed.

I remember the ear-piercing screams of my mother and the foul names she used to call me. And I remember the times when she would be silent, non-responsive and cold. I don't know which was worse. Both of them knew how to shake the floor with their presence. Both of them knew how to look at me like I was a disgrace to the universe.

But both of them also knew how to smile, praise me and play with me. And there was love there. To this day, I do not question if my parents loved me. They just couldn't show it most of the time, because they were trapped in their own trauma prison and could not contain the poison of it all.

As a child, this was incredibly destabilizing. I never knew what I was going to get. So I became good at staying in my room and sensing the energy in the house. Whether it was safe to come out of my room. I learned how to read their facial expressions and body language, to learn when it was safe to speak, or ask for the same new shoes as my best friend, or for $2 to go and buy some hot chips (one of my favorite self-soothing tools). I learned how to smile, even when I didn't want to. I learned how to pretend all was well. I learned how to focus my energy on school.

I got a part-time job in a supermarket the very day that I was old enough. It got me out of the house and gave me a chance to be with regular humans. I loved saying hello to the customers and even stacking boxes—it was a reprieve. Work was a place of safety and regulation. Work became my safe place. Later in life, I became a workaholic . . . I would turn to work as a means for self-regulation. It took so much perseverance to break this pattern because at one time, work had saved me. I learned to be quiet. A good girl. I learned how to illicit praise (which I mistook for belonging). I found a way to exist. By becoming the girl that would be hurt less and praised more. And that girl turned into a woman who did the same. Ironically, these survival responses started to backfire in my early adulthood. My unconscious desire for safety and belonging took me to some incredibly dark places. More abuse. More aloneness. More pain. More shapeshifting and survival. Until one day, my trauma made me physically sick. I had no idea that I was traumatized. I was just living my life. And no matter what I did, I couldn't heal. I saw countless doctors, therapists and healers, but I could not heal.

But the moment I connected my experience to origins of trauma, everything changed.

Invitation to Self-inquiry

- Do you feel a sense of safety or threat inside yourself? What does it feel like?
- Do you feel a sense of un-belonging in the world? That it is more jarring, overwhelming or threatening than it should be? Can you describe it?
- Do you spend a lot of time trying to create the life you think you are supposed to have, but still feel like something isn't quite right?
- Do you feel a sense of disease or tension in your body? Where? What does it feel like?
- Did you grow up in a family, culture or environment where you felt safe and welcome? What were your early days like? Did you have to learn to survive and belong? How did you do it?
- Now ask yourself: Is there truly threat all around me, or am I existing from a baseline of threat? Take a moment to feel what shifts with these illuminations.

Somatic Healing Practice

Welcoming Existence

Sit on the floor with your back against the wall. Be aware of how the floor and the wall feel against your body. Look around the space you are in. Orient here. Invite your body to relax a little more if it can.

Affirm to Yourself

'It's safe to exist here. I welcome my belonging in this world.'

Trauma-informed Note:

If you have been living in a state of threat, your body may begin to twitch and shake a little and you may get the urge to cry. If it feels safe to, allow it. If you do not feel safe with the practice, you can come out of it by looking around the physical space, rubbing your palms together and taking a sip of water.

2

Living in Fear

Fear is the primary emotion associated with threat. When we are threatened, we are afraid. Our fear helps us and it harms us. During times of trauma and oppression, it helps us survive, but when it becomes the foundation of our experience, it stops us from accessing our sense of aliveness. Our impulses. Our agency. Our choices. It makes vulnerability impossible. Connection and intimacy become inaccessible. Fear breeds powerlessness.

Our fear is the biggest block to our own healing. In order to heal, we need to look it square in the face and let it know that we are safe, that we don't need it anymore, and allow it to leave us. When it has become a part of who we are, the idea of letting go of fear can evoke even more fear. In order to begin the process of letting go of fear, we need to first build a sense of safety inside us. And we need to understand how fear is living and breathing within and around us. In its mildest form, fear exists as anxiousness or worry. In its most extreme form, it exists as horror. This kind of fear is reserved for those of us who have experienced or witnessed the most severe violations.

I. **The Psychology And Organizing Principles Of Fear**
Fear is rooted in the belief that 'I am not safe. Something bad is happening, or threat is imminent.'

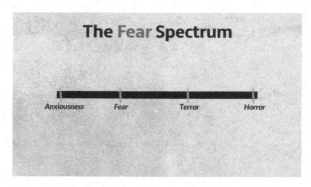

Image 1.2.1. The Fear Spectrum

II. *Relating from fear*
Fear is a direct response to threat. We may respond differently to fear depending on how acute/intense or chronic/prolonged it is. Two of these responses are:

A) Fawning

Above all, we seek safety. We will do anything we can to keep peace, maintain order, or avoid further experiences of harm. This often requires us to 'switch on' or 'fragment' and learn to engage in the best way to do that. In modern trauma terms, this is known as a 'fawn response'.[2] It is a psychological and relational adaptive response.

If we have learned to fawn to keep relational peace, we will often develop into someone who a) is a people pleaser, b) doesn't express their own thoughts and feelings, or in some cases cannot even identify them, c) finds it hard to make choices/decisions, d) learns to grin and bear it/smile when they don't

---

[2] Pete Walker, 'Codependency, Trauma and the Fawn Response', Pete-walker. com, January/February 2003, available at: http://www.pete-walker.com/ codependencyFawnResponse.htm. Accessed March 2022.

feel like smiling, e) becomes anxious when the people around them are experiencing emotional distress or dissatisfaction.

This is a key marker of co-dependency:

'If you're okay, I'm okay. If you're not okay, I am not okay. Therefore, I will make sure you are okay.'

Most of us who have unhealed trauma, exist in a state of co-dependence. We will abandon ourselves in order to seek relational harmony, because without connection and a semblance of belonging, we will be plunged into our existential aloneness . . . and that's simply not an option.

B) Aggression

Attempts to create safety can result in aggressive behaviour. This may manifest itself in actions such as raising voices, narrowing eyes, blaming and shaming others, threatening behavior or even 'aggressive silences'. These are all unconscious attempts to neutralize perceived relational threat and achieve safety.

We usually develop aggression as a response to fear when there has been a history of volatility or lack of boundaries in our early-attachment relationships. This may range from verbal abuse or violence in the home, to having a parent on the narcissism spectrum—that is, their emotional experience takes front and center, and ours becomes a byproduct or completely irrelevant. We learn: a) 'if someone threatens me, I can neutralize the threat with aggression', b) 'if I disallow the other person's experience, I will gain the upper hand, which therefore means I will be safe'.

If we develop aggression in response to fear, we become unable to respect the experiences, emotions and needs of others. Our need for safety and belonging becomes more important than anyone or anything else. There is a fine line between disrespect and abuse. Fear is the root of it all.

Apathy

When our attempts to remedy our fear are futile, we remain powerless in the face of it. Over time, this turns to apathy and hopelessness.

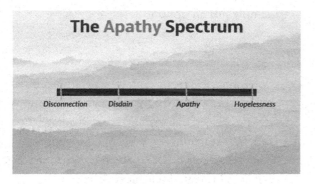

Image 1.2.2. The Apathy Spectrum

Apathy is the most dangerous state to live in, because we lose touch with our will. Our will is a direct manifestation of our life force. Our will is essential to our healing process. It is the light that keeps shining amidst the darkness. It is what keeps us going, searching, striving. The more apathetic we become, the more our will is diminished. Apathy ranges from feeling mildly disconnected from ourselves to feeling utterly hopeless. Once hopelessness sets in, we stop trying. We accept ourselves and the world as it is. Reality becomes fixed and finite.

When fear is our baseline, we are a rolling reaction to threat. When apathy sets in, we stop trying to change it.

The antidote to fear is safety. The antidote to apathy is movement. But when we reach hopelessness, all will to move is lost.

Personal Share

Threat was my baseline. My whole existence was a reaction to threat. But I did not have the words to articulate, 'I do not feel safe' or know who to turn to, to ask for help, 'Please help me feel safe; I am so scared'.

I felt wildly unsafe inside; and I was powerless to change it . . . but that was just normal. I had nothing to compare it to. My will was strong. I did everything I could to help myself build a good life. And I did. I had a husband, children, good job. All the trimmings. I had a good life. But I still had fear coursing through my veins. Sometimes, it would be mild anxiety. Sometimes, it would explode into full-blown panic. My blood pressure would shoot through the roof. My eyes would bulge. My own fear would terrify me further. There was a period where I used to faint regularly, and looking back, I am sure that this was an extreme response to my internal sense of threat. A lot of the time, I was so afraid that I would leave my body. I had no idea that I was doing it. But I would float up to the ceiling, or hang out next to myself. I later learned that this is known as dissociation. When the body is not a safe place to be, we leave it.

On paper, my life was fine. In my nervous system, my life was danger and chaos. I felt the pity and judgement of those around me. 'Why is she like that? What's wrong with her?' Of course no one ever said that. But they felt it. You can't mistake the stench of judgement. And I judged myself. Why couldn't I just be happy and 'normal'? Why couldn't I just get on with it and be like everyone else? 'Why am I like this? What is wrong with me?!'

I had such a strong will to find a solution to my dissatisfactory existence. I kept trying and trying to make a better life for myself and seeking people who could give me answers and help me do it.

Even though I saw countless medical and mental health professionals to try and 'get better', this deeper existential feeling was never expressed and no one ever asked me about it. Even though I read countless self-help books and practiced the tools they offered, it felt like I was trying to become a robot. The feelings inside me did not change. In fact, they just continued to get worse with time. The way my trauma was decontextualizing became more diffused and nuanced, harder and harder to make sense of.

Looking back now, from the position of a patient-turned-therapist, I wonder what would have happened if one person had noticed how unsafe I was feeling. What would have happened if they asked me if I felt safe or unsafe? What would have happened if they asked me if I was living inside my body or outside of it? And what would have happened if they could have helped me feel just a little bit safer with whatever tools they had? Even a smidge? But I realized, back then, trauma-informed care was not readily available. No one was talking about trauma. The people I was seeking help from had no idea what I was experiencing. They were just as powerless as I was. My pleas for help remained unanswered. Over time, fear and powerlessness become hopelessness. I just accepted that my life would remain like that, and made the best of it. My will diminished. My light started to dim. But it never completely went out.

Invitation to Self-inquiry

- Are you living in fear? Where do you sit on the spectrum?
- How does fear show up in your relationships? Do you fawn or aggress, or both?
- Can you recognize the sense of fear behind the actions/ expression of certain people in your life?
- What makes you feel safe in this world? Are there people, experiences or places that help you? Who/what are they?

- How is your will? Are you experiencing apathy? Where on the spectrum do you sit?
- Now ask yourself: By acknowledging my fear, can I allow it to dissipate a little? If so, is there a change in your level of will? Take a moment to feel what shifts with these illuminations.

Somatic Healing Practices

Inviting Safety

Create a cocoon for yourself. Get a pillow and blanket. Lay on your side on the floor, sofa or bed. Bring your knees close into your body, like in a fetal position. Let your body know that it is protected and safe in this place.

Affirm to Yourself

'I am safe now. There is nothing to be afraid of here.'

Trauma-informed Note:

You may find that this invites tears, or that your body wants to slump or twitch or gently shake. It this feels safe, you can welcome it. If it does not feel safe, remember, you have the power to exit your process. You can do this by sitting up, looking around the room, rubbing your palms together and taking a sip of water.

Igniting Life Force and Will

Sit comfortably. Place your hands on your stomach over your navel. Your navel is where you received nourishment and life in the womb. Breathe into it. Your breath is your life force. Reconnect your life force to your navel. If it feels right, you can let it naturally circulate around your entire body. Sit gently with this intention for as little or as long as you wish.

Affirm to Yourself

'I choose to be here. I welcome my life force. I am alive.'

Trauma-informed Note:

If your life force has been slowed or is stuck, it may reignite in a rush. If this feels overwhelming or too much, stop this process and lay on your stomach on the ground. Let the ground support and ground you. If you choose to go back to this practice, do so in small bursts and always follow up with connecting to the ground to integrate.

I learned about lying face-down on the ground when studying with a Qi Gong Master. She called it a 'Qi deviation', which means too much energy for us to metabolize. As we heal, we begin to cultivate more capacity for our own aliveness, but this takes time, patience and practice. Go slowly and gently.

3

The Absence of Trust

Fear makes trust impossible. It will drive us to one of the three experiences. In all of them, real trust is absent. These are:

- **Distrust and Suspicion:** 'I do not trust you even if you show me that you are safe and worthy of trust.'

  In this case, we are unable to create a sense of relational safety. Our trauma is telling us that connection was and always will be harmful. Because it is an unconscious trauma response, we have no idea that this is happening. All we know is that we cannot establish a palpable sense of trust.

- **Premature Trust and Naivety:** 'I trust you before you show me you are trustworthy.'

  In this case, the moment we feel any sense of resonance, we allow ourselves to be vulnerable and open ourselves to potential harm. Our instinct is telling us that we need to be in connection to heal. And this is partly true. But our trauma tells us to put belonging before safety. The urgency for belonging overrides the need for the discernment and time required for real trust to emerge.

- **Blind Trust and Denial:** 'I trust you, even when you show me that you cannot be trusted.'

In some cases, we might erase red flags altogether and give ourselves the green light to engage in harmful connections. Our trauma is telling us that love and harm co-exist. It fools us into thinking that we are being loved well, when really, we are being hurt or denied intimacy. Very often, the harmful people we trust feel similar to people who have hurt us in the past . . . people who were supposed to love us.

We have a biological imperative to connect. But when we can't trust, we are unable to fulfill it. The intimacy that we seek thus becomes unattainable. If we are distrusting, we may try very hard to work on learning how to trust . . . but we simply can't. Or we pretend that we do, when really, we don't.

If we trust people prematurely or blindly, we leave ourselves open to being harmed again and again.

Real trust is born from three core elements:

a)   safety,
b)   discernment,
c)   time.

In the case of trauma, we do not have access to safety or discernment. Without these, real trust cannot be born.

In order to truly trust others, we have to increase the sense of safety we feel inside us. If we learn to discern, read the signals that tell us when to trust and when to self-protect, slowly but surely, we can open ourselves up to the people and experiences that will nourish us, rather than hurt us.

Igniting Intuition

Before we can trust other people, we need to learn how to tune into our intuition. When we exist in a state of trauma, we lose touch with it, because we are taken over by our survival instincts. It is never truly gone. But we need to reconnect to it, allow its signature to

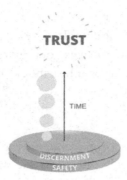

Image 1.3.1. Trust

become strong and unmistakable, and place it on the throne of our awareness, above all else.

Our intuition will always guide us in the right direction. Sometimes, we think we are connected to our intuition when we are actually connected to our trauma or survival self.

Our intuition is felt. It is somatic in nature. So in order to feel it, we need to be connected to our body. We need to learn how our body experiences danger. How it experiences safety. How it tells us when we need to say no, when we need to say yes and when we need to take time to pause before making a choice.

Igniting intuition is a journey of cultivating self-awareness within a dynamic environment. It develops through lived practice and patience, while we rewire our somatic self. It strengthens through making errors and course-correction. It strengthens through taking time to make sense of our experiences again and again. Because our intuition is a dynamic response, it will emerge in safe spaces with people who support our authenticity, sense-making, and invite us to be imperfect and ever-evolving within the connection.

Once we trust our intuition, we can begin to lean into the journey of trusting others.

There's a conundrum here: in order to trust others, we need to first trust ourselves. But its only through our relationship with others that we can learn to trust ourselves. Such conundrums and paradoxes that show up in our experience of trauma are what make it so hard to begin healing. It's like getting lost in a maze. If we are unsure of who to trust, or if we can even trust ourselves, we can start by trusting our own heartbeat. Our breath. Our body.

Personal Share

I couldn't trust. I was like a scared animal terrified of everyone and everything. And my fear made me susceptible to running into relationship traps again and again. It's like I would ping-pong between trusting no one and then unzipping my chest and handing my heart to monsters dressed up as fairies. Perhaps they were not even dressing up. Perhaps I dressed them up in my fantasy. In my fantasy, I was no longer alone and scared. I was connected, happy and loved. I would live in the fantasy, until it became enough of a nightmare to wake me up.

As a teenager, blind trust led me to be raped. Later on, it led me into the hands of a narcissist. After copious amounts of healing, I believed I could learn to trust again, but premature trust and naivety led me into the arms of an unavailable man-child. Each time I would exit a harmful dynamic, I would vow to keep myself safe. And I would for a time, but then I would find myself back in harm's way. Because underneath all the brilliance of my healing, my core was still rooted in fear and aloneness. And I was unconsciously looking for a remedy.

The inability to trust also kept me from developing deeper relationships with my family and friends. It kept me isolated, distrusting and suspicious. I didn't trust that my pain would be safe with them. I didn't trust that they would welcome me in my entirety. So I packed parts of myself away, and only showed the parts that felt safe to reveal.

My journey to cultivate real trust is ongoing. I think it will always be that way. I think it's meant to be that way. We are not meant to be able to click our fingers and know if someone or something is safe or not (if we do, that's just another fantasy waiting to reveal itself as a nightmare). It takes time to learn someone. It takes time to know what safety feels like. And it takes a whole lot of healing to choose it, again and again. To place boundaries before belonging. And to slowly open our hearts to the people that prove to us that they are safe and worthy of it.

Learning to trust my body has been the most profound experience of all. Through years of building safety and learning to listen to and discern its messages, my body has become my greatest source of trust. My temple of trust.

For so many years, I could not trust my body. My body that was so sick. That didn't 'work' the way it was meant to. I had to stop forcing and manipulating it and give it the space it needed to heal. I had to trust that I could live here. The beat of my heart. The expansion of my lungs. I had to trust that I would learn to walk again. That I could become strong enough to hold my children in my arms. That I could become vibrant enough to swim, walk and stretch. I had to give myself time. Patience. Self-compassion. And with these things, my body healed. And I started to be able to listen to it. Tune in to my intuition. Learn my capacity. Start making healthy choices. Making mistakes. Readjusting. Being kind to myself in the process.

The more I tuned in and trusted myself, the more I could start to trust others. The right people. I'm still learning when to trust and when to self-protect. When to move forward, take a step back or simply pause. And my journey continues through exploring my own body, trying new things, testing my limits and learning what is truly safe.

Trust can be terrifying. But it's the only way we learn to look after ourselves and welcome the care of others. The more I trust, the more alive I become.

Invitation to Self-inquiry

- Is trust present or absent in your life? If it is absent, how does this manifest? As distrust and suspicion or as premature trust and naivety, or as blind trust?

- Are you connected to your intuition? If so, can you describe your somatic signals? What does safety feel like? What does danger feel like? What is your 'no' signal? What is your 'yes' signal? What is your 'pause' signal?
- Are there people in your life that help you discern? Who are they? Do you connect to them with this intention?

Somatic Healing Practice

Initiating Trust

Sit or lie comfortably. Place your hands over your heart. Allow your breath to flow naturally. See if you can feel the beat of your heart, not needing to change it in any way. Just be with it. Trust it. It has been keeping you here from the moment you were born. As you feel it, allow the trust you have for your heart to expand to your breath. Inhale trust. Exhale trust.

Affirm to Yourself

'I trust the beat of my heart. I trust my breath. I welcome my trust to expand naturally.'

Trauma-informed Note:

- If you connect to a felt sense of trust that is new for you, this may bring about feelings of grief for all the times when you could not trust, or all the times when your perceived trust opened you up to harm. If it feels safe to, allow the grief to express itself the way it wishes to, perhaps through tears.
- If you are unable to connect to a felt sense of trust, and instead experience an increase in fear/threat, move out of the practice. Remember you are in-charge here.

In both cases, you may like to lay on your side and move through the 'Inviting Safety' practice at the end of Part I Chapter 2.

4

Belonging

When we are living in fear, and are unable to really trust, we are existing alone.

Our trauma exists in our psyche, our soma[3] and our spirit. It is often largely non-verbal, so it is impossible to communicate or share with another person, even if we try. We are alone with our shit. The aloneness is a big part of the problem.

We will make attempts to feel included. Others may make attempts to include us.

We may even feel included. But inclusion and belonging are very difference experiences.

Inclusion highlights our dissonance and asks us all to get along. We can be included and still feel different, separate and alone. Belonging, on the other hand, welcomes authenticity, individuality and our differences with other people are not experienced as dissonance. We resonate within our diversity.

When we belong, we begin to heal. Because it is safe to be vulnerable—to express and to share.

---

[3] 'The body as distinguished from the mind'. Medical Dictionary, The Free Dictionary, available at: https://medical-dictionary.thefreedictionary.com/soma. Accessed April 2022.

We are meant to belong from our first breath. We are meant to belong to our mother. Our father. Our family. Our culture. Our religion (if we have one). We are meant to belong to each other, as humans. If, in our formative relationships and human ecosystems, we are made to feel unsafe or unwelcome in any way, belonging is lost. We learn 'I am not safe or welcome here.' In this relationship. This family. This culture. This world.

At least, not in my entirety or authenticity.

Because belonging is an essential experience for our development, those of us who do not receive it will have an altered experience of the world.

The Shame Game

Shame is the result of not belonging—of not feeling welcome in our entirety. When shame and fear blend together, we become quiet. Together, these emotions are the enemy of intimacy. In this state, we can neither express nor share—not with any sense of authenticity.

Some of the questions shame brings include:

'Why am I like this?'

'What's wrong with me?'

'Why can't I be different? Like everyone else?'

'Why does it feel like I am outside looking in? Or a square peg in a round hole?'

'Why can't I be further along in my journey than I am?'

Psychology and Organizing Principles

'I am bad. Something is wrong with me.' Shame is a response to un-belonging. This feeling can often sit at the core of the psyche when we have been led to believe that we are anything less than a perfectly imperfect human. Shame arises because a person, group, culture or religion has either a) indicated that we should be ashamed, b) treated us in a shameful or inhumane manner.

Image 1.4.5. Shame

Shame can show up as a mild niggle of awkwardness, or a loud roar of internal disapproval that asks us to erase ourselves from existence. Shame dampens our ability to be creative, curious and playful.

Relating from shame

When we relate from a place of shame, it's as if we are waiting to be judged or excluded. We often feel like we are walking on eggshells, worried about saying the wrong thing, or about how others might perceive or respond to us. This usually manifests in one of two expressions:

a) *Reduced or altered sharing*

Because we are worried about how we will be received, we tend not to share how we really feel, or we minimize or segment our experience into what feels safe to share and what doesn't. This blocks our ability to cultivate intimacy and over time, leads to resentment. The people we are in a relationship with are often unaware that we are not sharing authentically, or what our unexpressed thoughts, feelings and needs are, so they cannot meet us in the way we are longing for. Our fear of exclusion causes our exclusion.

b)   *Braced sharing*

In this manifestation, we speak the truth, but we are bracing as we do so, waiting for an unfavourable response. Sometimes, our own authenticity causes us to be incredibly anxious. We have muscled through and spoken honestly, but we become worried about what might happen next.

Both relational manifestations of shame incite feelings of anxiety. While it is common to orient to one kind of relational adaptation, some of us swing between both states, which can be very energetically taxing. It can feel like we are going to burst from the pressure of holding everything in, and then we are shocked or appalled with ourselves when we speak honestly. Either way, we experience distress and this just triggers another layer of shame: 'why am I so bad at this whole relationship thing?'

In order to start healing, we need to address the layers of shame that cloak us. Take them off one by one, examine them, and gently discard them. Move through the anxiety that rises and allow ourselves to be received in our entirety. Through this process we will reconnect to our authentic, creative and complex self.

Vulnerability and De-armouring

The way through shame is bravely speaking what feels true—even if our cheeks are burning . . . even if we are worried what others will think . . . even if it triggers a sense of anxiety. We have to allow ourselves to be welcome in the world, just as we are. Vulnerability is the only way.

Expression ignites a natural transformation inside us and through it, we ensure we are no longer suppressing our truth. Sharing brings us into belonging. We are no longer alone. If we don't have a baseline of belonging, we won't know how to be vulnerable. It will be some foreign concept that we have no map for navigating. The shame. The fear. The inability to trust. They stop us from doing what we really need to do: belong.

In order to change this, we have to break the cycle, by taking off one piece of our armour at a time and saying 'Here I am. This is me.' The process is often incredibly confronting and our fear may rise in the process. But we have to do it anyway. Slowly. Testing the waters of vulnerability each time. 'Is it safe? Is it safe to show myself to you?'

When we are with the right people, time and repetition will prove to us that it's safe to keep de-armouring, little by little, piece by piece.

Healing happens in a social context.
We need each other to recover.

Belonging and the Body

Belonging is a felt somatic experience. Somatic means 'of the body'. It is not a cognitive process. When we do not feel a sense of belonging in the world, many of us will feel like we do not belong in our bodies.

If we have not been shown that our bodies are our sacred homes for aliveness and connection, why would we belong there? If we are excluded, neglected, oppressed, shamed or hurt, we may unconsciously do the same to our bodies.

Body exclusion shows up as the orientation to the mind. When we root our awareness firmly in the mind, we exist with a mind–body split. We can no longer truly connect to, listen or respond to our body. We know we have one, and we get by with it, but there is no intimacy with our own human vessel. Body neglect shows up as lack of care. Perhaps we don't eat well, exercise, bathe or groom ourselves as best we should. Perhaps we do the bare minimum to function, but we don't offer the level of care our body needs or deserves (and they deserve so much care—they carry us through life every day). Body oppression shows up as holding in or denying our own physical expression. Perhaps we do not let ourselves twitch, shake, stretch, rest, sleep or do whatever it is our body needs to do in any moment! We hold it in and brace ourselves, which builds up tension, stress and fatigue, until our bodies start screaming to be heard. Common markers of body oppression include pain and twitches and ticks.

Body shame is the practice of telling our body that it is not good enough; or worse, that we hate it. Too fat or thin, too tall or short, too slight or large, too much cellulite, too many wrinkles, not tanned or pale enough . . . just not good enough at all. We give ourselves complexes and some of us become dysmorphic, seeing ourselves through the eyes of shame.

Body harm occurs when we ignore or violate our body's boundaries. Perhaps we pour junk, alcohol or drugs into it. Or we overwork ourselves till we are run into the ground and burnt out. Or we push beyond our limits and ignore our body's signals that tell us it doesn't want these things. We may allow others to push beyond our body's boundaries, too. Our body is talking to us all the time, trying to set boundaries. Every time we do not listen and respect our body, we are harming it.

Transformation of the body as a healing response to un-belonging

In some cases, when our experience of un-belonging has been extreme, we may choose to deny our body's raw reality. We may deny our gender, colour, race. And we may do this by claiming another reality for ourselves. Or choosing not to exist in any fixed reality at all, as fluidity provides freedom. The choice to transform the body is an act of healing and reclamation. We may wrap ourselves up in costumes, dye our hair or cover ourselves in tattoos or have plastic surgery. Anything to paper over the tragedy of our exclusion or oppression. Our choices empower us. And allow us to transform exclusion and harm into beauty and belonging. The redesigning or reinvention of our bodies allows us to be new. Free from what it was. Liberated.

This process often follows a strong impulse to look physically different. It is rarely entered into with the awareness of the root of the impulse, which is to create a body-based reality where we are empowered, and can truly belong. We are seeking to create a loving home within ourselves.

True belonging is born through vulnerability. Not just with others, but with ourselves.

Belonging comes through sharing of our stories. We need to share them with each other.

But we also need to create a sacred channel between our beautiful bodies and our compassionate minds. Our bodies have stories to tell that will only come to us in the quiet intimacy of our solitude. They need to express and be cared for in ways that only we can provide. Before we begin, we need to be safe enough and strong enough to listen.

Personal Share

When I was growing up amidst so much trauma, I remember feeling like I had been born into the wrong family, at the wrong time in history. I felt like a weird blob amongst my peer group, and at some points, I even wondered if I would have been better off as a boy. I hated my body. I didn't feel like it was mine. I spent hours alone in my room in this existential crisis. But I never breathed a word of it to anyone. And no one would have ever known. I learned how to pack it away, put on a mask and simulate a sense of belonging. Many of us do that. If we look like a human, talk like a human and walk like a human, then we must surely belong to the pack. But even if others couldn't tell, I always felt like the black sheep. The odd one out. The third wheel. Different. And alone. Even when I was surrounded by friends. 'What's wrong with me? Why do I feel like this?' I would ask myself again and again.

But in those days, I had no answer. So I just had to deal with it. The only way I could express my feelings was in the way I treated my body. I felt like it was betraying me by not being 'the same' as other people's. Red hair. Fair skin. Freckles. Tall. A little podgy. Yuck! I hated it. Why didn't I belong?! I first learned I could change it by over-exercising. I learned that I could get it in a somewhat acceptable shape. Still not good enough (I would never be good enough). But acceptable enough to wear the short dresses my friends were wearing and not wanting to kill myself. But that was just the start. I found other ways to betray my poor body. I pierced everything I could. I got as many tattoos as I could afford. I smoked a pack of cigarettes a day for a while. I dyed my hair every colour of the rainbow. I did anything I could to un-belong from my body—to make it into something that I wasn't. I would swap one tactic for another, trying anything to feel different. For about five years, I became incredibly anorexic. Denying, denying, denying. At my worst, I was 40 kilos (for reference, I am 5'8" and now the fittest and strongest in my life at 70 kilos). No matter what I did, I didn't feel like I belonged in my body; in this world. And this just led to intense frustration and shame.

Everything changed the moment I knew I was going to be a mother. In an instant, I knew that I did not want my daughter to have a life anything like mine. I wanted her to belong. To be healthy. To be able to express herself. To know unequivocally that she was loved. Even before she was born, she belonged to me, and I belonged to her. In that moment, a lifetime of trying to make up for not belonging anywhere was no longer important. So I let that shit go. And I vowed to be the best mother I could. I knew that meant treating my own body with a lot more love and care. I started eating well, I let my long locks stay natural and wore it in its natural, curly state for the first time in my adult life. I started to look after myself, knowing that I needed to be strong enough to look after her.

As I prepared to become a parent to my daughter, I also started the journey of re-parenting myself.

While none of us are perfect, I think I am doing alright.

When Violetta was born, I was quite unwell. I was getting medical treatments four days of the month and was on lots of medication. Holding her was like holding pure love itself. I attuned to her breath. I mirrored her expressions. I showed her the world was a safe place she could belong in. And through that process, I began to heal. A few months after she was born, I told my doctors that I wanted to stop having plasma exchanges. They scoffed and told me it was a bad decision, that my nerve damage may return, and I would likely develop problems in walking again. I stood by my decision and stopped treatment. I became stronger. Happier. More engaged with my life. I started doing Pilates. I also started a blog about my insights on the human experience. I am sure that the love I felt for my beautiful little girl sent a wave of healing through my entire being. I am sure that when we belong, we begin to heal.

I don't, for a moment suggest we go out and procreate in order to belong and that was never my intention (please, please, please, do not do this!) but my lived experience taught me that love is the biggest healer of all.

My little boy Harlan proved it to me again, about two years later. When he was six months old, I ended up in the hospital for two months and in rehab for three. The kids would come to visit me in the hospital. Harlan would lay on the bed with me and look at me with his giant eyes. And I would feel better. We would eat sticks of raisin toast together and I would feel better. Later, when I went home, we would lay on the bed together, making sounds, and I could feel healing taking place. To this day, my son ensures I know how loved I am. Every morning, we cuddle in our rocking chair. He snuggles into me and kisses my cheek. He mirrors my words back to me, 'Do you know how much I love you?'

I belong to these kids and they belong to me. Because their sense of belonging is so innate, they can be radically authentic, shake their bodies any way that feels good, set boundaries and express their desires. I am so grateful and proud to be their mama. They teach me again and again how we should all belong in our bodies, in our families, in this world.

Invitation to Self-inquiry

- Do you feel a sense of aloneness, inclusion or belonging?
- What was your experience of belonging like as a child? Was it provided to you or not? To what extent? Consider family, culture, community and religion (if you have one).
- Do you tend to armour up around people? Or are you able to be vulnerable? Is it different with different groups of people?
- Do your mind and your body belong together or are they disconnected in some way? If so, how does this manifest itself?
- Now ask yourself: how can I invite a greater sense of belonging with my body, with people around me, in the world?

Somatic Healing Practice

Belonging

Lay down flat on your back. Bring one hand to your heart and place one hand on your belly. Breathe into your torso. Let yourselves know that you belong here. Stay here for a while. If you feel comfortable, open your arms out to the sides and breathe into your entire chest. You may feel more space inside and a sense of more breath capacity. See if it feels safe to extend your breath to your palms and fingertips. If it feels too confronting, bring your hands back over your heart space. You may like to try moving between the two hand positions and see what arises.

Affirm to Yourself

'I belong here. In my body. In the world.'

Trauma-informed Note:

The practice may evoke a sense of grief or a sense of the body wanting to contract/close. If grief rises, is it safe to welcome it? If the body wants to contract, or close, can you allow yourself to follow its impulses? Listen and respond! If you are not able to listen, you may like to lay on your side and move through the 'Inviting Safety' practice at the end of Part I Chapter 2.

5

The Agents of Healing

When we experience this existential shift, our traumatized selves cannot so readily access the agents of healing we need (which are the very things we were missing in the first place):

a) safety,
b) belonging,
c) expression and sharing.

If we could follow a simple formula to heal, we would. And that's why no self-help book or step-by-step healing guide is going to magically make it all better. They might bring us awareness, moments of epiphany and concepts to mentally integrate, but there is no formula to follow. Healing is about finding our way back to ourselves and each other. Stepping out of the warped reality where we reside and building a better one to live in.

Sometimes, it feels impossible . . . Like we are doing everything we practically can to be the best version of ourselves and a good human, but something is just not shifting.

That's because healing is more than practical. It is an existential journey of the spirit. Our trauma can leave us powerless, without the foundation we need to exist peacefully and powerfully. In this state, we are not able to access the choice and agency we need to create metamorphosis—to change ourselves and the world around us.

For our existential experience to change, healing needs to occur in a social context. Healing is dynamic.

We need each other to recover. Because our trauma stems from harmful relationships, so too does the remedy to it. This is why, no matter how hard we try to heal alone, it will be within the dynamic of safe relationships that transformation will truly become possible. When we have never been truly seen and heard without fear of judgement or harm; the remedy is just that.

The remedy is in the root.

The Human Catalyst and the Spark of Power

To be seen and heard without fear of judgement or harm takes us out of relational powerlessness. In one moment, we can pull back the curtain and peak into an entirely new reality.

In order to do this, we need another human who can sit peacefully with us in our vulnerability . . . unwavering, accepting and compassionate. Someone so strong at their centre that they do not react or repel—the very thing we fear.

In this moment, they show us that belonging is possible. That we are welcome. In this relationship. In this world. In our own body.

I call these people 'human catalysts'. They give us the spark of power we need to jump-start our innate healing abilities. They share with us their capacity for aliveness and compassion. Through these connections, we will take away either a sense of renewed hope, support, or expanded vision—whether intentionally or by design. The catalyzing human interaction triggers both a) an expansion of our own capacity for aliveness and b) a new impulse for change.

Capacity and impulse are the essential ingredients of power. Once we are empowered, change is inevitable.

In my time, I have met many human catalysts. Some in person, others via their books and teachings. Some knew exactly what they

THE SPARK OF POWER

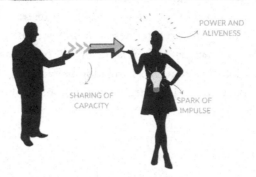

Image 1.5.1. The spark of power

were providing, whereas others were unknowingly lighting me up through their presence. Both kinds of human catalysts were equally as important to me. If we allow it, catalyzation occurs in every human interaction. When sharing becomes a way of being, we will always be giving or receiving, or both simultaneously—co-creating.

As we continue to cultivate our own peace, power and intuition, we become more and more receptive and responsive to welcoming authenticity, learning and growth through each interaction we have.

Choice—Empowerment and Agency

While human connection can increase our capacity and spark our impulse, healing requires *us* to grab hold of our newfound space and desire with reverence and intention.

We must choose to explore, to feel, to make sense and step forward to create new foundations and pathways. These new choices serve as stepping stones towards better realities.

Personal Share

I sought help everywhere for nearly twenty years. Doctors, therapists, alternative health, healers (a multitude of healing modalities), books and articles.

Along the way, there were some incredible human catalysts. There were women who showed up to cook for and cuddle my children when I could not—the purest form of unconditional kindness. There were others who would drive me to rehab, or go out of their way to bring me coffee when I was in the hospital undergoing treatment. There were certain healers who would hold or massage me while I wept silently, not asking me to be any other way than I was, or pushing their perceived wisdom or agendas on me. There was a trainer who helped stretch my legs when I couldn't lift them by myself.

These people met me where I was. They didn't ask me to change. Or push further or harder. There was no shame. Together, we belonged in the moments of my pain . . . and of my healing. Some of them, I met only once, while others supported me for years. Some of them renewed my fading sense of hope again and again, while some of them catalyzed profound experiences that sent me into periods of recovery and growth.

But there were also interactions with people who meant well, but were actually directing my attention away from my own curiosity, sense-making and intuitive abilities. When well-meaning family, friends, doctors, therapists or healers would tell me what was true and what was not, what was finite and fixed, dole out diagnoses and labels, or roll out a red carpet and 'show me the way', I would feel very hopeful and lap up the Kool-Aid, but inevitably fall down another messy rabbit-hole and end up back where I started, or into some other catastrophe or dead-end. And I'd feel confused and powerless all over again. 'Why am I like this? I am doing everything they tell me to do. I must be broken.' And really, some of the elaborate explanations and healing plans I was offered by healers were quite ridiculous, but I was so desperate to be well that I followed their guidance.

It took me a long time to realize that I was not broken. I was just looking at the wrong places. None of us are ever broken, we simply were not given the foundation we needed.

I had to go back to the origins of my trauma, the root of my existence, and figure it out from a place of empowerment and agency. I had to slowly piece together the answers to my 'why' and then I had to transform myself. Build a better reality, one moment at a time. I had to choose it again and again. I am still choosing.

This self-propelling exploration is what fundamentally re-patterns our existential experience. In fact, it is the only way to do it. There is no bypass available. I am very mindful of this, now, as a therapist and mentor. The client or student must want to do the work, they must access their own unconscious, their own somatic signals and their own pathways to change. They, too, must choose.

No one can do the work for us. No one can give us a checklist or treasure map that will speed us to enlightenment. If anyone tells you they can heal your life, they have not lived through their own embodied transformation. That's the whole point. It is ours. It must be ours. We must claim the right to live it.

We can invite a series of catalyzations. We can look for humans who increase our capacity for exploration, activation, choice, integration and inevitably, life. But we must do the work ourselves. This is my lived experience.

I truly believe that acknowledging the existential experience of our traumatized selves is a fundamental requirement to igniting the process of recovery and reclamation. Our existence is something we may have inherited, but we can all build a better reality for ourselves. We just need one moment where we know, without a doubt, that it is within our power.

I hope that this concept starts to materialize as possible for you. And that as you continue reading, you feel a growing hunger for it. Impulse. Desire. These are the agents we need to propel us into the life we deserve.

Once we are empowered to shift our existential reality, we can move to processing the unconscious self.

Invitation to Self-inquiry

- Do you have human catalysts in your life? Who are they? Can you connect to them with deeper intention?
- Have you been following people or processes that offer you a fixed or finite view on your identity or healing? What happens if you choose to expand your awareness?
- Based on what you've learned so far, do you better understand your 'why'? What can you make sense of?
- Now ask yourself: Am I choosing my healing? What can I do each day to choose it?

Somatic Healing Practice

Accessing Agency

Lay down on your back with your arms by your side. Take time to settle. Bring your awareness and the sensation of your breath in your palms. Open and close your palms slowly. Choose to open them. Choose to close them. Splay them open as far as they can go and then allow them to relax. Try the same process with your feet. Bring your attention and breath to your feet. Curl and splay your toes. Choose each movement. Come back to stillness for a few breaths.

Ask yourself: 'How does my body want to be now?' See if you can allow your body to move into a new position. It may be on your back, side, belly, sitting or standing. 'How does my body want to be now? Notice how it feels to connect to and follow your impulse. Move through as many poses as you wish. Stay for as long or as little as feels good. Let your body lead you.

Affirm to Yourself

'I choose me. I choose my healing. I choose my life.'

Trauma-informed Note:

The first time you try this, it may feel strange or confronting. You may feel 'this is silly' or stupid. This may be a sense of shame or un-belonging with the body arising. Notice if it feels safe to continue. Can you be vulnerable with yourself? This may bring tears. If it doesn't feel safe, you may like to move to the 'Inviting Safety' practice at the end of Part I Chapter 2. Remember, you can choose to end your practice at any time. Listen to your body. You can also come back to this as and when it feels safe to.

Part II

Prologue to Self

Who we are is a direct reflection of before—until we engage in a conscious healing process.

1. **Map for Love: Attachment and Attunement**
2. **The Nervous System and the Somatic Self**
3. **The Unconscious Mind**

There is nurture and there is nature. You can read several arguments about which one shapes us. My answer is that they both do, in unison. Understanding early attachment, the function of the nervous system, the development of the unconscious self and our tendency to fragment to self-protect, is essential to understanding who we are and why we are. We need to intimately know our messy, complex tapestry of Self, so that we can begin to heal and re-pattern, layer by layer, piece by piece. This conscious healing process allows us to be our own creator; to 'choose our own adventure' or even jump into another storybook.

What if I told you that you—your personality and your experiences—are a series of learned patterns? What if I told you that you had the power to change these patterns? One inquiry at a time. One conscious choice at a time?

How would that make you feel?

If someone had told me that when I was in the thick of illness, oppression and unresolved trauma, I would have felt rage! In fact, that actually happened to me. Back in the early 2000s, a friend gave me a book called *Meditation as Medicine* and it caused a huge rift to develop in our relationship. I felt like she was telling me that I could meditate away my illness and my pain that I had been coping with for over a decade. It felt insulting and dismissive. Not at all compassionate. 'Do not trivialize my pain or tell me I can think my way out of it! How dare you?! Do you think I want my life to be this way? Are you kidding me?' That was my unspoken response. But I thanked her for the book, flashed a fake smile, shoved it on a shelf and let myself know that this friend would never really be able to understand me. And at the time, she couldn't. No one could. Because the Natalia back then was a mess of decontextualized trauma responses—a reaction to everything that had been before. I couldn't understand why I was the way I was, and neither could anyone else.

But do you know what? My friend's sentiments were spot-on.

I couldn't meditate everything away, but I did have all the answers inside me. I just wasn't ready to hear that. It was too overwhelming for me to process. At that time, turning inwards was not an option. That is one of the fundamental things about trauma, we literally can't tune into the horrific events that have shaped us. We first need to cultivate enough safety and strength to start to explore ourselves with great compassion. But safety and compassion are often outside our reach in that state, until we start our conscious healing process and cultivate them little by little.

If you're reading this book, my sense is that you've already started exploring, illuminating patterns and igniting your own metamorphosis. Please go gently with this process. Sometimes, when we access new awareness, all of a sudden, we get a rush of understanding. Epiphany after epiphany. When our 'why' comes into vision, we may not know what to do with it. Read this chapter slowly and give yourself time to integrate. If you get flooded with illuminations, memories and dots start joining up, I encourage you to write. Get it out of your head, so you can look at it and make sense of it. Meditate. Cry. Breathe. Look after yourself as you heal. Slow down and give each piece of awareness time to integrate inside you and around you. Shift into self-compassion again and again. Self-compassion is the constant that will hold as we heal.

1

Map for Love: Attunement and Attachment

When we are born, we are somewhat pure. We enter this world receptive, ready to be nurtured, loved and guided, so that we can grow into happy, healthy, responsive humans.

The people we rely on to help us develop our sense of Self are primarily our parents, our family and to some extent, our community and culture.

In a perfect world, we would feel safe, seen, heard and encouraged at every expression—from the first time we open our eyes, to the first time we feed, sleep alone, laugh, speak and walk. We would be encouraged to be curious, to test our limits, set and express our boundaries, and also respond to others' boundaries. We would also be held, touched and cared for every day. These are the ingredients to developing a secure sense of Self and healthy relationships with others and the world around us.

To be honest, most of us don't get this. And if we have grown up in a family or environment where there was abuse, neglect, danger, shame or oppression, we have no chance of receiving the foundations for becoming a well-adjusted human who feels welcome and empowered in the world. We never got the chance.

Attachment is about attunement. When there is trauma, there is little to no attunement. Our caregivers are either not aware of our needs and expressions, or they are unable to respond to them (for a variety of reasons). In either case, this causes our little selves to adapt. We have to figure out how to exist here without the responsiveness, care and mirroring we need. We begin surviving from the very beginning. And in some ways, we are alone from the very beginning—at least existentially.

Survival and aloneness become the foundation of who we become. The way we adapt and evolve depends on many factors, including the way our parents connect (or don't connect) to us, other relationship dynamics in the family, the presence or lack of supportive people in our lives, our environment, culture and/or religious influences and our baseline of health and resilience in early life.

When it comes to attachment, these formative relationships become the blueprint for what we know as relationships—our map for love.

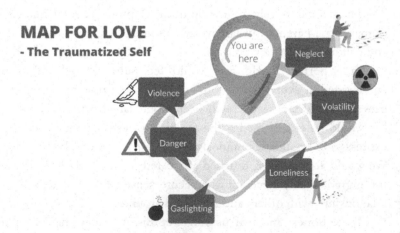

MAP FOR LOVE
- The Traumatized Self

You are here

Neglect

Violence

Volatility

Danger

Loneliness

Gaslighting

Image 2.1.1. Map for Love for the Traumatized Self

Our little selves learn: 'this is what love is' and 'this is how to relate.'

If we have been shown that love is shaming, harmful or altogether lacking, we learn that these are the hallmarks for relating to other people. Our 'map for love' is imprinted on our psyche (and in fact, our nervous system, too), and we go off and keep seeking out the same thing. It's all we know.

This often causes us to become one of the three different types of people in our relationships:

- **The Attachment Replica**
  We unconsciously seek relationships that mirror the way one or both of our parents loved or harmed us—or the way they showed love or harm to each other.
- **The Attachment Polarity**
  We ensure that we choose relationships that in no way resemble the parent that harmed us. We look for someone who our child-self deems as safe, who, in our assessment, will not recreate our trauma or oppression. In some cases, this can work out well, but in others, we are running so blindly from our trauma that we fail to see other red flags or we forge a connection based on what the person is not, rather than what they are, which can leave us feeling like we are 'misconnected' (not quite connected), and therefore we may still feel alone in the relationship.
- **Projection Looping**
  We continue to be attracted to people who are totally wrong for us. We seem to have a knack for choosing the wrong people, entering relationships with blinders on, completely sure that we have found our soulmate, and then end up in the same volatile or disconnected situation, again and again. It might be that we continue to choose the bad guy/girl that hurts us or cheats on us, or we might find ourselves with friends who are unstable, ungrounded and a mess, or we may continue to end up in relationships where we don't feel connected, either mentally or sexually.

In all of these manifestations, our little traumatized selves are running the show. We are, at once seeking the love and connection we never had and at the same time, protecting ourselves from healthy connection and love. They are unknown and therefore, foreign and terrifying . . . or just inconceivable and therefore, impossible.

Many of us live with some degree of attachment trauma. We assume 'I am just like this. This is the love and connection I am capable and worthy of.' Either we make the best of it and smile for our Instagram selfies, or we run from love altogether. Whether we are in a relationship or alone, there is often a sense of loneliness. We might feel it in the recesses of our heart or the pit of our stomach. But we usually don't breathe a word of it to anyone. It becomes a shameful secret that we carry in our existential backpacks. Sometimes, we pretend it's not there at all and convince ourselves that all is well. Our smiles become bigger, our eyes wider—like dolls on a shelf, or performers in a play that never ends. It's easier to pretend we are happy than to admit to discontent.

Personal Share

My map for love showed me that love was physically abusive, verbally abusive, chaotic, shaming and neglectful. Of course, as a young child, I had no concept that this was anything other than normal. I didn't know that I could (or should) expect anything other than volatility, violence and deprivation. Because that was my map. I grew up learning to pack parts of myself away in order to minimize harm, grab breadcrumbs of approval and care, and stay poised in a state of hyper-vigilance, waiting for something bad to happen. I also learned how to self-isolate—it was safest to keep to myself. Looking back, I was so deeply traumatized and neglected, and was simply yearning for a safe place to land (and that yearning still exists inside me, but now it is more of a gentle wish, rather than a life-or-death need).

The lack of love and care I experienced led me to choose a partner who was a) incapable of harm, b) wanted to care for and please me. When I met my husband, he became that safe place to land. He was (and is) a kind and gentle man that wouldn't hurt a fly and he did care for me through some very difficult years.

But I had come to the relationship from a place of deep need—from my little, traumatized self. And I believe he came to it from his own unconscious attachment wounding. This is known as a trauma bond. In a trauma bond, one or both people are entering the relationship from their little traumatized selves. This means there are not two adults engaging in a connection, but young children who are desperately looking for connection and care. Trauma bonds happen a lot, because so many of us have been harmed or neglected early on in our lives. The thing about trauma bonds is that the repair the little self seeks, cannot be tended to in the romantic relationship. Over time, this often leads to feelings of resentment, aloneness, betrayal, energy drain or even rage, for both partners.

My marriage had so much good in it. We were kind to each other. We cared for each other. We were companions as we travelled in and out of one hellhole to another. We built a beautiful life together. But as we approached stability, it became clear that it was all the caring and fighting and striving that had glued us together. It was a painful realization. Nothing bad had happened. We had just bonded from a place of survival. When there was no more need to survive, the connection became thin and unable to sustain. We drifted further apart. Our differences became more apparent. He knew it, too. I am so grateful that we were able to talk about what was not there and take steps to graciously move on and renegotiate our relationship as co-parents.

After we separated, my attachment trauma repelled me right into another trauma bond. But this one was incredibly abusive and harmful—a direct replica of my childhood map for love. It was after coming out of this second trauma bond that I started to heal my attachment trauma and find my true self. It has been an epic journey. I am still learning about my relational self and redrawing my map for love. It is an endless and profound journey. I have learned that as we heal, we can continue to redraw the lay lines of the heart and nurture relationships that are truly supportive, rather than use them as attempts to plug the holes in the heart of the traumatized child inside us.

It is not until we learn that we have the power to go back and redraw this map, that we can access the courage to say 'I want more for myself. I deserve more love. And I am going to do the work it takes to be able to receive it.'

The Relational and Dynamic Self

Humans are dynamic creatures. That is, our existence is largely a response to external stimuli. We exist in the context of relationship.

To truly understand the nuances of our relational 'why', we need to go back to the beginning, explore how we formed in those early relationships, and how that manifested and adapted over time in every attachment relationship after that. While attachment and attunement are commonly explored through the lens of romantic relationships, they may also show up in our close friendships, our relationships with employers or colleagues, and can also recreate itself in our relationship to a career or lifestyle pursuit, or within the internal dynamics of our fragmented psyche.

Wherever there is a relationship, there is a dynamic pattern to explore, because our relational self exists as a response to others.

A relationship is two or more people creating a shared, dynamic experience. This means it is never just about 'me', it is about 'us'. When exploring our relational self, we must always consider, 'why is my relational self like this?' and 'why is their relational self like this?' Our awareness must exist in two places at once—we require empathy.

Basic Attachment Theory Explained

Attachment theory[4] is a framework that allows us to understand how our adult relating patterns have been influenced by our formative attachment relationships with our parents. It was created by John

---

[4] Kendra Cherry, 'What Is Attachment Theory?: The Importance of Early Bonds', Verywell Mind, 17 July 2019, available at: https://www.verywellmind.com/what-is-attachment-theory-2795337. Accessed April 2022.

RELATIONSHIP

Your existential
backpack

My existential
backpack

Map for Love

Map for Love

ME
+
My love stuff

YOU
+
Your love stuff

Image 2.1.2. The relational and dynamic self

Bowlby and Mary Ainsworth.[5] They conducted an experiment called 'The Strange Situation', where they observed what happened to children after being separated from their mothers. It's important to understand that the experiment measured the response to connection after separation.

The study resulted in three key attachment styles. Here is my basic interpretation:

- *Secure Attachment:* The child felt safe both in and out of connection. As an adult, this translates to having healthy relating patterns, feeling secure and independent/whole in a relationship, and no sense of need or anxiety when apart from the other person, or suffocated or diminished in the presence of the other person. When it comes to trauma, secure attachment is not available, because it was not modelled by the parents.

- *Insecure Anxious Attachment:* The child felt anxious during experiences of separation or dissonance. As an adult, this

[5] For more information on John Bowlby and Mary Ainsworth's work on Attachment theory, see Cherry, 'Attachment Theory', 2019.

translates to feeling emotionally needy in relationships, mistrusting of one's partner when not together ('are they cheating on me?'; 'will they leave me?'). During arguments, feeling distressed or terrified of impending rejection or abandonment, which can cause volatile expression. There is often a need for a lot of affirmation from their partner, which can put strain on the relationship. This most commonly happens when rejection or abandonment have been present in early attachment relationships. The child is starved of the love they need and/or fearful that it will be taken away from them.

- *Insecure Avoidant Attachment:* The child felt overwhelmed with too much connection and required space or disconnection to feel safe and whole. Or conversely, there was a lack of emotional connection altogether. As an adult, this translates into feeling suffocated by relationships, 'checking out', shutting down, or avoiding too much connection, or high-intensity connection. 'Emotional flooding' is a common experience—when the threshold for connection is reached, it's impossible to stay connected and communicative, so the reaction is to disconnect, which often presents itself as stonewalling, ghosting, or even ending relationships. This most commonly happens when there has been a volatile or over-protective parent. The child feels like they cannot breathe or express themselves freely. Conversely, if the parent was emotionally absent, the child has no map for connection to draw from.

Developments in Attachment Theory in the Modern Trauma Paradigm

As modern research around trauma and attachment continued, it became clear that many who suffered from childhood trauma presented a different relational profile. Neither secure, nor anxious, nor avoidant. Mary Main[6] developed a fourth category called 'disorganized attachment'. Here's my basic interpretation of it:

Disorganized attachment creates a relational experience where continuity and peace are impossible, because love and harm co-exist. This causes a deep sense of relational confusion. As an adult, this presents with some traits of both anxious and avoidant styles, and having a generally confused and erratic pattern in relationships. There may be experiences of craving for connection during separation, feeling overwhelmed with too much connection and feeling threatened by certain expressions that trigger old experiences of harm or neglect. This presents itself as erratic behaviour, triggers, and feelings of unsafety or dissatisfaction in relationships. This most commonly happens when a parent has been either abusive (physically or emotionally), or there has been an experience of neglect. There is no consistent 'safe place' for the child to land.

As I have explored my own relating styles and worked with thousands of clients, without fail, those who have experienced childhood trauma, fall into the disorganized category.

When love is synonymous with harm, there can be no safety, only chaos.

A big piece of the trauma healing puzzle is to go back and look at our map for love, understand every twist and turn, explore the important landmarks and the insignificant pebbles, and then step by step, start redrawing the map. There is no formula, only a continued illumination and an expansion in our own self-compassion. In the process, we can choose to create a map for love that promotes safety,

---

[6] Mary Main's 'Disorganized attachment' theory, as explained in Lisa Firestone, 'Disorganized Attachment: How Disorganized Attachments Form & How They Can Be Healed', Psychalive, available at: https://www.psychalive.org/disorganized-attachment/. Accessed April 2022.

Image 2.1.3. Map for love for the Conscious Healing Self

respect, authenticity, vulnerability and care. In order to do this, we first need to learn to discern.

Discernment

Discernment is impossible when we are living in a state of trauma.

The ability to discern allows us not only to self-protect from harm, but to choose people and situations that nurture us. When we don't develop this ability, we often end up looping into difficulty after difficulty, wondering how we ended up there yet again. This is our trauma at play.

Discernment requires the following moving parts:

- A map for love that includes respect, empathy, vulnerability, care and compassion
- An understanding of our human rights
- A healthy nervous system that knows the difference between safety and danger
- Connection to our intuition

None of these are possible if we hold unresolved trauma. We grow up without learning how to protect ourselves. It is a fundamental human right to be able to say no. In the case of trauma, we either never develop, or lose connection to, our internal radar that is meant to steer us towards good, and away from harm.

Part of the healing journey is about learning to say no to harmful relationships and experiences, and yes to the people and experiences that will swiftly take us towards the kind of life we want. Early on in the journey, this can seem impossible. We may be met with choices and feel unsure which way to go; perhaps even paralyzed with the fear of choosing something new. When we start making new choices that go against our very ingrained organizing principles, it can feel like we are sinning against the world. Choosing the wrong thing usually becomes so normalized that it feels right. Choosing our own happiness feels inherently wrong or bad. This is often the unconscious core wound behind the constant destruction of our own happiness. Self-sabotage is a trauma response.

Before we can truly learn to trust ourselves with our choices, we may need to call in a 'human catalyst'—a guide who can be our anchor and compass; one who helps us orient and discern, in order to make choices that will be helpful, rather than harmful (see Part I Chapter 1). When we trust the voice of another, it can help us develop our own internal anchor, and reset our intuitive compass. With help, over time, slowly but surely, we begin to start to trust ourselves. It's through our own self-trust that we develop discernment.

Once we learn how to discern, we are able to protect ourselves and it becomes safer to take risks; to open our hearts to more and more love.

Invitation to Self-inquiry

- As a child, how were you shown love by your parents/ caregivers?
- Did your experience of love and connection include any sense of harm? This could include shaming, being quieted/

shut down or constantly questioned, neglected, denied connection, or physical abuse.

- How does your map show up in your relationships now? Consider the people close to you—your partner, children, close friends, employer, colleagues. This could include feeling imbalanced ('I give more than I receive'), rejected or abandoned, misunderstood, shamed or belittled.
- Are you able to discern and choose people and experiences that are good for you? Where does your intuitive compass orient?
- Now ask yourself: How can I begin to redraw my map for love? What do I want it to look like?

Somatic Healing Practice

Remapping the heart

Find a comfortable seat. Place your hands over your heart. Breathe into it. Acknowledge your existing map for love. Connect to one thing that you would like to let go of. See if it feels good to gently rock back and forth as you allow it to release.

Affirm to Yourself

'I let go of the kind of love that harms or denies me. I welcome a love that respects and honours me.'

Trauma-informed Note:

If you are currently in a harmful or neglectful relationship dynamic, or have experienced past relational harm, this may trigger feelings of grief or anger. You may also be met with memories. Please check your safety levels and capacity to process. If it feels overwhelming, remember you can come out of the practice at any time by opening your eyes, orienting to the room around you, rubbing your palms together and taking a sip of water. To help settle yourself, you may like to curl up on your side under a blanket. If you feel like doing so, you can integrate this with journalling.

2

The Nervous System and
the Somatic Self

The nervous system governs our entire experience so understanding and mastering it, offers us great power. This mastery comes through developing a deeply compassionate relationship between our somatic self, our mental/emotional self and inviting our unconscious trauma and little self to join the mix.

Because the nervous system largely exists and evolves in an involuntary state, most of us don't think about how its experience defines our greater experience, from our emotions and thoughts, through to the way we engage and relate in the world.

Learning about the nervous system, how to read our signals and consciously shift our state is one of the key components of healing and self-mastery. This is where science, psychology and spirituality meet.

While it can be helpful to understand the science, we do not need a degree in neuroscience, nor do we want to over-focus on the experience of the nervous system. While it is our central sensory-meter, it is only the starting point of awareness; not awareness in its entirety. We need to know just enough to be empowered to understand and look after ourselves and to be guided to the healing we seek.

Safety versus Threat

The first and constant question that our nervous system asks is: 'Am I experiencing safety or danger?'

All other processes, responses and reactions derive from the answer to this question.

When the nervous system senses safety, it has the capacity to process more complex information. Once it discerns a need or a desire, it can send signals through the body to invite a supportive action or expression.

We sense, 'All is well. I am safe in my body, in my mind, in my relationships, in the world.'

When the nervous system senses danger, it switches to survival mode in order to self-protect. All functions, actions or expressions that are not focused on regaining a sense of safety become unavailable. Complex processing and discernment become impossible.

We sense, 'Something is wrong. I am in danger and I need to protect myself from my body, my thoughts/emotions, my relationships, the world.'

Our thought process and actions that stem from safety are vastly different from those that stem from danger.

> Safety is the foundation for curiosity, vulnerability and receptivity, empathy, emotional intelligence and compassion.
> Danger is the foundation for reactivity, control, close-mindedness, selfishness and even stupidity.

External becomes Internal

Our nervous system is constantly picking up information from the world around us. It takes tiny pieces of information called 'qualia'[7] and sends them up to the brain for integrated processing. When we are existing within our capacity, it has the ability to process with incredible acuity. Our human body and its neuro-circuitry is incredibly sophisticated—we really are amazing creatures! This is why when we are feeling safe, calm and spacious, our perceptions become clearer and more precise, and our intuitive abilities crystallize. When there is chaos in the world around us, it is much harder for our nervous system to process complex or new information. Most of its energy goes into navigating the threat and trying to help us maintain some sense of equilibrium. When the level of external threat becomes more than our nervous system can equalize, processing becomes impossible. Our nervous system starts to register 'Danger, danger, danger!' and thus, external becomes internal. We begin to exist as a rolling reaction to threat, which we are powerless to change unless we learn to master our nervous system.

When it comes to trauma, the sense of threat and chaos we have lived through gets internalized. Our nervous system learns to treat threat as the normal baseline for existence. Our neurophysiological compass is miscalibrated. When we experience a miscalibration in the nervous system, our experience of the world changes. Threat appears everywhere. It becomes normalized and we are no longer aware that we are wearing threat-tinted glasses, let alone that we have the power to take them off and see the world more clearly.

The Past Becomes the Present

In the case of trauma, the nervous system perceives that past danger is still present, or that protection is required even when it is not. Threat is perceived where there may presently be none. When there are danger signals darting through our nervous system, it is near impossible to access a semblance of inner peace. It is also very

---

[7] 'Qualia are the subjective or qualitative properties of experiences.' See Internet Encyclopedia of Philosophy: A Peer-reviewed Academic Resource, available at: https://iep.utm.edu/qualia/.

difficult to see and feel others for who they truly are—empathy and compassion become inaccessible. Indeed, the world altogether can feel like a very threatening place.

When the past is taking up space in the present, it is harder for the nervous system to process new information and therefore, it can feel as if nothing we do really changes how we feel. Part of the nervous system's process is to match patterns. This means that when new information is presented to it—anything from a new food, to a new location, to a new person—our nervous system will scan its archives to see if it knows what this is. Once it registers that the information is actually new, it will refer to all the records it has that are similar to try and make sense of the new information.

Imagine a young child who knows what a dog is, but has never seen a wolf before. It's used to dogs being friendly and being able to happily pat them. When they see a wolf for the first time, they might think it's a dog and call out 'nice dog!' and approach the animal, expecting to pat it. The child will only learn that the wolf is dangerous and not safe to pat if: a) the wolf shows signs of being threatening (like snarling/growling or attempting to pounce/attack, or b) an adult teaches the child that this is a wolf, not a dog, and is unsafe to approach. The child's context of the world expands and they have more data points for processing in the future.

We learn through experience and guidance. Those of us who grow up and live with enough freedom to learn and guidance to keep us safe, will develop the optimum balance of courage and risk evaluation. Those of us who were oppressed and lacked guidance, will have a harder time understanding what is safe and what is dangerous. This can show up either as difficulty in making decisions, playing it very safe, or the tendency to make choices without the proper risk evaluation.

Because we are existing from our survival brain when under threat, the pattern-matching process often doesn't complete. The nervous system will take in the new information, send it up to the brain and the brain will often match patterns against old files and stop right there. It's a bit like trying to squish a puzzle piece into the wrong whole. The nervous system is busy doing all it can to survive, so the amount of energy it can give to finding discernment and clarity is severely reduced. We are likely to identify a wolf as a dog and put ourselves in harm's way. And this is exactly what happens to those who continue to enter abusive relationships—the ability to pattern-match is diminished and the abusive wolf looks like a welcoming puppy!

The inability to accurately process new information and discern, is what leads many traumatized people (myself included) into difficulty after difficulty. Conversely, it is also what causes our inability to notice new positive changes and allow personal and relational evolution.

We will feel an inherent amount of shame when we can't process new information, and our nervous systems are stuck in the past. Something feels generally wrong, but we can't quite put our finger on it, or change it. And something is wrong. We are straddled between two worlds, unable to step fully into the present, and unsure how to escape the nameless limbo.

Healing and Change Cannot Integrate

When we are living in a 'state of trauma', healing often cannot integrate with embodied change.

We may be making strides with our physical health, or our ability to show up in the world may be improving a thousand-fold, but we may not be able to see it. We can only see who we were before the improvements. This is really common for those with body image issues—we may be looking healthier and eating better, but the image we see in the mirror and the way we feel inside doesn't change. Similarly, when it comes to those with anxiety or illness—we may have our symptoms under control and be coping with more situations for longer periods without imploding, but we still feel like a hot mess. In relationships, our partner or friend may be making changes to be more supportive but we simply may not be able to see them. We may be viewing them based on their past behaviour and disallowing a new dynamic to emerge. This, I believe, is one of the fatal flaws in most relationships that keeps people stuck in the blame game and a loop of dysfunction.

In all these instances, we feel stuck like a hamster on a wheel. No hamster really wants to be running on that wheel for an eternity. Some of us will continue to look for a way out, but over time, resentment will build up—we become angry and powerless. Some of us will reach a point where we might begin to believe that there *is* no way out of the existential wheel, so we might stop trying. We might accept our fate, after which life would become a mindless and futile exercise.

Acceptance can be a dangerous thing. This strong belief I hold counters most modern spiritual teachings about acceptance. Acceptance is meant to be the doorway to inner peace. When it comes to trauma, however, it is often the very thing that keeps us trapped. In order to access its power, we need to break free from the state of trauma, to bring our poor nervous systems out of the sense of threat and start to heal—we need to access non-acceptance and admit, 'This doesn't work for me anymore, and I'm going to choose to create a different reality for myself.' Non-acceptance begins in the present. The moment we choose something different in the present, we are already breaking free from the chains of the past and our nervous system registers something new.

One moment of intention can unleash enough momentum to fuel an incredible transformation process.

Personal Share

After more than three decades of living as a rolling reaction, a traumatized mess, I came to a moment where I decided 'I don't want this life anymore. I do not accept this as my story!' I had been physically unwell for eleven years by that point. I had become a hamster in a wheel for about seven of them, simply accepting that I would require intravenous infusions three times a month and that putting together my pill box with forty-two kinds of medications each day would be an eternal weekly duty.

I had accepted that I would have limited physical capacity and that my role as a mother would be difficult, devoid of dancing, ball-kicking and play. Life was hard. The doctors had said there was no hope for anything better and it was now about making the best of life that I could, under the circumstances. I had severe anxiety and anything new or outside my routine caused me to feel overwhelmed or even panicky. I really couldn't process anything, and the things I could, still felt generally challenging, upsetting or infuriating. I was doing my best to keep myself in check and be the best person I could, while my nervous system was on fire—I literally had inflammation in the brain and spine that caused pain and reduced my mobility. Danger signals were coursing through my veins 24/7.

My family had to make an unexpected move to Singapore from Australia. Naturally, I was terrified of the move to a foreign country. But we went, and it was the best thing that ever happened to me. I believe that had I not moved, I would still be sick and traumatized (and the version of myself writing this book wouldn't exist). Something happened when I took away some of the old stimulus from my nervous system. The same hospitals, doctors, family that were part of my story weren't there anymore. There was space to process new information. It's like I'd emptied my cup and could start refilling it with something new.

I chose rest, sunlight and meditation, to start. I also started going for regular somatic treatments. I got a new neurologist who encouraged me to relook at my medications and see what we could cut out. And all of a sudden, a little bit of light started to peek through the darkness. That little bit of light shifted my entire neuro-circuitry. I started to feel that something was different and the ability to truly feel a change inspired hope and action. I quickly realized

that I had the power to input information in my nervous system
that would help me feel better, and exclude things that made me feel
worse. I also realized that the better I felt, the more tolerance I had
for things I wouldn't have dealt well with before.

I became more and more resilient. My tolerance for stress and
just life, in general, increased. My sense of peace and vitality grew
daily. All of these small life changes became the foundation of a
complete rewiring of my nervous system and led to what doctors
called 'a miraculous recovery'. The doctors had expected I would
continue to deteriorate and have a decreased life expectancy. In their
eyes, I was doomed. And for a time, their eyes had become my eyes.
The biggest epiphany was that I had the power to heal myself. The
second was that I had to look after myself and make my healing and
self-care a way of life. The latter was hard to get my head around,
as self-deprivation was part of my personal and inter-generational
make-up. I had learned to not look after myself. But if I wanted to
live a healthy and happy life, there was no other choice. So I chose.
I chose life.

Healing the Nervous System

Healing the nervous system is a big piece of the trauma-recovery
puzzle, and takes place in layers, over time. We need to learn how to
a) identify threat responses; b) self-care to increase safety; c) separate
past from present; d) deactivate trauma triggers; e) develop curiosity
and capacity.

The manifestation of threat is complex and completely unique
for us all. The ongoing exploration is: 'How is threat showing up
inside and around me? In my body, my thoughts, my relationships,
my engagement with the world?'

Before we can start to answer these questions, we need to
understand the nervous system at a basic level. I will purposely keep
the following explanation as simple and as non-scientific as possible,
because rather than become scholars of neurophysiology, I believe

we need to become scholars of our own experience, so we can decipher the messages and find ways to self-care and regain a sense of peace and equilibrium.

Nervous System Basics

To understand the concept of safety vs. threat, we need to know that we are exploring how the autonomic nervous system responds to safety or threat. This is best outlined by *The Polyvagal Theory* by Dr Stephen Porges.[8] In essence, the theory explains that the autonomic nervous system is constantly trying to equalize our experience. It wants us to feel safe, balanced and able to cope with the world around us. It has two branches—sympathetic and parasympathetic.

Our 'Doing' Accelerator—The Sympathetic Nervous System

The sympathetic branch is like our accelerator. Whenever we need to engage with the world, it activates so that we have enough energy to do what we need to do. When we exercise, when we work, when we have a conversation, whenever we are 'doing', our sympathetic nervous system is at work.

Our 'Being' Brake—The Parasympathetic Nervous System

The parasympathetic branch is like our brake. It looks at our energy expenditure and is constantly helping us slow down, stay within our limits and maintain a sense of coping in the world. It helps us to stay present and return to a state of 'being'.

Personal Capacity—Window of Tolerance

In a healthy nervous system, these two branches are best friends forever (BFFs), chatting all day long to keep us within our capacity

---

[8] For more information on Dr Stephen Porges' Polyvagal theory, please refer to https://www.polyvagalinstitute.org and https://www.stephenporges.com.

to cope with the world. Just enough doing and just enough being to function well and navigate the changing state of the external world. We all have a certain capacity to cope with the world as individuals. In nervous system terms, this is known as our 'window of tolerance'. When we exist beyond our capacity, the two branches of our nervous system can no longer work together to keep us feeling balanced. This is when we enter survival mode and either one or both of them signals danger, unleashing their army in response, in an attempt to regain a sense of safety and equilibrium. The best friends either stop talking to each other or begin fighting with each other.

In the end, all we want is to feel safe—inside our bodies and within our relationship with the world around us. This is a need, rather than a desire, and our nervous system will do absolutely anything to return to it again and again.

Survival

States of survival can range from mildly overwhelmed, to anxiety, fear and panic. They can also cause us to feel immobilized, frozen and helpless.

In a healthy nervous system, when the sense of danger passes, the BFFs will make up and start working together to get us back into our sweet spot where all is well in the world and we can function as normal.

In the case of trauma and thus, a miscalibrated nervous system, this doesn't happen. The danger may have passed, but the perception of threat remains and the nervous system stays stuck in survival mode. Left unhealed, we start to live in the world from a baseline of threat. This can either be felt and is constant, or hidden and intermittently lifted into felt experience by certain triggering experiences or stimuli.

In order to start our journey of mastering the nervous system, we need to learn to listen to the clues that show up to tell us when we are experiencing threat. They are largely non-verbal and somatic in nature. They are felt. Threat decontextualizes through us physically, mentally/emotionally and relationally. There are three main physiological states of survival. These trigger a range of intricate psychological and relational adaptive strategies. Understanding our primary neurophysiological threat responses is incredibly helpful for going on to decode and repair our psychological and relational self.

Fight or Flight Response

This is the most commonly talked-about survival strategy. This happens when our sympathetic nervous system becomes too stimulated and the parasympathetic nervous system can't equalize it.

The nervous system senses: 'Threat is imminent. I either need to run away or fight to protect myself.' It then triggers a relational response, which falls into one of the two main categories:

a) *Fight*: The signal to stay in the thick of the danger and find a way to win, prevail and conquer the situation;
b) *Flight*: The signal to run away from possible harm at full speed.

While the relational adaptation may vary, the physiological response is the same.

Signs and Symptoms of Fight or Flight Responses

Physical	• Elevated heart rate/blood pressure • Quickened breath • Narrowing of the eyes or furrowing of the brow • Tightness in the jaw, neck, shoulders and upper back • Insomnia • Upset stomach/digestion issues

Mental/Emotional	• Anxiety/panic • Racing thoughts • Emotional peaks or outbursts (particularly anger or bursting into tears) • Confusion/inability to make a decision

Relational	Triggers occur quickly and the response will depend on which relational response activates first:
	
	• *Fight*
	  ◦ Becoming defensive
	  ◦ Starting arguments
	  ◦ Blaming others
	  ◦ Aggression in voice
	  ◦ Empathy and compassion decrease or the person is not able to listen and respond to what the other person is expressing
	  ◦ Awareness narrows and the person can no longer consider greater context, but can only respond to what they feel in the moment
	• *Flight*
	  ◦ Retreat/disconnection
	  ◦ Unavailable for clear communication and conflict resolution
	  ◦ Unable to maintain responsibility for tasks or agreements
	  ◦ Avoids dealing with issues and places attention elsewhere; with some level of urgency

Freeze or Shut-Down Response

This happens when the threat seems too much to even try neutralizing. The sympathetic nervous system tells the parasympathetic nervous system: 'The danger is too great, there's no chance for me to neutralize it, you better take over.' So the parasympathetic nervous system responds with immobilization. It says 'Let's hide until the danger passes. Maybe if we are quiet and still, we will survive.'

Signs and Symptoms of a Freeze or Shut-Down Response

Physical	• Reduced heart rate/blood pressure • Reduced breath capacity • Fatigue • Constipation • Lymphatic slowness or blockages • Thyroid/hormone imbalance • Numbness and circulatory issues
Mental/Emotional	• Lack of motivation/apathy • Hopelessness/depression • Thoughts of 'I can't . . .' • Feelings of unworthiness such as 'I am not good enough'
Relational	• Withdraws/disconnects from relationships • Becomes non-responsive • Self-blames/shames other people for their experiences • Empathy and compassion decreases/ cannot listen and respond to what the other person is expressing • Unable to make sense of or verbalize their own experiences

Co-activation

Co-activation is the simultaneous or intermittent triggering of both a fight-or-flight and freeze or shut-down response. It is as if the nervous system can't decide which survival strategy is better, so it keeps darting around, trying to find a route to safety, unable to find a safe place to land. Signs and symptoms of a co-activated threat response will be a disorganized mix of both the fight-or-flight and the freeze or shut-down indicators. Those of us with unresolved trauma have a primarily co-activated threat response. Just like our attachment style, it is disorganized.

Relational

Most people with a co-activated or disorganized nervous system present as unstable and unpredictable in relationships. In more extreme cases, like in case of Dr Jekyll and Mr Hyde, they may be lovely and balanced in one moment, and volatile in the next. This makes for really difficult relationship dynamics. So usually, one of three things might happen:

a) Relationships become unstable, full of conflict, confusion and pain
b) Relationships continue to end due to the dysfunction
c) A Fawn response develops

Understanding our tendency to fawn as part of co-activation

Our instability and fluctuating distress levels bring us a lot of existential shame. We know something is deeply wrong and is stopping us from having the sense of peace and the relationships we desperately desire, so we have to find a way to sort it out. We develop a strategy to ensure that we can create and maintain connection. Because in some deep, unconscious place, we know that our ticket to some sense of safety and sanctuary comes through human connection.

Belonging is the only bridge to a better world. So we do anything we can to belong.

If we were to walk around sharing our co-activated, disorganized, traumatized selves, we would be at risk of exclusion—by way of rejection or abandonment—and this simply isn't an option. So we push it down and simulate a good, kind and responsive self. In order to do this, we have to abandon what's really going on and learn how to behave in a way that will please the other person. Our nervous system may be firing on all cylinders, but we smile sweetly and behave as if all is well. This is known as the fawn response. It is largely unconscious and is often the product of growing up in a threatening or unstable relationship or environment. The problem with being a fawner is that a part of us knows that we are going against ourselves, and over time, this breeds disconnection, resentment and relational burnout.

We all have tendencies towards different threat responses. They are all in attempt to feel internally and relationally safe, nothing more.

If we have grown up with trauma or under oppression, most of our life has been about desperately attempting to create a sense of safety. It's like we are fumbling around in the dark looking for something. We have no idea what it looks or feels like, but we know we need it, so we keep searching blindly, without reference.

If our baseline of existence is threat, we have no idea what safety really is, nor do we have a map to get there. So our search is somewhat futile . . . until someone gives us a flashlight and a map to help us on our way.

The Prolonged Effects of Threat and Trauma

Threat begets threat. Trauma begets trauma. We are not meant to survive forever. Even though we have an incredible neuro-circuitry and a cunning psyche that's always trying to protect us, there is a limit to their powers. We may reach our limit when one too many things go wrong (the proverbial straw breaking the camel's back), or we may simply reach it over time. When our capacity to survive, adapt and simulate safety is exceeded, we will spiral into chaos. This may show up in different places. Our fragility is unique, and it is in those fragile places that our trauma will find a way to express itself. It may start to seep through the cracks of our façade, or it may explode it in one fell swoop. The three key places that our trauma may show up are:

Physical Health

Milder imbalances may turn into complex illnesses relating to the nervous system, immune system and endocrine system. Some of the more common diagnoses include: auto-immune conditions like Hashimoto's, chronic fatigue, fybromyalgia, Crohn's Disease, Cancer.[9] There may also be a complex set of symptoms that are non-diagnostic and non-responsive to treatment. When a physical health condition stems from a chronic state of threat, mainstream and symptom-focused treatments are often ineffective as remedies.

Mental Health

Initial experiences of anxiety or depression may develop into more complex conditions as our nervous system becomes more dysregulated and our psychological attempts to seek safety become more creative and intricate. When our nervous system is co-activated, there will be experiences of dissociation and fragmentation that can cause us to feel or be labelled as 'crazy'. Diagnoses that are commonly doled out include: borderline personality disorder, bipolar, dissociative identity disorder, schizophrenia and psychosis.[10] In all

---

[9] Chang, Xuening et al., 'Associations between adverse childhood experiences and health outcomes in adults aged 18-59 years', *PloS one*, vol. 14, 2, 7 February 2019. https://doi.org/10.1371/journal.pone.0211850.

[10] 'Linking childhood trauma to mental health', UK Trauma Council. Available at: https://uktraumacouncil.org/resource/linking-childhood-trauma-to-mental-health. Accessed May 2022.

these cases, the psyche is trying to deal with extreme experiences of threat that it is unable to process and integrate. Modern trauma research is only now waking up to realize that these diagnoses may all be unrecognized trauma and fall under the newer classification of 'Complex Post Traumatic Stress Disorder' (CPTSD).[11] Just like with physical health conditions, the root exists in threat and trauma, so medications and cognitive-driven treatments often act as bandaids, rather than addressing the root cause.

Relationship Troubles

One of the most common places trauma shows up is in our relationships. Sadly, when this happens, our trauma begins to spread like poison into the lives of those around us. The most obvious ways that trauma shows up is through disrespect, volatility and lack of empathy and compassion. As with all trauma responses, this exists on a spectrum from mild disrespect and disconnection, to full-blown abuse and neglect. Often our left brain's attempts to shift our trauma-fuelled relationship dynamics prove futile. If we could be stable, balanced and kind, we would. Nobody enjoys relationship dysfunction. No one is an asshole on purpose. We develop our shitty relationship patterns from the terrified unconscious and the threatened neurophysiological self. It is only when we go back to look through the archives of our relational why and invite a felt experience of growing safety, that we can really start to shift it.

Personal Share

Mental Health and Me

I entered a 'state of trauma' from a very young age. At home, there was grief, anger, resentment, disconnect and drama all around me.

---

[11] Shirley Davis, 'What Is Complex Post Traumatic Stress Disorder (CPTSD)?', CPSTD Foundation, 3 September 2019. Available at: https://cptsdfoundation. org/2019/09/03/what-is-complex-post-traumatic-stress-disorder-cptsd/. Accessed April 2022.

So it became the foundation of my world—internally and externally. I remember knowing that something was wrong, but not having the words to articulate it. Over time, I learned how to deal with the threat around me—how to act in a way that would minimize harm. I also learned how to mask and hide the sense of threat inside me. This ranged from learning how to dissociate and see energy, to self-soothe alone in my room at age seven, to distracting myself with studies and part-time work in later years.

My survival strategies were manageable, maskable and acceptable. I appeared like any other girl in the neighborhood, but inside, I was a mess of emotions—the biggest one being a sense of shame that something was wrong with me and a feeling like I should never have been born . . . that I was a disgrace to the planet. No one knew that shame was a daily disease I was living with because I hid it so well. In my final year of school, I developed depression and anxiety. This was the trauma starting to leak out, and my poor nervous system was no longer able to even pretend to fake it.

With the anxiety and depression came 'unacceptable' behaviours. I had no urge to study and be the best student ever anymore. I started talking back to my mother, who had been volatile, shaming and verbally abusive towards me for years. This resulted in me being taken to the doctor's office and given a garden-variety anti-depressant. I was the problem and I needed to be fixed (or so I was told). After a couple of weeks on the anti-depressant, a manic reaction was triggered in me. Instead of dulling my experience, it sent me into overdrive and I became confused, angry and unstable. Upon being dragged back to the doctor, I was sent to a very expensive psychiatrist, who, after a short assessment, labelled me as having Bipolar 2 on the spot and prescribed me a triple cocktail of meds to 'make me better'. This included a stronger anti-depressant, anti-anxiety and an anti-psychotic.

I dutifully took the cocktail morning and night, and proceeded to travel further and further away from myself. It didn't really fix anything, but took me into varying states of being a zombie, being hyper-anxious and scared, and in the end, just hopeless. It was not long after this diagnosis and medication that I left home after a particularly awful row with my parents, and ended up in all kinds of traumatic experiences, including two counts of sexual abuse. I won't get into this story here as it's an entire book on its own and I hope to write in the future. After four years of mental health madness and medication, my spirit whispered to me: 'Natalia, this is not who you are!'

I checked into a private mental health clinic and proceeded to detox from the drugs. It was one of my darkest times and I entered suicidal and psychotic states. But out the other end . . . came me. After six weeks of detox, daily Cognitive Behavioural Therapy (CBT) and the safety of the clinic bubble, I was deemed as 'normal', stripped of my diagnosis and sent on my way to have a happy life. I had a brief insight into an unaltered version of myself, and the future looked a little brighter. Unfortunately, two years later, my trauma started to show up in the physical body and I was plunged back into darkness.

Physical Health and Me

About two years after I came out of my mental health manifestation, my trauma found a path to express itself through my physical body. I had been a very healthy child—robust and resilient. So the onset of mysterious symptoms came as a shock. I'd just landed my dream job in an advertising company after struggling in a toxic work culture, the year prior. My boss was an amazing woman, who had been on her own path of healing and the company environment really supported work–life balance and authentic connection. All was well in my world. By all rights, I should have started to thrive. But the opposite occurred. Based on what I know now, the increase in safety allowed my body to start coming out of co-activation. The safety allowed me to drop into illness. You know those long days where you are rushing around in full speed like an Energizer Bunny, and when you finally end the day and take a pause, you realize how exhausted you are or that you forgot to eat or that you've got a sore back? It was like that. I had been running in full speed, on survival mode for twenty-three years, and the moment there was a bit of space and a few compassionate people around me, it's as if my body realized it was okay to let go.

The first thing that happened was that my gut shut down. About two weeks into the new role, one morning, I just started vomiting and having diarrhea. And it didn't stop. Hours of it later, I had passed out on the toilet seat. When I finally woke up on the floor in a daze, I knew something was wrong and went to Emergency. That was the first of hundreds of hospital visits over the next decade. I was tested for everything. Hooked up to a drip. About ten doctors passed through my room, all observing, nodding, shaking their heads and mumbling. Occasionally addressing me with a few disjointed questions. I was a specimen. During the two-week hospital stay, I developed a spindle-like rash on my belly and lost 10 kg. I left without answers, incredibly weak and unable to eat anything, other than a few spoonfuls of soy custard at a time. I was told to carry on with life as normal and see the immunologist in a month.

So I went back to work. My team was shocked at how much weight I had lost. My boss was supportive. She knew I needed to pause every two hours to eat a few spoonfuls of custard and then vomit it out in the toilet. And so I did. I adapted to this new way of living and working. 'I'm just like this now.' About a month later, the next symptom presented itself. I was sitting at my desk doing client calls and all of a sudden, my right foot dropped and froze. I couldn't move it. It felt heavy and it was pulling on my ankle. When I realized I couldn't move it, I became terrified. I hobbled over to my boss's desk and let her know that I needed to go to a hospital. And off I went.

This time, tests showed that I had nerve damage in my leg and I was told I would never walk again. A line of purple bruises appeared on my shin. These were the first of the bruises that would later cover my legs and also start to appear on my chest and arms. After every test under the sun, there was still no diagnosis. They even put me in a university training lecture hall and had 100 student neurologists assess me. I have never felt so dehumanized in my life. For them, I was a curious assignment, but I was a terrified young woman who had no idea what was happening to her once-healthy body. Just like the first time, I was sent home with no answers, a leg splint and told I needed to adapt to life without the use of my right foot. This was something I could not accept!

I just knew that I would walk again and with the help of a gentle physio/craniosacral therapist, I was walking within two months. The nervous system has an incredible ability to repair and regenerate. I returned to work during this time and had to figure out how to function with my leg in a splint and a temperamental gut. And I did. I learned how to drive to client meetings with my left foot (very dangerous but it was the only way I could do it.) I learned to pull over and vomit on the side of the road when I needed to. And I learned how to switch on and smile, even when my nervous system was screaming for rest. Ignoring the cries from my beautiful body led to my symptoms getting worse. I started getting alternating foot drops and then my hands and wrists started being affected too. One hand lost all power and ended up in a hard splint for some years. Bruises started to cover my shins and appearing elsewhere on my body. I started to lose weight and my luscious hair started to thin. And I felt tired. So tired. But I kept going, accepting that I had to make life work, even with my deficits . . . especially because of my deficits. And I became known and rewarded for my efforts. Labels of 'strong' and 'brave' became the gold stars that fed me to keep pushing through the illness. I was proud of my ability to continue to fight.

Once the pain started, it became much harder to grin and bear it. The pain crept up on me until it engulfed me. Looking back, I wish that I had been able to link it to the trauma stories and emotions that were trying to express themselves. But I didn't have any context for it. Trauma was not in the spotlight as it is now, and most of the books that now serve as a roadmap to recovery had not yet been written. So pain was just pain. Pure and physical. That's when the heavy medications started. Oxy, Endone, Valium, Lyrica. All the hard stuff. They became the only way I knew how to dull my body's chaos—and the only thing the doctors could do to keep me from crying about my extreme discomfort from the other side of the desk. Countless visits telling them I couldn't go on like this anymore. And each time, just a new script. Up the dose. Add another medication to the list. I felt so much shame sitting in the doctor's office, begging them to make it better. Some of them were kind. Some of them looked at me like I was a nuisance and referred to me the psych department. But the hospital psych couldn't help, other than hold space for my tears and say something encouraging. They looked at me with pity—and oh, how I hated to be met with pity. It only made me feel worse.

No one could help. So again, I learned how to live and do as best I could in the situation. And I did. I always had a strong spirit. I left my full-time role and started a content marketing business that could revolve around my illness. I worked in small bursts from home each day, delivered high-quality written content and then spent the rest of the day in pain, either dissociated in a dark room or at the doctor's office. I built a pretty successful business. But I was sick as hell, confused, angry and exhausted. Over time, my symptoms became worse. One day, both my feet stopped working at the same time, so I went to the hospital for the umpteenth time, and that's when the intravenous treatments started. The doctors were clear that they were only experimenting now. They couldn't figure out what the hell my body was doing. My scans showed inflammation through my brain and spine and a marked reduce in bone density. Fire and depletion. Not a good combination. I committed to a new medical regime of plasma exchanges, immunoglobulin and steroids. At first, it was two days a week, but over the course of a year, it moved to four days a month. So I adapted my life to revolve around a week of hospital stays and the side-effects—the high doses of steroids had me bouncing off the walls and then crashing. I learned the pattern and then I worked around it. I kept this up for seven years. And during that time, I grew my business, had two children (with the help of an amazing surrogate) and learned to live the best life I could. Inside, I knew something was so wrong. And that shame engulfed me on a cellular level. At times, the grief would rise up like smoke and I would allow myself a few tears in the safety of my solitude. But then I would stuff it back down and smile. Until one day, I couldn't. When my son was six months old, my body broke. The pain became so high in my right hip, I was rushed screaming to the hospital. My legs weren't moving and I was just screaming and crying. They shut me up with morphine. I remember lying on the cold gurney in the ER, just wishing for it to be over, in and out of consciousness. At some point, they wheeled me to a ward and my neurologist arrived. He told me that we were going to try a new treatment to get a hold of the pain and reset the nervous system. Ketamine.

Ketamine is medical-grade horse tranquilizer. The intention of it within mainstream medicine is to reboot the nervous system. I was informed that it can make a patient feel 'unbalanced' in the process.

I remember being moved to the ketamine ward and hooked up to the special drip. I could hear the screams of other patients. Either screaming to themselves or barking at nurses. One threw a chair at a nurse and security came with their restraints. My screams were internal. It was as if my voice had disappeared, and instead of contributing to the mayhem, I got lost in the incessant berating internal voice of my psyche. I felt cold, fragmented and terrified. I could feel my spirit trying to check out as I moved further and further away from my body and dissociated from the horrible truth of the world. The ultimate freeze response. And then I remember blackness engulfing me and I was sure that I was closing my eyes to die.

Being in the blackness was neutral. It felt like a holding space. An in-between. It felt safe. I didn't have these words at the time to describe it—in fact, as I feel back to it, there was no judgement or making sense of the blackness. It just was. And it was okay. Although I think the method of using Ketamine to reset is torturous and abusive, something did shift. In the blackness, I came back to nothingness, just for a moment, and I believe in that moment, something profound changed.

I could hear muffled voices. And I started to tune into them. As I did, I began to float above a series of scenes. As I continued to tune into the experience, I saw my children. But it was not them in the past, it was them in the future. I saw various scenes of their life without me. Some were happy, some were sad, or difficult. An incredible desire to go back smashed through my neutrality. 'That's not the life they are meant to have! I have to go back!'

Then there was nothing.

The next thing I knew, I was coming to in the hospital bed. I was frozen and couldn't move. For some time, I just lay blinking. Calibrating. At some point, movement and voice became available to me. I buzzed the nurse and told them to take me off the ketamine, that I was done. I also asked to be connected with a counsellor, I wanted to talk. The last thing I asked for was to be taken in a wheelchair into the hospital garden—I needed fresh air.

These were my first empowered acts of self-care. I accessed agency and choice. I sought out compassionate human connection.

While there were still eighteen months with my illness ahead of me, everything had changed. I wanted to be here. My will re-ignited my life force, and allowed my nervous system to slowly start thawing from its frozen state. My body would later learn to follow.

After spending two months in the hospital, I spent another three months in rehab, and then some months at home, learning to listen to my body, to move, to walk, to rest . . . and once I was strong enough, I had to tune into the stories that it had been holding. A place where there were no words, only sensations and feelings.

> In order to heal, we need to go to our roots and reconnect with our felt primitive self. That's where the trauma is embedded.

A Note on Mainstream Healthcare

I am very grateful for the privilege of medical health insurance and constantly wonder what would have happened if my father had not invested in it for me. Would I be a 'crazy person' living on the streets? There were plenty of such folks wandering the streets in Sydney. Or would I have been found dead in a ditch somewhere? Quite likely.

I am grateful to my father for protecting me in this way . . . one of the only ways he knew how.

While the mainstream healthcare system did not offer me a path to healing, it did keep me safe when I most needed it—it became both my saviour and my oppressor.

These are the thoughts that fuel my philanthropic heart and inspire me to keep educating people on trauma and empowering care-providers to understand and respond in supportive ways as early as possible. I hope, one day, trauma-informed education will be available for all so that trauma healing can take place within this well-intentioned system.

Our Felt, Primitive Self

When we are surviving, the more evolved parts of our brain that help us make sense of our experience don't function as well. Instead, we operate from the primitive part of our brain that is based on first order reality.

First order reality is all about space, movement, direction, speed, texture, smell, taste and colour. Imagine a reptile trying to navigate its way across a rainforest. Let's call him Fred. Fred is simply going to feel his way through moment by moment. He will sense the world around him, detect safety or danger and continue to respond to those signals. Fred is not processing on a complex emotional level. He doesn't consider what he looks like as 'travelling', nor does he consider how the other reptiles in the jungle might be seeing him or judging him. There is no judgement in first order reality.

As babies, we start out in a similar way; sensing, feeling and finding our limits. However, very early on, we start to develop second order reality. The moment we form judgement about our experience, we enter the second order. 'I like this.' 'I don't like that.' 'This is good.' 'This is bad.'

Our second order reality inspires impulse—desire or repulsion. Impulse naturally evolves into agency, choice and action. If we grow up with enough safety and freedom, we develop a natural instinct to reach for what we want and move away from what we don't want, as we assess the level of risk and danger involved with every action. When it comes to trauma, however, this natural evolutionary process isn't possible.

Our second order reality is largely influenced by our parents, the people we spend time with in our early years and our environment.

Have you ever seen a small child fall over and hurt their knee and for a split second, there is no reaction? They often look to their parent to know how to react. There are three ways in which the parental response and situation may play out here:

a) The parent looks distraught and makes a fuss, and the child bursts into tears.

b) The parent smiles calmly and says, 'oh dear, what a fall, let me take a look and give you a hug', and the child will explore the graze while feeling safe.

c) The parent shrilly says, 'You're fine, it doesn't hurt, never mind, look at this nice shiny thing and distract yourself', and the child learns to ignore his/her signals of injury and carry on.

Which kind of parent did you have? And if you're a parent, which kind are you?

The point here is that the way the child's nervous system learns to respond to threat is heavily influenced by external factors—through nurture (or the lack of it). And this isn't even about trauma. This is about how we learn to respond based on what we are shown—trauma or no trauma.

If, as a child, there has been threat all around us, we learn that the world is an inherently threatening place. Threat can look like anything from violence to aloneness. As children, we need the kindness and care of those around us to let us know that the world is a safe place. If we are neglected, we will be quite scared about our ability to survive. Of course, as children, we can't yet make sense of these experiences, nor do we know that we deserve better. They are normal without question.

Threat is normalized and becomes our trauma.

Our neurophysiological, psychological and social development are impaired or coloured by threat. Fear becomes the baseline for how we experience the world. And we have no idea that there is any alternative available. There are three important things to note here about the impact of such a context:

a) Our perceptions and deductions will be skewed as they are filtered with a neurophysiological experience of fear.

b) Our social manifestation of fear will go in one of two very different directions—either we will be terrified of everything, or terrified of nothing. Fear becomes safety. And safety becomes fear. I call this second one 'The Trauma Paradox'.

c) Our ability to assess and respond to threat or safety is severely impaired. For some of us, we don't even know what safety really feels like.

As threat decontextualizes through our experiences, it will be met with shame. The meeting of these two survival-fuelled states is complex, and often unnameable. We just feel like something is wrong and 'Why am I like this?' is often as far as we get. When we don't have an answer, we will quieten our spirit and march on.

As we grow up, we have to learn to fit in with our peers and social expectations. So we do our best to follow suit. But for many of us, there is an experience of masking—learning what is acceptable and performing in order to belong. It's a bit like we are scared wild animals, dressing up in human costumes for fear we will be outed and either eaten alive or cast out of the pack.

When we are bracing against our own sense of threat, everything feels hard. We are constantly expanding against our impulse to contract, hide, curl into a ball and protect ourselves; or the impulse to run, rant, dance and howl at the moon. We can't help but feel like we don't belong. A huge amount of energy is exerted trying to override the nervous system's signals. This often leads to seemingly unexplainable exhaustion. But the fatigue really makes sense if we know what's going on in our circuitry.

The fear and the shame that sit at the heart of our inner world become the locks that keep us trapped, unable feel authentic, expressive and free in the world. Because we can't make sense of our feelings, we shove them down. But the fear and shame live on in the nervous system—non-verbal pantomimes that perform their stories through our physical bodies and our social interactions.

To start to heal, we need to orient away from our human costume and return to our first order reality—the place of feeling, sensing, exploration and navigation. Once we understand our somatic signals of threat, we can meet them with the most compassionate intentions. It's like going back to our young nervous systems and bodies, and being the good kind parent that acknowledges the difficult experience and provides just the right amount of care.

Tuning into Somatic Signals of Threat—Fear and Shame

Once we begin to tune in to our somatic signals of threat, we can start to care for ourselves in a new way. Threat is commonly linked to the emotion of fear. I believe for us humans, there is also the secondary emotion of shame at play.

When we are unable to respond to the impulse of fear, we split. A part of us wants us to respond to our fear, and another part of us tells us that it would be bad or wrong to respond to ourselves. This part of us is shaming us for feeling the fear.

Threat is the amalgamation of shame and fear. In order to start processing the two, we need to first detangle the threads and feel each aspect on its own. Because we often have no words for these experiences, it can help to listen to the story of our body, by exploring our somatic experience.

Somatic Signs of Fear

Fear most commonly presents as different bracing patterns through the body. As with all emotions, fear exists on a spectrum and so the level of adaptation through the body will differ, depending on the degree and duration of the survival response. Bracing is our body's survival protection mechanism. If we fall or if we are at risk of harm in any way, our clever body will contact or 'brace' the muscles required in order to protect from greater harm.

In the case of trauma, we often have old bracing patterns that stay in contraction/protection, or that are triggered intermittently either by trauma triggers, or simply experiences of high stress. To the body, threat is threat, and excessive stress may not be registered any differently than trauma because to the body and the nervous system, it's all about survival. So, experiences of stress can trigger old, hidden trauma.

- Prolonged bracing can cause pain, reduction in mobility, flexibility, agility, and a reduction in oxygen and blood flow.
- We commonly hold fear-bracing patterns in the neck, jaw and shoulders, as well as the hips/psoas. There may also be contraction at the diaphragm or lungs and stomach.
- If we have experienced terror/horror, bracing patterns are often deeper and extend into the toes, fingers, eyes and the deep muscles of the pelvic floor.
- Fear may also affect our posture. Either there will be a tendency to curl forward and self-protect or there will be a tendency to remain rigid.

When we are unaware of our somatic responses to neurological threat, we are often unable to change them. We usually respond in one of three ways:

- Being unaware of the adaptions. 'Bracing patterns? What bracing patterns?'

- Being aware of the adaptions, but ignoring them. 'Yes I have these clinks and twinks in my body, but I'm just like that'.
- Being aware of the adaptations and trying to physically treat them. 'I have a pain or a tightness and I am going to go back to my chiropractor/physiotherapist again and again, but the issue keeps coming back.'

Once we start to explore our bodies through the lens of threat and trauma, we can start to heal and transform in ways that we have never dared to imagine.

- *Sensations often associated with fear:* Swirling, tingling, pounding, buzzing, exploding, tension, or freezing up.
- *Colours often associated with fear:* Black, purple, red, blinding white.
- *Location:* Fear can live anywhere in the body and sometimes feels like is inside our cells, everywhere.
- *Direction:* Fear may want to expel in an upward or downward direction. It may also feel like it wants to emanate out from the entire body in every direction.

Safety is the antidote to fear.

Inviting our bodies to safety can have a profound impact on our ability to come out of bracing and shift out of somatic adaptation and into somatic evolution. As we listen to our bodies, we want to scan for areas of brace and tension, as well as the experience of the spine—is it curling forward or has it become rigid or stiff?

We may affirm again and again to our beautiful bodies, 'You are safe now. The threat is over,' and invite them to slowly unfurl from their trauma-fuelled holding patterns. Depending on the nature and duration of the threat, this may take years of gentle attention and patience.

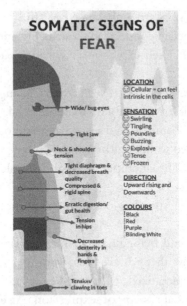

SOMATIC SIGNS OF FEAR

Wide/ bug eyes

Tight jaw

Neck & shoulder tension

Tight diaphragm & decreased breath quality

Compressed & rigid spine

Erratic digestion/ gut health

Tension in hips

Decreased dexterity in hands & fingers

Tension/ clawing in toes

LOCATION
☺ Cellular = can feel intrinsic in the cells

SENSATION
☺ Swirling
☺ Tingling
☺ Pounding
☺ Buzzing
☺ Explosive
☺ Tense
☺ Frozen

DIRECTION
Upward rising and Downwards

COLOURS
Black
Red
Purple
Blinding White

Image 2.2.1. Somatic Signs of Fear

Somatic Signs of Shame

Shame asks us to hide and be quiet.

There can be bracing patterns/holding in the rib cage, diaphragm and abdomen, as well as constriction in the thoracic inlet (upper chest area) and throat. It's common to feel like we have something stuck in our throat or that it closes when we want to speak authentically. We may also tend to cast our eyes down or away to avoid making eye contact, because to show someone the doorways to our soul feels too confronting . . . they may not like what they see. We may also experience a curvature of the spine, tilted or tight hips, and rounded or hunched shoulders. This is a somatic self-protection that occurs to help us feel less exposed in the world and quieten unwanted expression.

When shame runs deep inside us, it feels as if it is in our very cells. Some of the ways somatic shame can show up include:

a)   Feeling a sense of un-belonging in the body or like the body is inherently flawed.

b) Feeling awkward, unbalanced or stiff.
c) Imbalance in connection to sexuality and sensuality.
d) Feeling like self-expression is wrong, bad or impossible.

- *Sensations often associated with shame:* Closing inwards, exploding outwards, or the inability to sense at all.
- *Colours:* Shame often doesn't have a colour, but sometimes is associated with a murky brown colour.
- *Location:* Throat, upper chest and shoulders, spine and hips, and the cells.
- *Direction:* Expanding outwards from the cells.

Acceptance and belonging are the remedy to dissolve shame. We need to know that we are welcome in our bodies and in the world. For the traumatized self, this takes invitation upon invitation, followed by tiny baby steps of expression. At each step, there is a requirement to pause and inquire, 'Is it safe here? Is it safe for me to show myself?' Shame and fear process in tandem; a delicate dance. It is only through time and repetition that our bodies learn that here and now, it is safe to exist, to express, to explore and to create. That we are welcome in the world.

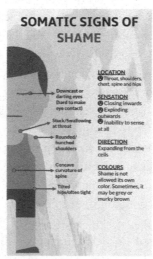

Image 2.2.2. Somatic Signs of Shame

Reclaiming A Sense of Safety and Belonging through Self-Attunement

To heal our fear and shame is a great act of self-love. It requires us to listen, question, welcome, challenge and create safe spaces inside and around us.

The level of compassion we need to hold space for our multi-dimensional, layered and nuanced experience, will test our limits for patience and kindness and ask us to soften our hearts in service of ourselves. We will meet resistance to our healing again and again. It is so much easier to run from ourselves. That's what we know. And the running protects us from having to feel and be with the truth of our trauma. To welcome a transformation that is real and true, we have to choose the process. We have to be accountable for our healing journey. And we have to take care of ourselves with the utmost reverence. This level of attunement and care is often the very thing that we were missing at the time of our trauma; self-attunement is the only thing that will truly help us heal.

Our bodies need to know: 'I hear you. I see you. I welcome you.' And 'It's safe to be here. The danger is over.'

They also need to be asked: 'How would you like to express in this moment?'

The traumatized body is often exhausted, frazzled and fragile. It may also have a desire to simply go wild for a time and then drop into a deep state of rest and repair.

One of its biggest desires is to repair its relationship with the mind. After being disconnected for so long, a series of meaningful conversations are in order. When the soma and the unconscious mind meet, a pathway to incredible healing emerges. We can start to come home to ourselves.

Personal Share

When my healing journey began, the newfound awareness that threat (fear and shame) was present in my body, my mind, and my relational nature, was very distressing to sit with. It bought up huge amounts of grief and anger. It felt a bit like I had been robbed of my life. This distressed, fractured, half-human that I had become was a manifestation of my trauma. 'It's not fair!' I would feel.

As I started to listen to the many layers of fear and shame, they unlocked layer upon layer of deeper emotions to feel, express and integrate. In this way, my process became very nuanced and complex. Each time I would tune into the presence of threat in my body, I would create a safe space to welcome it and explore it. As I sat with my bracing patterns, my racing heart, or my listless, dissociative self, my body would start to express . . . and so would my aching heart. To start with, much of my healing happened in my bed, or on a yoga mat in my healing space at home. I would tune into the places of tension or charge in my body and tell myself, 'I see you, I hear you. I welcome you . . . What and how do you want to express right now?' I would often find my body entering spontaneous twitching sessions, or it would move and arch, or stretch. Sometimes I got the urge to push the wall or the floor or wring my bedsheets or pound something with my fist. And with these movements of the body, often came tears, sighs, screams, growls and occasionally, phrases that I had never uttered before.

'Go away.'
'Get off me.'
'I hate you.'
'Fuck off.'
'I wish I was dead.'
'I wish you were dead.'
'I didn't deserve this.'
'I just want to be held. Please.'

The early stages of my healing were often intense, with high activation and release of trapped energy and emotion. But sometimes, I went into a space of deep rest, hibernation and regeneration. I would allow myself hour upon hour of being curled up in a fetal position, or rocking and staring into space.

There was always a point when I knew the process had completed. I would then spend some time breathing into the spaces and changes, allowing them to become real.

And they were.

The spaces allowed me to feel a little safer—remedying the fear. The changes allowed me to start expressing in new ways—remedying the shame.

Over time, the processing became gentler, and more manageable. I was able to bring my inquiry into two new phases. Firstly, I started to check in with my threat response in real time. I could notice my signs and signals of threat in the present and question their place—'Do I need to feel threatened right now? Or is this an old or unneeded response?' If it was unneeded, I could simply invite my body to switch out of survival mode. My compassionate invitation would include deepening my breath and relaxing the misplaced bracing patterns in my body. Secondly, I started exploring movement as a way to tune into the many bracing patterns that were so ingrained. I started with Yin Yoga and Qi Gong. I would take time to feel into the brace, let my body know it was safe and invite it to let go. 'You're safe now. The threat is over. You're safe.' This would take me into experiences of twitching and shaking, often accompanied by tears. And after each process, I would have a little more ease, a little more flexibility and a freeing up of energy. My vitality began to increase day by day. My capacity for life and connection started to self-correct. It was like coming home to a place inside me that was at once familiar and completely new. Coming home to myself again and again led to incredible feelings of gratitude and deeper layers of grief at the lost years, where there was only the traumatized self.

My process went on to inform the way I work with trauma clients now, and the core of my modality, 'Trauma-informed Relational Somatics'. These days, I tune into myself daily with such normalcy and intention that healing has become a way of life. There is nothing painful about it. It is simply a daily practice of self-attunement, authenticity and compassion, that allows me to stay present and integrated in the world.

Invitation to Self-inquiry

- What is your go-to survival response? Is there more than one? How does it show up physically, mentally/emotionally and relationally? Use the lists above as a reference.
- What are your somatic indicators of fear and shame?
- Do you perceive threat when there may be none? What are some of the instances when this occurs?
- Now ask yourself: How can I enhance my self-attunement? What practices can I put in place?

Somatic Healing Practice

Self-attuning to the nervous system

Lay down on your back. Place your hands where it is comfortable. Become aware of your breath, not needing to change it. Now see if you can tune into your nervous system. If you are a visual processor, you may like to visualize spindles and roots existing throughout your entire being. If you are a kinesthetic processor, you may simply feel the gentle flow of energy moving through you.

Tune in. What state is your nervous system in right now? Fight or flight? Freeze? Co-activation? Or is it resting peacefully? Just notice. Now tune into any areas of tension or charge in the body. Bring your compassionate awareness and your breath there. Does your body want to let go of any tension? Does it simply want to relax and soften, or does it want to twitch or shake a little? Is it safe to allow it? Spend some time letting your body gently let go of the tension or charge in the ways that feel right for you.

Affirm to Yourself

'It's safe to let go of tension. I welcome peace in my nervous system and space in my body.'

Trauma-informed Note:

If you have been holding a lot of charge or tension in the body and this is the first time you are tuning into it, a couple of things may happen:

a) You may become hyper-aware of tension or charge that you were previously unaware of, which you may find confronting.
b) You may find that your body wants to twitch and shake quite a lot. This is okay as long as you feel safe with the process. Remember, as with the other practices, you are in charge and can choose to end the practice at any time.

If you do go into an experience of release, take time to settle afterwards, either by curling up on your side with a blanket or laying on the floor on your stomach. Breathe into the spaces and changes you feel. Self-attune to your nervous system again. By the time you end the practice, you should be feeling an increased sense of safety.

3

The Unconscious Mind

Very little of the way we express in the world is conscious or intentional, until we start to tap into our unconscious mind and expand our awareness. This is the work of self-mastery. The concept of conscious awareness is explored in many self-help paradigms, from hypnotherapy, to psychology, spirituality and somatics. The language each framework uses is different, but the message is the same:

Many of our impulses, feelings and actions are a response to the subconscious or unconscious. If we can understand ourselves and others at this level, we theoretically *should* be able to 'rewire' the way we perceive and engage in the world. In essence, the more we illuminate our unconscious, the greater our capacity for inner peace and relational harmony. When we are conscious, we can move with awareness and intention. This is a powerful and liberating state of being.

The difference between the subconscious and unconscious is not clearly defined.[12] The sub-conscious is historically defined as the part of our consciousness that we are not readily aware of, but can tap into, through self-inquiry. The unconscious is historically defined as the part of consciousness that we are unable to tap

---

[12] Michael Craig Miller, MD, 'Unconscious or Subconscious?', Harvard Health Blog, Harvard Health Publishing, 2 August 2010. Available at: https://www.health.harvard.edu/blog/unconscious-or-subconscious-20100801255. Accessed May 2022.

into. However, I believe that our consciousness exists in layers and pathways that we can continue to illuminate, the more peaceful we become within ourselves and the more masterful we become with our perceptive powers.

When I first started learning about the subconscious as a young hypnotherapist, I was fascinated by our innate power for change. Simply talking to the subconscious could 'cure' all kinds of things, from stress and insomnia, to pain and phobias. However, I quickly became aware that while this was an important piece in healing, it isolated the mind from the nervous system and body. Something was disconnected. I could see incredible mental or emotional changes in my clients, but I could still feel a sense of disease in their bodies. And sometimes, the changes they would experience would be impermanent. Something would trigger them back into their dysfunction. This was true of my journey also—I'd make some progress, but then I would loop back into distress of some kind.

I also found the methods to be ineffective when it came to unexplained anxiety. I later learned that's because the anxiety is an unconscious, felt, somatic experience, as opposed to a cognitive one. Our trauma is unconscious—in the mind and the body, until we begin to bring it into our awareness.

When we address the mind and forget the body, we split ourselves in two.

> The unconscious and the nervous system co-exist. What we experience in the unconscious mind we will also experience in the nervous system.

If we work with one and not the other, we are leaving part of ourselves behind, often causing more internal confusion. We may cognitively understand our experience, but we may not feel any different. And this can make us feel crazy, like something was wrong with us, circling back to the question 'why am i like this?' Or we may be able to calm our nervous system, but still experience triggers and trauma responses that take us into states of survival again and again.

These days, when it comes to healing from trauma, there is a strong focus on healing the nervous system. This is a wonderful development in the modern trauma paradigm; however, there can be a tendency to forget about the unconscious mind and all the unprocessed stories that are playing out again and again. The stories of the body and the stories of the mind need to find a way to reunite. The more we learn about our unconscious, the greater our capacity for internal union.

The Unconscious Library

Our unconscious learns through experience. Every time we experience something, the mind files it away as a reference. When experiences are repeated again and again, the file becomes incredibly thick, and harder to edit or rewrite. These files become the organizing principles that are the blueprint of the internal and relational self. We are nothing but a series of files, pathways and patterns, running on a loop. Our healing journey is about decoding ourselves and returning to a state of curiosity and evolution.

We learn from the people and environment around us. When we are born, we are pure little babies that are primed to learn and form. In fact, ages zero to eight are known as 'the formative years'[13] because we are at our most malleable, in a constant state of learning and development—physically, emotionally and socially. However, the brain does not fully develop until our mid-twenties,[14] so our unconscious foundation is still being set during this time. Scientific findings in neuroplasticity[15] inform us that the brain has the most

---

[13] 'The formative early years of a child's life demand a nurturing environment and attentive care', Early childhood Development Overview, UNICEF, December 2015. Available at: https://data.unicef.org/topic/early-childhood-development/overview/.

[14] Staff Writer, 'At What Age Is the Human Brain Fully Developed?', Reference. com, 3 April 2020. Available at: https://www.reference.com/science/age-human-brain-fully-developed-b909a4ffd8d4f75d. Accessed April 2022.

[15] 'Neuroplasticity', Psychology Today, available at: https://www.psychologytoday. com/us/basics/neuroplasticity. Accessed April 2022.

incredible power to change itself, heal and reform, which would suggest that our capability to alter our unconscious pathways is also infinite.

While the nervous system's primary eternal question is: 'Am I safe or unsafe?', the unconscious is much more complex in its processing. It makes many micro-assumptions, based on its experience to answer the bigger existential questions:

'Who am I?'

'Who am I in the context of this dynamic/relationship?'

'What is a safe and acceptable way for me to exist?'

'What do I need to do in order to belong (or is that even possible)?'

'Where are my limits/boundaries?'

These are all developmental enquiries that are part of our evolutionary process as individuals and as a collective. The answers derive from the external world. Here, external creates internal.

Those of us who grew up within a traumatic family life or facing greater oppression, never had a chance to have a peaceful inner world. Our external world was chaotic, harsh and in some cases, violent. And so our inner world (our unconscious) was born out of these foul ingredients.

EXTERNAL BECOMES INTERNAL

Image 2.3.1. External Becomes Internal

Personal Share

My early life was full of learnings that created a reality where I felt worthless, alone, undeserving, unlovable and unable to express my true nature. My mother was stuck in her own mental health nightmare, depressed and bedridden one moment, volatile and screaming the next, and smiling and loving when we had company. On the one hand, this was totally destabilizing. On the other hand, it was all I knew. There were times when she would tell me she wished I had never been born, call me 'stupid cunt', 'silly little bitch' or 'foul child'.

My father was a prisoner to his own rage. He held it in most of the time, trying to be a good provider and caretaker (and in many ways, he was), but sometimes it would be unleashed upon me through physical violence. The triggers were often untrackable. I remember once, I simply laughed when he was cutting the mulberry tree and a branch snapped back at his face. My uninhibited expression resulted in the worst beating of my life that left bruises all over my legs and hips.

Interestingly, later in life, my hip became incredibly painful and my leg stopped working due to nerve damage. I was told I would never walk again. While I did a lot of body-based work to increase my mobility and learnt to walk, my hip and leg were still very braced and painful. It wasn't until I started processing the physical violence I endured that the pain completely disappeared and I started to access new layers of mobility and flexibly that had never been available to me.

Some of the key learnings imprinted on my unconscious included:
'I am worthless'
'I do not deserve love and care.'
'I deserve to be harmed.'
'My expression is not welcome.'
'My existence hurts others.'
'I am alone in this world.'
'The world is a horrible place.'
These unconscious organizing principles set the foundation of my internal and relational experience in the world.

Who was I? I was a disgusting animal that didn't deserve anything at all, and I had better be grateful for any crumb of kindness or connection. I had better pretended that everything was fine, not only to keep peace, but for my own safety.

Of course, back then, I had no words for this experience. But it silently propelled me. Aside from the very clear relational trauma, there were other learnings that I took on, about what it meant to be an acceptable human being.

a) Work hard, so hard that you run yourself into the ground. Play is for fools.

b) Be the best and when you think you've done well, know that you can do better. Do not rest on achieving anything other than excellence and perfection.

c) Be quiet. Don't speak unless you are spoken to, and even when you are spoken to, remember to be polite and say only the things you know others want to hear.

d) Know your place—this is your culture, your family and the right way to live. Anything else would be wrong and bring shame upon the family.

e) Be afraid—sickness, poverty and exclusion await you, unless you do everything in your power to run from them, which may mean becoming a human pretzel and staying in the lane you've been put in.

How should I have existed? I should have put my head down and focused, studied hard, got a good job, married a nice man, bought a house, had babies and saved for a rainy day, because every day is raining and one day, it will be pouring so hard, I might drown, so I better build a life raft and learn to swim in this bleak fucking world.

While these beliefs permeated my unconscious, they were closer to the surface than the earlier existential trauma learnings, hence easier to access and dismantle.

I had no idea that my experience was unique, or malleable. I didn't know I could change, so I just was. Until I learned that

I had the power to change it all. Delving into the unconscious was an important piece of my healing journey, and it continues to be.

Organizing Principles and the Traumatized Self

Organizing principles are the internal laws that govern the way we experience in the world. They are unconscious and involuntary. They tell us who we are, how we should relate and what is possible (or impossible). They develop based on the way we answer those unconscious existential questions. They are our identity in action.

When our organizing principles originate from trauma, they go against our true nature. Our true nature is to be curious, malleable, compassionate and sharing. None of this is possible in the face of threat. And that's essentially what trauma is: internalized threat.

But on some level, we know that the human we are existing as is not who we are meant to be. It's a very existential feeling—and one that we push down again and again, because we cannot so clearly articulate why we feel this way, nor have any tangible plan to find the version of ourselves that we know exists somewhere . . . just not here in the reality we are living in.

> Our organizing principles dictate the way we express and relate in the world. Expression and relation are the fundamental processes of existence.

Some of the ways our trauma-born organizing principles show up include:

- *Judgement:* We may be quick to classify things as right or wrong, good or bad. This causes us to bypass any process of learning or discernment and can lead us to making poor decisions or closing ourselves off from people and experiences that may bring wonder, beauty and joy into our lives.
- *Ability to Give and Receive Love:* We may have a very specific unconscious understanding that tells us what love should

feel like, and how it should be expressed. This is one of the biggest reasons we may either remain alone or be in a relationship but feel unloved. We simply do not know how to receive love in any other way than our despicable blueprint deems right. We may also be hell bent on giving love in a way that can't be well received by others. (This is something that I have experienced and also witnessed again and again. There may be a feeling of having so much love to give and nowhere to put it, or finding that it simply cannot be received . . . like we are speaking in a different language).

- *Capacity for Risk:* This often goes one of two ways: either 'I will risk everything' or 'I will risk nothing'. So we are either playing with fire (and getting burned again and again) or we are sitting in a prison where nothing ever changes. This most often plays out in the realms of love and money.

- *Self-respect or Self-abandonment:* Those of us with trauma often lack self-respect or the ability to truly care for ourselves. We abandon ourselves again and again, because we don't know what it is to be cared for. And we give in to the demands of others, because that's what we have been taught to do, or because we are so desperate for connection, that we will give up our self-respect in order to taste it…even for a moment…. Even if it hurts us.

As long as the organizing principles remain unconscious, we are powerless to change them. Once we understand the tyrannous laws that drive us, we can start to dismantle them, slowly, surely and with a lot of self-compassion.

Trauma Wounds and Trauma Threads

Our traumatized selves evolve in a complex process, but we can illuminate them by understanding the link between:

- Trauma Wound

- Belief/thought
- Emotion
- Somatic Experience
- Current manifestation

As we continue to unpack the experience of our unconscious trauma, we can illuminate the trauma threads that have created us. An example of a trauma thread may be something like this:

- *Core Trauma Wound:* Psychological abuse by mother
- *Belief/thought:* I am unworthy
- *Emotion:* Shame
- *Somatic Experience:* Feel like curling forward and disappearing into nothing, or hollowness in the chest
- *Current Manifestation:* Feel awkward and uncomfortable in social groups, imposter syndrome, self-sabotage

Most of us have multiple trauma threads at play. We may also have complex trauma threads that combine multiple thoughts or emotions within the same experience. These are often harder to work with because complex emotions are more difficult to make sense of. We may also have multiple trauma threads that stem from the same relationship or experience. Taking time to identify all of our threads in detail creates a blueprint for our healing journey.

It is often the case that either:

a) Trauma threads are hidden from us when we do not have the capacity to process them. Our psyches are very clever that way—we will only reveal to ourselves what we can handle.

b) Trauma threads illuminate in stages so we may feel we have processed a thread and then at a later date, it is retriggered for deeper exploration and healing.

Illuminating our trauma threads is an exercise in self-mastery, compassion and patience.

The more tender a wound, the more self-compassion we need to witness, soothe and repair it.

To Prove or Disprove, That Is the Question

When we seek to understand why our past manifests a certain way in our present, it is important to understand that our traumatized selves will either seek to prove or disprove what we have learned through our trauma. Either we plunge straight into the trauma wound, proving it true, or we rebel against it, desperately trying to prove it untrue. In some cases, we may do both at once, which again causes a feeling of inconsistency, chaos and confusion.

If we continue with the example of shame or worthlessness:

a) *Proving Shame/Worthlessness:* 'My expression and relationships show me that I am not good enough/not worthy, and that other people are always better or more valuable than I am, because this is what my trauma wound told me.'

b) *Disproving Shame/Worthlessness:* 'My expression and relationships are an attempt to show myself (and everyone else), that I am worthy and in some cases, I will show others that I am more worthy than them, because this soothes my trauma wound.'

Quantum psychology suggests that we have one core wound, called the 'false core', and we create a 'false self' trying to disprove it. I found learning this framework incredibly helpful; however, my experience in processing my own trauma and working with clients has been that we have many trauma wounds that create an incredibly complex self, which will seek to either prove or disprove each wound. The manifestation of each wound may change over time. Whether we tend to prove or disprove our trauma wounds will depend on the ever-changing stimulus around us and what our psyche deems is a 'safe way to exist' at any given time, within each relationship dynamic.

Image 2.3.2. Proving or Disproving Our Trauma

Identifying Core beliefs

Core beliefs are the identity statements we learn about ourselves as the result of our formative relational experiences. They go on to shape the way we relate to ourselves, other people and the world, in general.

Some of the common core beliefs that may shape us if we grew up with trauma or under oppression include:

'I am worthless'
'I am unlovable'
'I am undeserving'
'I do not (or cannot) exist'
'I am alone'
'I am weak'

These core beliefs are our external relational experiences internalised. 'You are' becomes 'I am'. In order to heal, we have to illuminate the harmful core beliefs and the trauma wounds they derive from, and make a conscious choice not to allow them to lead the way we live and relate in the world. In my experience, in addition to illuminating them, healing requires us to feel them deeply, let them rise into our awareness, our hearts and our bodies and compassionately release them. Only then can we truly let go and create a new template of beliefs.

Internal Does Not Create External—Spiritual Bypassing

Looking through the lens of spirituality, one is often taught that our inner world creates our outer world. Many mainstream self-help and spiritual teachings encourage us to simply think differently in order to manifest a better reality. 'If I say that I am worthy again and again, I will feel worthy.'

The truth is, when our unconscious derives from trauma, this is not possible. And in trying to simply will our way into a new life, a new self, we leave our traumatized selves trapped even deeper inside us. It's a bit like playing dress-up. We put on a costume and simulate a different reality. But our tragic truth still exists beneath the surface. We may manifest a brilliant external world, but our inner world either does not change, or we become experts at internal shape-shifting, compartmentalizing, hiding from ourselves; until something comes along and triggers the trauma in the form of such a violent expression that we can no longer pretend that it's not there.

We spend a lot of energy emulating the energy of an angel running from the demons inside us.

Many of us who go down the route of spiritual bypassing still have that pesky voice inside us, shaming or berating us. Another common symptom is reactive behaviour, volatility and disrespect— almost as if we had a Jekyl-and-Hyde personality. Love and light one minute, rageful monster the next.

The path to healing begins not with shaming ourselves into denying our inner world. In fact, healing asks for the opposite. It asks us to acknowledge the painful truth of our trauma and nurse ourselves back to some kind of baseline where it's safe to be truly authentic. Rather than project love and light into the world, we need to direct it inwards towards ourselves.

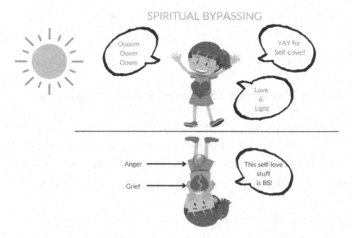

Image 2.3.3. Spiritual Bypassing

Personal Share

I've had a very interesting relationship with my spirituality. Today, I would say that I am a deeply spiritual person, but I do not lead my life through it, nor do I seek to impress my beliefs on others. In the depths of my illness, meditation was offered as a solution to me and as I have explained earlier, this made me incredibly angry. How dare someone tell me that I could meditate or pray away my pain?

Later on in my journey, however, I did turn to spirituality. It started to creep into my awareness through receiving massages. Gentle massage was one of the very few things that could ease my pain and also turn down my anxiety—which back then, was incredibly debilitating. The therapists that I connected well to and returned to again and again were spiritually inclined and had trained in energy healing modalities from Reiki to Quantum Healing, Kinesiology and all kinds of other obscure spiritual frameworks. I didn't understand any of it, but I knew that a certain therapist's touch and presence made me feel better. I was still poo-pooing the idea that I could love myself to health and happiness, but I could not deny the facts—when I had the treatments, I felt better, even if for a short time. I would leave the sessions feeling so much relief and an onset of peace. But it would only be a matter of hours, or as much as two days, before I was plunged back into pain and distress. I didn't know what else to do, so I just kept going back to be soothed, hoping that at some point, it would stick. It didn't. But any reprieve was a welcome one.

Some of the therapists that I never ever went back to, adopted the role of healers and spiritual teachers. They would tell me things like 'You need to practice self-love,' or 'send healing light to your chakras', or tell me that they could feel my anger and my pain. This was the most incredibly harmful and triggering thing to hear! It caused me to feel more pain, more anger and a heightened sense of shame that I was already trying so hard to stuff down. Some of the more egoistic ones told me that by the end of the session, my pain would be gone, that they would pull out some dark energy or spirit and in effect, be my saviours. This, of course, was really confusing for me at the time. What? I have a dark spirit inside me? I am possessed? You are going to do psychic surgery on me? I didn't know whether to run for the hills or get down on my knees and thank these mortal godsends. Most of the time, I just nodded and smiled, lay there while they completed the healing, lied and said that it was a profound experience and left feeling a sense of hopelessness and disconnect. I never returned to those therapists. Now as a teacher, I place a strong emphasis on power dynamics, ego and the role of the therapist and the importance of not telling a client who or what they are, as it is incredibly re-traumatizing and disempowering.

At that stage, I still did not feel connected to the concept of spirituality. I was fumbling around in the dark, trying anything and everything to feel better . . . just enough to keep going.

The first time I opened myself up to spirituality properly, was after my blackest shut-down period. I had asked the doctor for special leave from the hospital to have a Reiki massage. I remember even travelling to and from the healing centre was so incredibly painful. Every jerk of the car sent shockwaves of pain through my fragile body. I needed to be taken in a wheelchair from the bed to the car, then be assisted a few steps from the curb to the healing centre. As a regular client, the owners knew me and had strongly advised for me to see their resident shaman. I had no idea what a shaman was, but I was so desperate to feel better that I would try anything at all. In the first session, the shaman waved white sage all around me and started chanting. I had never heard chanting before, so I felt a bit overwhelmed, but something unexplainable told me that I was safe. When she finished, she gently placed her hands on my shoulders, and I immediately started to cry. For the next hour, she gently massaged my body and the tears started to flow and I trembled gently.

After the session, she told me that I had the capacity to heal myself and that she would like to support me. I had no idea what this meant, but I already felt an incredible trust with her. She asked me to opt for a series of sessions over a few months, once I got home from the hospital. She offered to come to my home while I could not travel due to my pain and immobility. When I mentioned that money was tight due to all the medical bills, she offered to reduce her rate by a huge amount. She made the treatment completely accessible to where I was in my journey. She didn't promise to heal me, but she offered to guide me, to walk by my side while I learned about myself. And so we set forth on a journey together. Every session was different. Sometimes she would massage me and I would cry and shake. Sometimes, she would take me on a past-life journey. Sometimes we would talk. She also equipped me with homework after each session. I remember one of the first things she asked me to do was to lie on the grass each day and see if I could listen to the heartbeat of the earth. I found this incredibly preposterous. But I tried it anyway. For about an hour, I felt nothing and felt all kinds of stupid! But then there it was . . . The ba-boom of the earth's heart.

Life—I was connecting to life. And as I lay there, I began to notice that my own heartbeat was synchronizing with the earth's. And my breath deepened and my body relaxed a little. While she never explained why she was prescribing these things, looking back now, I understand that this was an exercise in belonging. For the first time, I belonged to the earth and I felt a sense of relational harmony. And I believe this was a pivotal moment in my journey— to no longer be an alien in the world. The changes I experienced through this time were small, indescribable but palpable. I just felt a little bit more at ease with being here. My journey with the shaman came to an abrupt end when my family relocated to Singapore for my then husband's job. But I believe she had removed what I fondly call 'my healing plug'. The healing was in motion, and I just needed to follow the path that was unfolding before me.

When I got to Singapore was when my journey of processing my trauma began. It was an intuitive process that at the time, I could not explain through the lens of trauma, psychology, neuroscience or somatics. I chose to categorize it as a 'spiritual awakening'. I found myself exploring spirituality with intention. Reading books, going to meditation workshops, yoga classes and engaging with spiritual social circles. I travelled through Asia, studying all kinds of modalities that were steeped in spirituality. But something felt incomplete. The intention towards enlightenment felt forced and false. It felt like one giant simulation. One of the side-effects of my trauma healing was that I became incredibly intuitive—it was like I could feel, sense and foresee (it scared me quite a lot, actually), so when I was met with these spiritual beings, it was like I could see the truth beneath the surface: the shame, the anger, the confusion and the fear. At the time, I didn't know what spiritual bypassing was or anything about the traumatized psyche, really, I just knew that I was uncomfortable and that something was wrong. The more I learned about trauma healing and the fragmented psyche, the more I understood that this kind of spirituality was a trauma response—nothing more than suppression and a psychological adaptation in order to belong to another group, culture and reality.

Initially, my presentation as a young hypnotherapist and craniosacral therapist was a spiritual one. People came because they thought I was some magic human nymph who could heal them. I spent a lot of time telling them that they needed to go on their own journey as projections do no favors. While everyone wanted a healer, I knew they needed something else. So I decided to distance myself from spirituality.

Not long after this repulsion from spirituality, I decided to partner with a prominent Chinese doctor to open a health clinic in Singapore. The idea was to make trauma healing mainstream and use the medically adjacent and accepted clinic as a trojan horse. Our mission meant that I had to give up any spiritual expression in order to be accepted by the medical world. And so I did . . . for a time.

Being a clinic director served to ground my work as a trauma therapist and create a footprint for trauma and somatic healing in Asia, but it asked me to deny a big part of myself—the part that believed in the magic of the spirit, the interconnectivity of everything and the soul's purpose.

Through my years as a clinic director, I noticed the collective world becoming more and more open to the idea of trauma, spirituality and healing, and it is only more recently that I have felt safe enough to move more authentically and claim my complex identity as a well-respected therapist and educator *and* a deeply spiritual being. Perhaps this is a part of my own healing journey—to claim who I am in my entirety. Perhaps it is a function of our collective evolution. Perhaps these things are one and the same.

The reason I share about my spiritual journey here is to encourage an inquiry that seeks for hope, transformation and light, but does not avoid or bypass the dark. In fact, these polarities can only exist in relationship. Our capacity for light is a direct replica of our capacity for darkness. Healing asks us to allow our pendulum to swing into the unconscious and carry us into the light, the conscious. In the end, whether we classify ourselves as spiritual or not, doesn't really matter. What matters is that we are seeking to understand the unconscious. To answer the question 'why am I like this?'

My biggest takeaway from exploring my unconscious through multiple lenses was that I was not so singular—the external and internal did not match. And my internal self seemed to lack cohesion and clarity. I later learned that this was called fragmentation.

Invitation to Self-inquiry

- What are the organizing principles that live in your unconscious library?
- What are the trauma threads that you can identify? Identify the trauma wound, the belief/thought, the emotion, somatic experience and its current manifestation.
- Do you prove or disprove your core beliefs?
- Do you tend to bypass your pain to share love and light in the world?
- Now ask yourself: How can I start to turn all my love, light and compassion towards myself? How can I begin to heal my trauma wounds with this intention?

Somatic Healing Practice

Letting Go of What Does Not Serve and Welcoming What Heals and Supports

Recycling Energy

Lay down on your back on the floor or on the bed. Connect to your breath. Once you feel settled, connect to your inhalation. Breathe in energy that heals and supports you. Connect to your exhalation. Release what no longer serves you. Continue inhaling and exhaling, thus recycling your energy.

Affirm to Yourself

'I breathe in what heals and supports me, I let go of what does not serve me.'

You may like to stay with this process for some time (even stay here for some weeks or months) as you begin to shift your core experience. Once you feel ready, you can move on to a more advanced practice of working with your trauma threads.

Releasing Trauma Threads

Identify one of your trauma threads to work with. Find a comfortable position on the floor or in your bed. If possible, bring your hands to the part of your body where the experience is most present. Breathe into it with compassion. Connect to the somatic sensations, the emotion and the thoughts that go with it. If you are able to link it to a past memory or relationship dynamic, allow it to enter your awareness. Acknowledge that this wound has shaped you until this moment. Breathe in to connect with it, and as you exhale, let it go. Send it out of your breath, your body, your being. Repeat the inhalation to connect, and exhale to let go. Do this a number of times. If it feels like your body wants to move, twitch or shake, allow it. If tears come, welcome them.

Affirm to yourself

As you exhale: 'I let go of the wound that does not serve me. I let go of <insert the word here, e.g. unworthiness>.'

As you inhale, welcome the new core belief you wish to instill in yourself: 'I am <insert new core belief, e.g. worthy>. I welcome a new way of being that embodies this.'

Repeat this a few times (e.g., exhale unworthiness, inhale worthiness).

You may reach a point where you feel that there is a natural ending or pause in the experience. At this time, move into a position to integrate, either laying on your side under a blanket, or laying on your stomach. Take time to find a sense of peace in the body, then orient to the room around you, sit up, rub your palms together and take a sip of water. You may like to journal about the experience to integrate.

Trauma-informed Note:

This practice may be highly activating if you are holding unprocessed trauma. Before beginning, it is important to gauge your capacity and readiness for processing at this level. To practice with intent not to re-traumatize, you need to have enough capacity to stay present in the body and the room around you, and ensure that any memories remain as memories and you do not regress to re-experience them.

If you are unsure, you may like to test this practice out by starting in a seated position, with eyes open. If you feel any sense of fear about proceeding or moving to a laying down position, this indicates that you are not yet ready for this process. If possible, now is a good time to seek support from a professional somatic therapist or you may wish to continue building safety in the nervous system with the somatic practices from Part I. Remember, healing cannot be rushed or forced. When you are truly safe enough to process, it will emerge easefully, without any need to force it out. Please place your sense of safety above all else. There is healing simply in the embodiment of this intention.

Once we understand our unconscious nature, we can begin to explore our complexity. We can welcome the existence of re-integration of our fragmented selves.

Part III

The Fragmented Self

Those parts of ourselves that we hide from the world, are aching for a place to be seen, heard and held.

We are not singular, linear or sensical. Trauma or no trauma, we are all fragmented. We are an amalgamation of many fragments (or parts) that co-exist to create our complex selves. Many of us try to exist in a singular or formulaic and congruous way, which takes us away from the beauty of our natural nuance and the creative, evolutionary nature of the self. We block ourselves from being the fluid and ever-regenerative creatures that we inherently are.

We do this because something tells us that to exist in the glory of our complexity would be wrong. Therefore, we invalidate the true nature of our own existence. We fragment.

1

Fragments

Fragments are aspects of our psyche that form in response to external stimuli. We have many influences; therefore, we have many fragments. Our fragments often develop in early life, when we are at our most malleable. However, my belief is that we are always susceptible to developing more fragments when we are faced with acute or prolonged states of threat; when we are traumatized. We are generally not taught to understand ourselves as fragmented, or as having parts. The lack of education and awareness about the fragmented self often leads to a warped sense of identity and disconnect, and the disallowing of our innate complexity. We become dis-integrated.

When fragments are integrated and accepted within us, we can hold them gently with conscious awareness and care. We can allow ourselves to be complex, textured and rich. We can be forgiving and welcoming of our incongruity. When we are integrated, we are internally inclusive and self-accepting. We hold an internal sense of belonging.

When fragments are dis-integrated, they become suppressed and distressed, jostling around for a space where they feel safe, seen, heard and welcome, both inside us, and in the world.

When we are dis-integrated, we are internally exclusive and self-abandoning. Existing in a state of dis-integration, we may feel like we don't make sense. We may feel a sense of internal conflict or chaos (which can show up as incessant internal chatter, discord or argument). Externally, we may find ourselves rebelling without clarity, or acquiescing into submission (even when we know something or someone isn't good for us). Our unconscious disintegrated fragments will often lead us to make decisions that take us further away from ourselves, sometimes leading us into the most dangerous and bleak situations. Most often, we will feel incredibly alone because when we abandon parts of ourselves, they do exist alone in the dark corners of our psyche; like naughty children who have been put in a corner with dunce hats on.

Our disintegrated fragments may exist in three different states:

- **Unconscious and Hidden**

  These fragments have been packed away so deeply within the right-brain unconscious that we cannot even sense them. They lead us, and haunt us like ghosts. The reason that they are unconscious, is because we do not have enough capacity to witness their experience or process their origins, which often lie in childhood experiences of abuse or neglect. These fragments will only become available for processing once we have established a greater sense of internal safety and belonging in the world.

- **Conscious and Unexpressed**

  This is the most common kind of fragmentation. We are aware of a constant internal negotiation, or a disconnect between what we feel and how we express. We can hear the fragments' voices, but we either ignore them, or tell them to be quiet. Essentially, we are at war with ourselves, often re-enacting the dynamics that have caused us to suppress these parts of ourselves in the first place. We become our own oppressors. Our real oppressor's name is shame. In order to reintegrate these fragments, we need to not only invite the fragments into expression, but we need to work with our shame and transform it into self-compassion. Only then will we allow these fragments an opportunity to express themselves.

- **Hijackers**

  Hijackers are fragments that exist unexpressed just beneath the surface of our external self. They may be conscious or unconscious. They are often triggered by people and situations that are energetically similar to past experiences of disempowerment, abandonment or shame. When we have hijacker fragments, we tend to appear as inconsistent, unstable or manic. Our switch can flip at any time and both ourselves and those around us are often powerless to navigate around potential volatility. It may feel as if we need to wrap ourselves in cottonwool in order to maintain a sense of equilibrium, and for others, there may be a feeling of walking on eggshells so as to not trigger us. In my opinion, these are the easiest to process as they are already expressing themselves, and merely need a safe place to tell their stories.

A large part of our healing journey is about understanding our fragmented selves and welcoming all our parts into the compassionate care of our conscious healing self. The goal is internal coherence.

Personal inclusion is the cornerstone of inner peace.

Somatic and Relational Signs of Fragmentation

Until we bring our fragmented selves into conscious awareness and begin integration, we will only know of them through our unconscious, somatic and relational experience. Janina Fisher's work on fragmentation informs us that our fragmented selves live in our right unconscious feeling brain, and often cannot be made sense of by the logical left brain.[16] This is because when we experience trauma, a functional split occurs between the two hemispheres of the brain. Our felt experiences can no longer be made sense of. They speak to us in code: through sensations, movements, colours, images and behaviours or actions. When an unconscious fragment is either seeking a place to express, or has been triggered, we will sense it and we will express it in a dynamic relationship (though often without conscious meaning or reason).

Our role in healing our fragmented selves is to decipher the code from the right brain and make sense of it with the left brain. Essentially, we help the two parts of the brain to start communicating again.

When a fragment is seeking expression, somatic sensations may include tingling, buzzing, heat, cold, upward or downward moving energy, pressure from the outside coming in, pressure from the inside exploding out, tension in the body (particularly the hips, back, chest, neck and head, tinnitus, dizziness or unexplained pain). We may also start to see or feel colours, symbols or images in our mind's eye.

Relational manifestations may include:

- Neediness/clinginess
- Disconnection (stonewalling or pushing away)
- Picking a fight
- Power-mongering (shaming or manipulating)

When we can assign ownership of our organizing principles, reactive and incongruous behaviour, to a fragmented part of us, we begin to make sense. And it is only then that we can begin to release our shame and access the self-compassion we need to start the journey towards re-integration, cohesion, personal inclusion and inner peace.

One of the most profound things I realized (and that I often tell my clients) is: 'In the context of trauma, I/you/we make perfect

---

[16] Janina Fisher, *Healing the Fragmented Selves of Trauma Survivors: Overcoming Internal Self-Alienation* (Oxon: Taylor & Francis, 2017).

sense. There is nothing wrong with me/you/us.' The moment that there is a perfectly good reason to explain how maladjusted we feel, shame immediately begins to dissipate and we can start to welcome ourselves into our own compassionate care.

Fragmentation and The Inner Child

Re-integrating the fragmented selves is an extension of inner child work. The term 'inner child' was first used by Carl Jung (one of my greatest influences).[17] However, the term is now used across many therapy, healing and spiritual modalities, and has been somewhat diluted in its meaning. In the simplest frameworks, we are asked to consider what our inner child wants and needs that it didn't receive. The problem here is that because we are fragmented, communicating with a singular inner child often misses the mark.

Rather than speak to one child, we need to learn about each fragment: who they are, when they developed, what happened to them, what they would have needed and what may be supportive of them in the present moment. Most of us will have many aspects of our inner child that need attention and a safe place to tell their story.

Not Everything Is Trauma . . . Or Is It?

When I first learned about fragmentation, it was in the context of the traumatized self.

Re-integrating the fragmented self is one of my areas of specialty as a therapist. When it comes to trauma, these can be so deeply cemented, unconscious and expertly hidden, and it is only through a truly safe therapeutic dynamic that these traumatized parts will emerge to tell their story, which is essential for healing

---

[17] For an accessible explanation of Carl Yung's 'Inner Child', please see Isabelle Pikörn, 'Noticing, Healing and Freeing Your Inner Child', InsightTimer Blog, available at: https://insighttimer.com/blog/inner-child-meaning-noticing-healing-freeing/. Accessed April 2022.

to occur. There's a requirement for the therapist to be able to sense the unexpressed fragmentation and 'reach in' to communicate with it, and invite it to start expressing and integrating. If you consider a scared child, it takes an incredible amount of safety and trust for it to come out of hiding and start to speak. If you consider a super soldier in combat, it is going to take the wisest peacekeeper to encourage them to put down their weapons and start peace negotiations.

However, in recent years, I have been noticing that deep fragmentation exists in most of us, and that this is a function of the modern world, which is, sadly, a traumatized one. The markers of the traumatized self show up even in people who had seemingly safe and loving early lives. Here, the stimulus causing fragmentation has nothing to do with early attachment. It has nothing to do with lack of environmental or social safety. It derives from a world gone mad.

Invitation to Self-inquiry

- Are you aware of a sense of fragmentation?
- How do your fragments show up somatically? Relationally?
- Are you aware of your 'inner child'? Expanding your awareness to fragments, can you consider that your inner child perhaps has multiple fragments?
- Now ask yourself: Am I welcoming my fragmented self? Or am I denying or excluding parts of myself?

Somatic Healing Practice

Remembering the Forgotten

Lay on your back on the floor or in your bed. Allow yourself to settle. Breathe into your entire body. Into the cells. Acknowledge which parts of your body tend to get the least of your attention. It may be a forearm or wrist, the tops of your feet, your pinky finger or the ribs right under your arm pits. Choose one part to share your time and attention with during this practice. Gently place your hand over this part of your body. Tune into it with your compassionate awareness and your breath. How does it feel to care for this part of yourself? You may like to keep your hands still and soft, or gently stroke this area. Does this part of you have a story to tell? Can you listen to it? You may like to journal your experiences.

Affirm to Yourself

'I remember you are here. You are no longer forgotten.'

Trauma-informed Note:

If you are not used to receiving care, or have grown up with a lack of emotional or physical care, this practice may bring about feelings of grief. Ask yourself if it is safe to welcome them. If you feel overwhelmed, you can move into the 'Inviting Safety' practice at the end of Part I Chapter 2. Remember, you can come out of the practice at any time by orienting to the room, rubbing your palms together and taking a sip of water.

2

Fragmentation in the Modern World

The modern world asks us to fragment. It asks us to deny so many aspects of ourselves, not only to belong, but to merely survive. Survival and inclusion equal 'success' in the modern times.

Over time, as humanity, we have lost our way. It wasn't always like this.

In recent centuries, the importance of creativity, beauty, community and belonging has become secondary to the desire for money, power and status. As we have shifted away from the realms of the felt, and into the very mental, left brain-driven quest for modern success, we have created hustle. We have created polarity. We have created 'every man for himself'—aloneness. Ironically, the world that we have created denies us the things that we need and crave for to live life with internal peace and relational harmony.

And therein lies the existential confusion that exists in most of us—the feeling that we can't quite put our finger on . . . that something is wrong here.

The reason we feel like things aren't quite how they are meant to be is valid. They aren't.

The world we created asks us to stray from our humanness and become focussed and somewhat singular in our quest for 'success' (aka survival and inclusion). Modern-world 'success' can only be reached if we block out a lot of our feeling state—our impulses for curiosity, creativity (aka diversity), play, rest and reprieve. To 'make it', we need to abandon parts of ourselves. We need to fragment. And in order to make peace with this gross state of self-deprivation, we have to pretend that we have chosen this—that we are happy with our lives and who we are. To admit the truth would be too devastating. The truth is that most of us are not happy at all. We don't want this life in this survival-forged world. The truth is also that most of us don't have the power to change it, because we live within structures or systems that will not allow us to be complex, intuitive and evolutionary. They ask us to be singular and work towards their goals, rather than our own. We are oppressed.

In order to belong here, we have to orient only to the parts of ourselves that are deemed as worthy of inclusion by modern-world benchmarks. These parts are steeped in survival—fear and shame. They are obedient and co-dependent. They are repressed. And they are often impatient and frustrated.

Belonging vs. Individuation

To belong and to individuate are two of our biological imperatives. We need each other in order to survive and thrive. But we also have an in-built impulse to diversify, individuate and be unique. Sadly, many systems in the modern world ask us to forgo our individuation process (either partially or entirely), in order to belong. When this existential ultimatum is presented to us, we will have one of the two main responses:

a) We choose belonging; we forgo or adjust our individuation.
b) We choose individuation; we run or rebel from the pack.

In either instance, there are consequences because on a primordial level, we need both experiences to feel like all is well in the world.

The consequences of belonging over individuation may include:

• Feeling stifled/unexpressed

- Misconnection (feeling a sense of aloneness, even when in relationships)
- Loss of self (not knowing who we really are)

Over time, and left unaddressed, these experiences compound into either resentment and anger, or apathy and depression. Sometimes, a strange mix of both. Without existential inquiry, we feel like something is wrong with us (shame, again!) and we either internalize it, which sends us deeper into our fragmented experience, or we begin 'acting out' and leaking our distress into the world, which often hurts others. When our expression incites harm, we are perpetuating the continued chaos and trauma in the world. Our inability to contain and transform our own turmoil is the foundation of war.

In my opinion, it is our inability to metabolize our individual and collective trauma that is at the core of all suffering.

The consequences of individuation over belonging may include:
- Ostracism/rejection
- Misconnection (feeling a sense of aloneness, even when in relationships)
- Self-righteousness/lack of empathy

Over time and if left unaddressed, these experiences may lead to a feeling of being misunderstood or excluded, which in turn leads to the same end state of either resentment and anger, or apathy and depression. Sometimes, a strange mix of both. Either way, we feel like something is wrong with us. In this manifestation, it is more common to blame the system rather than the self, but underneath, we likely still feel inherently excluded and alone—which no matter how much we tell ourselves is fine . . . it simply isn't. It goes against our prime biological imperative.

In a world that asks us to fragment, deny our impulses and pack parts of ourselves away, we can never truly be valid. Not in our entirety.

This is why so many of us feel like something isn't quite right. We may meet all the markers of success, but inside, we may still feel some kind of dissonance, and then tend to shame ourselves for not being happy with what we have. This is typically known as 'existential crisis'.

Misconnection and Existential crisis

Misconnection is a term I use a lot. It is the experience of being in relationships, but not feeling true human connection. The kind that allows us to soften, attune and resonate in our vulnerability and complexity. The kind where we can be just as we are, without armouring or shape-shifting. The kind where we feel true belonging.

When we are fragmented and disconnected from our true nature, true human connection is an impossibility. Intimacy is elusive.

After prolonged states of living as a version of ourselves and engaging in relationships where we can't receive the human connection we desire and need, we *are* going to feel like something is wrong. We *are* going to crave for more. The question is: What we do with that craving?

There are three ways in which we may respond to our deepest desires for something more:

a) **Denial**

We deny it and slip into a deeper state of apathy and self-abandonment. This option often brings with it a false expression of 'detachment and acceptance'. In order to protect our fragile psyches from the truth of our experience, we convince ourselves and the world that we are practising detachment and acceptance—being mindful and grateful. When our spiritual enlightenment comes with a feeling of loss or lack, and we keep having to tell ourselves we are content, we are not detached—we are delirious.

b) **Self-soothing**

When we cannot quieten the cravings, but do not feel safe to really listen to and follow them, we may self-soothe or scratch our itch in other ways. This is most commonly seen through expressions of substance abuse, infidelity or love addiction, spending sprees and other behaviours that are either self-sabotaging, or relationally sabotaging. Most of us know these behaviours are harmful, but we engage in them anyway, because it's the only way we know to shift the feeling of internal discord.

c) **Disruption**

When we choose to honour our cravings and follow our impulses, there will be some kind of disruption. This may be to leave a job, end a long-term relationship, disconnect with our family of origin or move countries. This is the only response where we choose ourselves. The decision to choose ourselves often creates turmoil for those around us. Because we require belonging, above all, many of us don't ever go to disruption, because we fear the relational disharmony it will ensue.

Personal Share

There have been two occasions in my life when my existential cravings were strong enough for me to enter a state of disruption. The first was my decision to leave the mainstream medical system within which I had been operating for nearly two decades. The second was to leave a marriage with a good, kind man—the father of my children.

Both decisions were terrifying and seemingly nonsensical in the context of their lived paradigm.

Both decisions went against all trusted advice.

Both decisions led to temporary chaos and destruction.

Both decisions led to incredible healing, transformation and self-reclamation.

The thought that went with the felt experience was 'I don't want this life anymore'. It was a quiet voice that over time, became a distinct bellow that could no longer be ignored.

I had experienced this feeling many times since I was a young girl, but I had regularly quashed it. I was disempowered and held no hope of a different reality, until I developed enough internal safety to reconnect to a very wise part of myself.

When I started to do my healing work, I noticed the emergence of a new part of myself that was calm, strong, kind, compassionate, intuitive, discerning and brave. Over time, she became present and powerful enough to hold the space for all my other parts. I call this part the 'conscious healing self'. Some people say that this is the 'true self' or 'essence' or 'god self'. On reflection, I believe that I was starting to form a healthy human centre that I had never had an opportunity to cultivate because of the lack of safety and emotional support in my early life. She was able to hold space for all of my fearful fragments and lead the way as I exploded my world and found a new way to exist. Twice.

Disruption has consequence.

Here, I will share about my decision to leave the medical system.

I'll reserve my sharing about leaving my marriage, perhaps, for a later book, because to be honest, I am still processing this change, and I have found it is best to wait to share until clarity of expression arises.

I bravely made the decision to end medical care after eleven years on hardcore medication and seven years on intravenous treatments. At the time, I was taking forty-two pills per day (putting together my prescription-junkie pill box was a weekly nightmare), and I was having monthly intravenous treatments—three days per month as an in-patient in a hospital. While I was incredibly scared of what would unfold, I knew that I had to do it. My conscious healing self guided me through the fear. As I started to delete medications from my 'diet', my body went into huge withdrawals and ultimately, a healing crisis. There was everything from opioids to nerve blockers, blood thinners, immunosuppressants and more. The intensity of the pain, the heart palpitations, the gut detox, the swelling and rashes were insane. My eyes also started to swell up and close over. My body was literally going crazy.

There were many moments that I thought I was going to have a heart attack or that my violent trembling would turn into a fatal seizure. But that new part of me—it's like she was watching over me with her warm hand on my shoulder, letting me know that I would be okay. I spent hours every day meditating, having warm baths and sleeping. I also started having memories about my experiences of abuse—my trauma was coming up to be processed. I wanted to shut it all back down, but again, my conscious healing self told me that this was the pathway to a better reality . . . that this process was essential. So I went with it. I let my body have its experience for the first time in my life. I let it writhe. I let it contract. I let it sleep. I let it heave. I let it sob, wail and scream. I held the space for my truth to emerge, with no tactics to deny, avoid or suppress it. No medication, no work, no distractions at all. I was present with myself. Over the course of four months, my body found equilibrium. Homeostasis. Peace. All my symptoms vanished from my inflamed brain and spine, to my bruised legs, to my fluid-filled lung, my bloated lymph system to my narrowed eyesight. I had been wearing three different pairs of prescription glasses for years, and all of a sudden, my vision was crystal clear.

Through the destruction, I re-emerged as a healthy woman with no trace of illness. No pain. Nothing. Just life. It's like I was new. Breathing air for the first time. And I was grateful for every single breath. In that moment, my health and my body became the most sacred things of all . . . and I believe this orientation will remain for the rest of my days on earth.

As I've referenced earlier, in the context of a spiritual framework, this process is called 'spiritual awakening' or 'death and rebirth'. In a non-spiritual context, I can see that I just had to learn to listen to my beautiful body. That the orientation to my own lived experience was the essential ingredient to learning to live well.

Claiming my health and my life redirected me into a new reality. One where I was self-aware, self-loving, intuitive, kind and caring, and able to choose to start building a better life for me and my children.

This was never about existential crisis . . . it was about existential recalibration.

Existential Grief and Highly Sensitive Individuals (HSI)

Knowing that something is inherently wrong with the world and our place within it may illicit a feeling of existential grief. This presents itself as unexplained bouts of sadness that have no tangible trigger. Some of the manifestations of existential grief include:

- Unexplained bouts of crying
- Feelings of loss that don't make sense (like someone has died when nobody has died)
- Experiencing a perceived pain of the earth
- Deep connection to the plight of animals
- Over-empathizing with others going through hard times (it is as if their grief is our grief)
- Longing to have been born at a different time in history (either resonating with past centuries or envisioning a better future)

These experiences often cause us to be labelled (whether by others or ourselves) as highly sensitive. Perhaps we are not highly sensitive at all, perhaps we are simply in touch with the reality of our traumatized world, choosing to process it in a way that is palatable and possible.

Understanding these experiences allows us to welcome them with more grace. Of course, we are grieving in this world gone mad.

Invitation to Self-inquiry

- Do you deny parts of yourself in order to survive and belong in the world? Which parts?
- The parts that you deny, what do they crave? Are you equipped to give it to them? What would the consequences be? Are they manageable? If not, why not?
- Do you feel misconnected in your relationships? Which parts of yourself are you holding back? Can you invite them into expression? If not, why not?
- Have you experienced existential grief? How does it show up for you?
- Now ask yourself: What can I do to find a little more authenticity and peace amidst the world gone mad?

Somatic Healing Practice

Invitation to Peace and Harmony

Choose to either lay on your back on the floor or sit upright against a wall. Settle into the position and be aware of your breath. Shift your attention to become aware of the floor beneath or the wall behind you. Notice if you are bracing against it in any way. Ask yourself if you can soften into the surface. Can you harmonize with it? Notice if your body is able to soften/relax a little further. You may stay in this practice for as little or as long as you wish. Notice if the passage of time allows a continuing softening, or is there a point when you cannot soften anymore. What is it like to rest in this place? You may like to journal about your experience.

Affirm to Yourself

'I invite peace inside me and harmonize with the world around me. I invite a new way to exist here.'

Trauma-informed Note:

If you have been bracing against the world or denying your authentic self, this practice may bring about feelings of grief and tears. Alternately, you may find that you are unable to soften against the surface, which may illicit feelings of frustration or anger. If it feels safe to do so, welcome your experience, or you can choose to come out of the practice at any time by orienting to the room around you, rubbing your palms together and taking a sip of water.

Before moving on, let's take a moment to acknowledge that even if there has been no trauma in our early life, there is trauma now because we live in a traumatized world.

Trauma exists on a spectrum, and for those of us who have survived experiences of abuse, neglect or oppression, the experience is compounded, simply by living at this time on the planet we call home.

3

The External Shell

We all have a personality that interfaces with the world. I call this our 'external shell'. We construct a personality that is safe for us to share. Our relational sense of safety comes from our ability to belong. We create a self that will be included, rather than excluded. While our unconscious self-creating decisions will partially come from our organizing principles and early-life relational blueprint, they will also be impacted by the people, culture and environment that we exist within at any time.

When we exist in a world where we feel welcome to express, explore and evolve, it will be safe to include more of ourselves in our external shell.

When we exist in a world where we feel at risk of shame or harm, we will pack parts of ourselves away, creating a very clear split between our inner self and our external shell.

The paradox here is that by unconsciously trying to belong and escape rejection and exclusion, we reject and exclude ourselves. We fragment and lose touch with who we are.

The Suppressed Internal Self

The internal self is made up of all the parts of ourselves that we dare not share with the world. Either because we perceive that it is not safe to do so (learnings from the past), or because it truly is not safe to do so (because of the present). When we are either a) unconscious of our external shell, or b) unable to discern past from present, we will remain in a state of suppression in order to maintain safety and belonging.

Most of us can sense when there is a defined split between our external shell and internal self. But we don't know how to name it. It just feels existentially wrong. The common sentiment is: 'The "me" that the world sees, is different to how I feel inside.'

This experience can exist in one of two polar manifestations:

a) 'The world may see me as a failure, but I believe that deep down there is a different version of myself who is capable and worthy of so much more . . . it's just that I can't find or express as that person.'

b) 'The world may see me as a shining star, but inside, I feel like a hot mess or a failure.'

Both experiences bring with them feelings of shame and disconnection. The latter is the essential experience of imposter syndrome, and often leads to self-sabotage.

Imposter Syndrome and Self-sabotage

Imposter syndrome is the widely popularized term that describes the split between the eternal shell and the suppressed internal self. It was first coined by Suzanne Imes and Pauline R. Clance in the 1970s.[18] These days, imposter syndrome appears in the personal inquiry of the masses, from young adults to new mothers, middle managers, to the world's greatest leaders. The experience transcends gender, class or culture. It is a symptom of our internal

---

[18] Imposter Syndrome, Psychology Today, available at: https://www. psychologytoday.com/us/basics/imposter-syndrome. Accessed May 2022. In my view, all existing definitions of imposter syndrome seem to miss the mark, as this section strives to establish.

and relational disconnection. Those of us who can tolerate the feelings of discord, unworthiness and shame that arise with this experience, move through life with them packed away in our existential backpacks. Those who can't, turn to self-sabotage. The part of us that feels unworthy hijacks our experience and ensures that we never attain the things we truly desire.

The remedy to this collective sickness is to be seen and heard in our entirety—to exist and express as one cohesive complex whole, and be accepted as such. We will no longer be an imposter, therefore, the associated shame will disappear. And there will be nothing to sabotage us.

While the concept is simple, the level of healing and self-mastery to attain it is immense, perhaps a life's work, both for us as individuals and as a collective. In order to access this remedy, we have to a) reach inside ourselves and find out who we really are, and b) exist within dynamics that truly welcome us—the whole of us.

Because our world is polarized, traumatized and built upon systems that demand our fragmentation, most of us do not have the safety and space to reach a state of cohesion.

Before we can be welcomed to the world, we need to create a world that welcomes us.

Modern Spirituality and the Rise of the Diversity Equity and Inclusion (DEI) Movement

Over time, there have been those of us who have been brave enough to stand up and say 'this world doesn't work for me!' and 'this system is floored and it's time to change it'.

Both modern spirituality and the more recent DEI movement, demand that we create a more inclusive world. But at the same time, they damn the system. Damnation and dissonance are the enemy of alchemy, which is essential for transformation of any kind. Once the decision has been made to separate oneself from the exclusionary world, two potential paths unfold:

a) *Acceptance:* To remain within the exclusionary system and push back against it, eternally trapped and excluded.
b) *Rebellion:* To self-exile from the system and search for or create a new one.

Spiritual circles and communities that promise love, light and inclusion form, but in the end, they remain separate from the majority.

DEI activists demand that minorities are included (just enough to check a box), as a result of which, in the end, there is still separation through labelling and categorization. Inclusivity is not inclusive at all.

The only path to inclusion is authenticity. If we are authentic, we will say: 'I am hurting. I feel alone. I am grieving. I am angry. I want to be seen and heard and welcomed into the fold. Please welcome me just as I am!'

To be authentic requires incredible vulnerability. While vulnerability may be terrifying, it builds a multidimensional bridge—between our fragmented selves, as well as with the people and communities we co-exist with.

In order to break the cycle of separation and exclusion, we don't need to create a new system. We need to be authentic within the one that's here, and transform it from the inside out. If we don't say how we really feel, there is no opportunity for our internal and external worlds to meet.

The Spiritual Bubble

The bubble of closed spiritual communities protects those within it from the realities of the modern traumatized world. But can true healing really occur within the realms of the bubble?

There is no doubt that the bubble provides a reprieve—a place to recover, be introspective, curious, playful and without some of the responsibilities that 'real life' demands. Within the bubble, we can find the peace that we have been lacking. The authentic expression that we have been longing for. But is it real, or only a fantasy?

I'm reminded of the old Berkeley and Locke adage: 'If a tree falls down in the forest and no one is around to hear it, does it make a sound?'

The complex answer is both yes and no.

A self-proclaimed guru may be enlightened as they sit in the peace of a temple, the silence of a forest, or a circle of their peers, but what happens when they leave the bubble and come back to the mainstream world? Can enlightenment be maintained or not? Can it be shared with the rest of the world (which is the pure purpose of all spiritual practice—to become light and to share light)? To me, this is the true mark of integrated healing. Is my peace impervious to the chatter of the world or is my peace existing in a state of co-dependence with my spiritual bubble?

A true test for many spiritual seekers is to return to the world that was the source of their triggers and discontent and see, 'Is it safe for me to be here? Can I maintain my peaceful, loving self, or not?'

For many, the answer is no, so they return to their safe bubble. There is nothing wrong with this.

The choice to exit any dynamics that bring about a sense of harm is heroic and self-loving. In fact, we should all be creating bubbles where we feel safe, seen, heard and held.

The point is that if we stay in our bubble, the world doesn't really change. It is still exclusive, and we are still not truly welcome.

When it comes to attachment healing, the goal is 'earned secure attachment'. That is, we feel safe and whole both in connection and aloneness. Most of us feel safe in one state and threatened in the other. So we may crave the safety of connection and be terrified of our aloneness. Or we may feel safe and 'free' in our aloneness, and overwhelmed or threatened within connection. Some of us are triggered by both states in one way or another. Healing asks us to learn to orient to both states as safe and welcoming.

Spiritual healing and the quest for inner peace asks the same of us. To feel peaceful in the bubble and outside the bubble.

However, the fundamental problem is that the world as we know it, is not safe and welcoming. So the quest for this level of spiritual healing seems impossible and futile. At this time in history, I believe the work of the spiritual seeker is to view their bubble as a cocoon for healing, and when they are ready, step out into the big bad world, and light it up with their healing presence. As more and more humans choose their healing and emerge into the world, the system will change. It is created through our collective embodiment.

Ego vs. Consciousness as a Form of Self-abandonment

The concept of ego vs. consciousness is commonly explored through many spiritual psychology frameworks. As with most popularized teachings, over time, it has been simplified and maladapted through human interpretation.

The intention of the teaching is to master our reactive triggers; to stop us from leaking harmful behaviour into the world—to stop spreading our trauma. While this intention is well and good, the simplification of the psyche into ego vs. consciousness (good or bad) stops us from welcoming our fragmented selves into our own care. This creates another version of our external shell—we swap one costume for another.

The teaching says that when we react, we need to notice it, pause and then move beyond the reaction to act in a way that embodies love and kindness. While this ensures that we 'do no harm' in the world, we are often doing harm to ourselves in the process. When we deem our ego reactions as bad, two unhelpful processes occur:

a)   We shame ourselves (yet again!)

b) We move into singularity, denying our complexity and the origins of our reactions, which always derive from an unhealed part of us; a fragment asking for a safe place to express and receive some form of care.

Our failure to listen and respond to ourselves with self-compassion tells that part of ourselves that we reject it. In many cases, this mirrors the reason this fragment exists in the first place. It was never safe or welcome for it to be here. Our fragmentation intensifies. We are still imposters in the world.

Rather than abandon our ego and move into consciousness, our ego needs us to listen to it more deeply, to the stories of all its fragments, and help them heal. Until we create a safe place to look to the roots of our reactions, our fragments will continue to be triggered until they reach a state of aggression, which will result in some kind of harm—either to others or ourselves.

Personal Inclusion

Our external shell exists for a reason. It was constructed to protect ourselves from harm and abandonment. It has brought us to where we are today. Some of the resistance around reintegrating our fragmented selves comes from the fear of being left unprotected if we discard our external shell. Over time, I learned that the point was not to discard our shell, but simply to soften it and create space for our fragments to integrate. Something about this reframe is incredibly comforting. It is no longer about exile or exclusion. It is about a reverent process of personal inclusion.

It is my belief that our individual journeys of personal inclusion will light up the path for a truly inclusive world to emerge.

Embodiment is the only path to a new world.

Personal Share

I've had two external shells. The first was a function of my trauma. The second was a function of my spiritual bypass. To be fair, the second one was very short-lived.

My initial external shell presented me as a strong woman who could handle anything at all. It presented me as successful, determined and driven. It presented me as confident, self-accepting and grateful. Inside, I was none of those things. I was exhausted, angry, grief-stricken and desperate for a safe place to land and dissolve into the disgusting mess of my truth. The tension between my inner and outer worlds continued to mount over years, and after becoming a mother, I would find myself having angry outbursts. One moment smiling and peaceful, the next, roaring at my husband or even my sweet baby boy, who would be crying. Over time, the tension became insurmountable. I could not hold this external shell up to the world anymore. Parenthood is a common turning point that causes our external shells to crack or shatter.

The day my body broke down was the day that my external shell dismantled. Entering a state of vulnerability and authenticity was my only option. There's something incredibly humbling about being physically weak, immobile and dependent on others for help. There were times that I needed help to shuffle to the toilet. There were times I needed oxygen to breathe . . . help with the most basic act of aliveness.

If I wanted to exist, I had no choice not only to accept help, but to ask for help.

As a mother, I had to allow other people to care for my children. This was perhaps more painful than allowing the oxygen from the tank to enter my nostrils. As mothers, we have a primal impulse to care for and protect our children. So primal that we often forget to look after ourselves.

Not too long ago, we lived in communities where there were multiple women to help us hold and care for our babies, so that together, the women of the community could find balance.

During the thick of my illness, that community appeared. And it was in the net of the community that I could acquiesce, let go of my external shell and be honest about how sick I really was. Each person offered small acts of kindness that combined to create that net. From food delivery to childcare, to those who would sit with me or bring me some small treat to brighten my day.

As I yielded to my authenticity, I softened. My heart. My body. It was like I felt my vision change . . . like my eyes were refocusing. And I could feel the warmth of these humans in my cells. My own gratitude bought tears to my eyes again and again.

As I started to recover, the support started to thin out and rather than a net, there were a few shining lights that continued to brighten my weeks.

In those few months, I felt what it feels like to be held by community. I also learned that vulnerability is the only path to any real kind of healing. And I learned that to be the best mother I could be, I had to look after myself and welcome as many people into the fold to love my children well as possible; that there can never be enough love and it was not my place to be the sole source of it.

As I started to strengthen my physical body and heal, I unknowingly built another external shell.

This one wanted to prove that she was an angel—love and light incarnate. Moving in spiritual circles, I unconsciously learned that the more I emulated love and light, the more praise I would receive and the more successful I could become.

Back then, I had not learned about trauma or attachment. It was in the very early days of my healing journey. All I knew then was that I was healthy, well, vibrant and peaceful. And people in these circles loved my newfound energy. I felt so wanted. Looking back, I know that my desire to belong was at the core of so many of my relational choices, as is the case for most of us.

So this new external shell emulated peace, love and wisdom.

This time, I was very quick to notice that something was not quite right in this paradigm. The main thing that alerted me to it was the sense of competition that quickly emerged among the other healers. Love and light one moment, backhanded compliments and psychological manipulation the next. The moment I realized what had happened in and around me, I dropped the shell.

I exited the spiritual world, put my head down to focus on my continued healing and hone my work. I created a safe bubble where I could do my healing work and prepare to share it with the world. That bubble served me well, but I was very alone in it. I needed to be alone to figure out who I truly was. It is only in the recent years that I have emerged from this self-constructed cocoon to step into the world and step up to share from the most authentic place I've ever been in.

The thing about external shells is that they are meant to keep us safe. But they also keep us trapped. They block us from what we truly seek, which is to exist and be met with an unbridled sense of complex vitality. I'm still learning how to exist with this level of complexity and authenticity, and continue to do the healing work that keeps me here. My dedication makes it more and more graceful by the day.

Invitation to Self-inquiry

- How much do you understand about your external shell? List the qualities that it possesses and what you understand about their origins.
- Do you feel a split between your external shell and your internal self? What parts of you are unexpressed? Why do you think they are quiet?
- Have you experienced imposter syndrome and/or self-sabotage? What have you learned of this experience?
- How do you handle your triggers? Are you managing the same ones again and again, or are you working with the root cause? Considering that your reactions derive from a fragment, which part of you do you believe is being triggered? What is this fragment's story?

- Now ask yourself: What parts of my external shell can I soften? And what parts of my inner self can I welcome into expression? Which relationships are safe enough for me to begin exploring this?

Somatic Healing Practice

Softening the Somatic Shell

On the floor, position yourself in child's pose (or a similar pose that feels comfortable, where you feel protected and safe). If it feels comfortable to cradle your forehead in your palms, do so. Allow your breath to settle. Notice the arc of your back, your shell. Is it safe to allow the arc of your back to soften? What about your hips? Can they relax a little more than before? And your head, can it relax into your palms? Allow the muscles in your neck to let go a little. Notice how it feels to soften your somatic shell. Is there emotion that rises? Thoughts? Can you welcome them? Stay in this posture for as long as it feels right. Before coming out of the practice, you may like to lay on your stomach for a while to integrate. You may wish to journal your experience.

Affirm to Yourself

'It is safe to be soft here. I yield into the safety of my body, on the ground, in this place.'

Trauma-informed Note:

If you hold a lot of tension in your body, you may find that it is not possible to soften. You may wish to revisit the 'Invitation to Peace and Harmony' practice at the end of Part III Chapter 2. Find the softness where it is available, rather than force it.

4

Trauma-born Fragmentation

While we are all experiencing modern-day fragmentation, those of us with unresolved trauma have the additional experience of living with trauma-born fragmentation.

When we have experienced trauma or oppression in early life, we have to learn to survive through it. We have no choice but to develop and form as a reaction to threat. Trauma is at our core. Our little psyches, hearts and bodies, shapeshift in order to a) survive, and b) belong.

This is trauma-born fragmentation.

Because this happens during our formative years, these adaptions become the blueprint of our self. We don't know any different. Life is just like this. We are just like this. Again, there may be this existential inkling that something is wrong, but we ignore it because we don't know what it means. We chalk it up to our own insufficiency or craziness. Really, we are experiencing trauma-born fragmentation. Parts of ourselves are lost, hiding or screaming. Our healing asks to find and care for them all.

Feeling Crazy in a Non-trauma-informed World

For those who have experienced developmental trauma, the feeling of being crazy is a common one. We have no idea why we are dysfunctional, why we experience the world differently, why we feel like an alien or why we exhibit strange behaviours and triggers. The shame that we hold with this is often cemented when it is echoed in the world through the dismissive or non-trauma-informed expressions of family, friends, colleagues and sometimes, even random strangers. The lack of trauma-informed care is a large part of the reason that, as a collective, we keep re-traumatizing each other again and again. My lived experience of this and witnessing the unintentional but ignorant re-traumatization of many clients, is what drives me to write, speak and teach in this area.

We have to break the cycle! Once we co-create a trauma-informed world, we will all be able to heal together.

Personal Share

In the midst of my illness, I felt such a sense of terror. My body was breaking down, my anxiety was high and I was completely powerless in front of it. My level of distress was off the charts to begin with, and when new symptoms arose, they would trigger unmanageable states of fear. I was worried I would die multiple times a day. Because of this extreme internal terror, I developed a number of coping mechanisms. Some of these included:

- **Agoraphobia:** I was scared to leave the house. The world seemed like a scary place that was likely to cause a worsening of my symptoms. I was worried that if I worsened when I was outside, I would spontaneously combust.
- **Obsessive Compulsive Disorder (OCD) Tendencies:** I would check everything before I either went to sleep or left the house six times. Six was my magic number. I would check every window, every door, every light switch, the stove and the oven (even if I hadn't been using them). For some reason, fear of fire was a really big one. Perhaps this was because my nervous system was basically on fire.
- **Leg Shaking:** Whenever I was sitting, I would shake my leg. It would annoy the hell out of my parents, but I couldn't stop.

I now know that this was my body discharging threat energy from the nervous system.

- **Skin Picking:** I would find any imperfection in my skin and pick at it until I bled. My face, my arms and shoulders. I couldn't stop and I gouged out some pretty big sores. Later, I would look at myself in the mirror and send hate rays through my eyes towards my reflection.

- **Anorexia:** While I couldn't control my body, I could control what I put in it. I became incredibly fastidious about what I put in it. I would count six pieces of vegetables and six tiny bites of meat, or six pieces of salmon sashimi. No carbs at dinner. I would eat slowly and try and make this mouse-meal last for an hour and drink pot upon pot of tea to fill my belly. On days that I had hospital treatments (when I should have been priming my body with goodness) I 'treated' myself to raisin toast. I would shame myself with every bite, but I loved that warm toast with gooey butter.

Looking back, I know that all of these things were attempts to deal with what was really going on. Severe fragmentation. A wild sense of threat. A ton of suppressed emotions and no pathway to express them.

I was pretty great at pushing all the emotion down. I never wanted to show anyone how distressed and awful I felt. To everyone else, I was 'the strongest sick person' they had ever met, but I could also feel pity pouring out of them and the unspoken (or sometimes spoken) sentiment, 'Just get your shit together, Natalia.'

There was one occasion that I showed up at the doctor's office in a particularly dire state and just burst into tears. I was so scared. I had bruising appear all over my legs and chest, one of my legs was not moving and I had a rash all over my chest. Very clearly physical symptoms. He looked at me like I was a nuisance. He looked at me like I was already dead. 'The emotions are all in your head. Perhaps some anti-depressants will help'. The subtext was 'oh gosh, another crier. Get her out of my office now. Psych! Call the psych team!'

Another doctor looked at my charts, then looked me up and down and told me, 'There's nothing more I can do for you. The condition is getting worse, and you'll just have to make peace with a life like this. I'm so sorry for you.'

'I'm so sorry for you.' Pity.

'You'll have to accept this life.' Hopelessness.

'It's all in your head.' Accusation.

The relational experience I had (not just in the medical system, but from well-meaning friends and family) triggered surges of red-hot anger and slate-grey grief. They would well up inside me, and my fragments would start chattering or battling inside my head. I let the war stay inside me. I braced. Smiled. Polite and accepting on the outside, exploding on the inside. Fragmented. Alone. Crazy.

Traumatized Fragment Archetypes

While our experience of trauma-born fragmentation is incredibly personal and unique, I found that over time, there were clear archetypes available. I'd notice similar patterns of fragmentation within my clients, and would be able to resonate clearly with each one. Fragments would emerge as a response to specific kinds of trauma and traumatic relationship dynamics. Having a map of archetypes to refer to can be helpful for initiating a process of self-inquiry and 'clicking in' to the experiences of our fragmented selves, so that we can care for them and transform our experience in the world. Archetypes are a common way for analysts and teachers to categorize psychological information for transmission.

To me, it feels important to tie all archetype work to a disclaimer:

These are categories that one person or group (in this case, me) has deciphered. Rather than accept them as a direct match or replica for your experience, let them open a personal inquiry, and take time to delve into what is true for you. In other words: Don't let anyone tell you who you are or what your trauma is. The whole point of healing is to learn this for ourselves. To be curious, to feel, to experience and allow our truth to emerge . . . not to let someone else try to do it for us.

Below are six key fragments that may occur as a result of trauma or oppression, and how they may decontextualize, depending on if our psyche seeks to prove or disprove our experience. These are the parts that were not safe or welcome to express at the time of the trauma, or within a particular relationship dynamic.

a) The Runner Fragment
b) The Fighter Fragment
c) The Heartbroken Fragment
d) The Needy Fragment
e) The Denier Fragment
f) The Vanisher Fragment

Each fragment experiences an existential paradox, that causes them to feel stuck in their experience. Our healing asks us to resolve or transform the paradox.

The Swing of the Pendulum

If we consider the attempt of our traumatized fragments to prove or disprove their existential paradox on a pendulum, the fragment is likely to swing from one end of the pendulum to the other, while it searches for resolution and equilibrium. My belief is that this is only possible once a) the existential paradox is illuminated; b) the fragment has its core needs met by our conscious healing self.

Without these key components, it is very common for us to become either stuck in one polarity of the pendulum, or swing in between the two ends, with no ability to find a centre. This may feel like we are making progress in our healing journey, but at some point start noticing that something still isn't right, or new dysfunctions are emerging.

For example:

One of the most common experiences that comes along with trauma is the feeling of not being able to speak up, say how we feel, set boundaries, or ask for support. When we start our healing journey, we may find ourselves swinging to the other end of the pendulum, feeling a strong need to express ourselves and set boundaries, so much so that we become rigid, inflexible and less compassionate to other's experiences. Here, we have attempted to remedy one dysfunction with its polarity.

Healing requires time, space and intention to allow the pendulum to settle. Resolution and equilibrium allow expression to become neither impossible, nor imperative. Expression simply becomes a dynamic and peaceful choice.

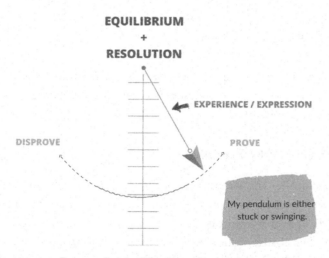

Image 3.4.1. Healing Pendulum

When there is no more urgency to express or exist in a certain way, we are free.

The following archetype breakdowns outline the cause of fragmentation and share the 'existential assumption' formed, as well as the suppressed emotions, decontextualized experience for both ends of the pendulum (to prove or disprove) and the existential paradox that plays out.

Understanding when these fragments are experiencing or hijacking our experience can be incredibly helpful for shifting into a state of self-compassion, which is required to ignite our healing.

1)   The Runner Fragment

Reason for Fragmentation: Unable to leave an abusive or neglectful situation or relationship (e.g. physical or emotional abuse, prolonged emotional neglect, poverty or oppressive family or cultural dynamics).

Assumption: 'I am trapped.'

Initial Suppressed Emotions: Fear, powerlessness.

Secondary Emotions: Resentment/anger, grief, apathy, hopelessness.

Decontextualized:

a)   *Proving 'I am trapped'*
  - Life-force energy is heavy, sluggish, unable to regenerate.
  - Feeling stuck, blocked, powerless to change our situation (whether it's a relationship dynamic, career or a lifestyle habit).
  - Sense of suffocation in relationships, groups and physical spaces where we don't feel ample spaciousness.
  - Wanting change or space, but being unable to affect it, and actually seeking situations and people where we feel bound by responsibility/duty/burden.

The paradox: 'I want to run free, yet I bind myself in chains.'

b)   *Disproving 'I am trapped'*
  - Life-force energy is overly expanded, diffused and uncontained.
  - Freedom above all (seeking a life with little responsibility or burden).
  - Avoidant in relationships or choosing non-committal relationships; being triggered by other people's needs, requests or desires.
  - Sabotaging potential long-term love/career prospects
  - Craving deeper, lasting relationships but unable to cultivate them. Freedom comes at the expense of roots.

The paradox: 'As I run from my roots, I crave roots.'

2) The Fighter Fragment

Reason for Fragmentation: Unable to fight back against disempowerment or violation (emotional or physical abuse, witnessing the abuse of others, poverty, cultural or racial disempowerment).
Assumption: 'I am violated.'
Initial Suppressed Emotions: Fear, powerlessness, anger.
Secondary Emotions: Rage, grief, terror.
Decontextualized:

a) *Proving 'I am violated'*
   - Life-force energy is low, prickly, unstable and 'hot'.
   - Feeling harmed by other people's actions, words or presence easily.
   - Hypervigilance and hypersensitive to personal boundaries/space, yet unable to set and maintain boundaries.
   - Perception of the world as a terrible place.
   - Unconsciously seeking disrespectful relationships.
   - Unable to experience self-love and potentially engaging in self-sabotaging or self-harming behaviours.

The paradox: 'As I desire peace and sovereignty, I seek chaos and enmeshment.'

b) *Disproving 'I am violated'*
   - Life-force energy is dense/heavy, contracted, impermeable.
   - Strong-willed and defensive (boundaries become defenses).
   - Lack of empathy, sometimes bordering on selfishness.
   - Distaste for weakness, vulnerability and emotional expression.
   - Outcome-oriented/goal-driven; 'nothing will stop me' attitude; often using subtle manipulation to stay in power or on track.

- Yearning for deeper connection, quiet and rest, but putting them second to hustle, goals and force.

The paradox: 'In order to escape the violator, I become the violator.'

3) The Heartbroken Fragment

Reason for Fragmentation: Incredible pain experienced due to violation or neglect (often connected to birth trauma, maternal abandonment/neglect, or betrayal, or being unprotected during an experience of abuse).

Assumption: 'Existence is impossible with this level of pain.'
Initial Suppressed Emotions: Grief, fear, powerlessness.
Secondary emotions: Anger, apathy, hopelessness.
Decontextualized:

a) *Proving 'Existence is impossible with this level of pain'*
   - Life-force energy is low, non-renewing, permeable/ easily disrupted.
   - Unable to enter a state of creativity or productivity.
   - Sadness, grief and loss are present regularly.
   - Unable to feel joy, even when it is seemingly available.
   - Tendency to co-dependency or seeking healing and happiness from others; sometimes manipulating others into caring for us: 'I am not okay unless you behave/ express in a certain way.'
   - Feeling alone, even when in connection.
   - Unconsciously seeking people who will abandon or betray; yet surprised and devastated when they do.

The paradox: 'I seek existence without pain, but the pain is my existence. I break my own heart through self-abandonment.'

b) *Disproving 'Existence is impossible with this level of pain'*

- Life-force energy is sharp/staccato, yet dense and impenetrable.
- Orienting to pain as a means of aliveness and regulation (adrenaline-seeking behaviour).
- Creating dissonance and separation between self and others through judgement.
- Utilizing possessions, money and power as a means of gratification.
- Triggered by or judgmental of displays of affection, softness and fluidity.
- Unconsciously enters relationships where they are in a position of power; often using manipulation to maintain or bolster it.

The paradox: 'I create a life where I am not susceptible to heartbreak, yet my heart is already broken.'

4) The Needy Fragment

Reason for Fragmentation: Unable to have their needs for connection and attunement met—physical, emotional, mental, spiritual (often connected to neglect, or mis-attunement by a caregiver due to their own trauma manifestation).
Assumption: 'It is imperative that I cultivate more connection to survive.'
Initial Suppressed Emotions: Grief, fear.
Secondary Emotions: Anger, terror, hopelessness.

a) *Proving 'It is imperative that I cultivate more connection to survive'*
- Demanding in relationships; sometimes emotionally manipulative.
- Distressed in relational dissonance or space (the hint of conflict signals the end of the relationship and incites fear).

- Feeling of 'there's never enough love', even when love is present.
- Unconsciously engages in relationships with people who are avoidant/stonewallers/emotionally unavailable.
- Sees any kind of mis-attunement as a threat and picks fights that ends in relational dissonance, withdrawal or break-up.

The paradox: 'I crave connection and belonging, but no matter what I do, I experience disconnection and aloneness.'

b) *Disproving 'It is imperative that I cultivate more connection to survive'*
    - Unconsciously seeks relationships with needy/demanding partners.
    - Loner mentality; 'I don't need anyone else'.
    - Self-oriented, bordering on selfish, 'I don't care if my existence or expression harms others.'
    - Feels overwhelmed by too much connection; often labelled an introvert.
    - May take on a caretaker, coach or mentor role in order to cultivate connection that maintains a sense of separation.
    - Triggered by or judgmental of people with needs (aka everyone).

The paradox: 'Need is repulsive yet unavoidable, so I exist in eternal repulsion and aloneness, unable to acknowledge and meet my own needs.'

The Denier Fragment

Reason for Fragmentation: Unable to make sense of heinous abuse or injustice (often a result of physical or sexual abuse, incest, cultural or historical trauma, or being a witness to crimes against others), therefore dissociation and/or delusion kicking in.

Assumption: 'This reality cannot be true.'
Initial Suppressed Emotions: Horror, terror, powerlessness.
Secondary Emotions: Grief, anger, confusion.

a) *Proving 'This reality cannot be true'*
    -   Unable to accept other people's boundaries—either gets deeply offended or pushes back against them.
    -   Often hears something completely different to what has been expressed (experiencing rejection, or offence when none is intended).
    -   Stays in situations and relationships where there is clear disrespect/abuse at play.
    -   Projects fantasy onto people and experiences and is often blindsided when reality kicks in.
    -   Difficulty with discerning the meaning of others actions or making healthy decisions.

The paradox: 'I want to create a better reality, but I am unsure what reality is to begin with.'

b) *Disproving 'This reality cannot be true' (Over time, 'I will create a finite and true reality')*
    -   Hyper-rational. Logic must exist at all times.
    -   Only what is true and tangible now is possible; no space for imagination or dreaming.
    -   Lacks empathy—cannot shift awareness to perceive experiences that may be different to our own.
    -   Rigid with plans, timeframes, budgets and rules. No space for flexibility.
    -   Perturbed by others' sensitivity—the subtle makes no sense to them.
    -   Maybe labelled as on the spectrum, high-IQ; or may experience social ostracism.
    -   Thrives on simplicity and is overwhelmed by complexity.

The paradox: 'Reason creates my reality, but because reality often has no reason, I feel lost.'

6) The Vanisher Fragment

Reason for Fragmentation: An inability to escape or rectify the harmful or unwanted situation (often arises from either low-grade chronic abuse or neglect, a narcissistic parent, or acute experiences, such as sexual abuse or torture).

Assumption: 'It's not safe to exist.'

Initial Suppressed Emotions: Grief, fear, powerlessness

Secondary Emotions: Terror, desolation, imprisonment

Decontextualized:

a) *Proving 'It's not safe to exist'*
   - Life force is contained, quiet, diffused.
   - People-pleaser; puts other people's needs above their own.
   - Finds any kind of dissonance/conflict highly distressing.
   - May find it hard to articulate personal or original opinions, often draws on the ideas of others.
   - Doesn't like to take up space.
   - Hypervigilant of others' emotions.
   - Seeks out relationship dynamics where their needs and desires are not respected/welcomed.
   - Often perceived as happy, amenable, kind, but internally holding in resentment/anger.
   - May be secretly competitive in nature, but tries not to show it.
   - May feel shame and alarm following authentic expression or amidst experiences of intimacy.

The paradox: 'I want a safe place to exist, but existence is not safe.'

b) *Disproving 'It is not safe to exist' (Over time, 'I will show the whole world how full of life I am')*

- Life force is expanded, uncontained, fluctuating.
- May present themselves as big-energy, bold, brash or gregarious.
- Overly expressive/needs to express regularly.
- Takes up space in a group dynamic.
- Questions other people's reality/pokes holes in their story (or even picks fights), in an unconscious attempt to bolster their own sense of power.
- Unconsciously engages in relationships with people who have less energy because the comparison makes them feel an increased sense of existential safety.
- May feel competitive or anxious when others are displaying success or originality that incites acts of 'one-upmanship'.

The paradox: 'I continue to prove the validity of my existence, yet my existence continues to be invalid.'

Complexity and Blending

Fragmentation is a complex and common experience, for all of us. When trauma-born fragmentation is at play, the level of distress and confusion around our sense of self is heightened, not only because there are multiple fragments in the mix, but because every single one of them is hurting and desperate to find a way to feel better. In fact, the desire to feel safe and connected is the unified goal of all our fragmented selves. Unfortunately, our fragments are often misunderstood in the world, and by our own psyches.

Misunderstanding is the trigger for our perpetual shame cycle. When we take time to explore our complex experience, we can find understanding, which is the seed of compassion.

Because our fragments have been existing in the same psychological space for so long, they have a tendency to blend and experience together, but react differently, causing a hybrid expression. This can make it harder for us to untangle and we can appear to others as confusing, nonsensical or even crazy.

Healing asks us to hold space for our own confusion, and gently untangle our fragmented selves and invite each one of them to stand up and speak.

Trauma Triggers and the Rise of the Personality Disorder

When we are triggered, one or more of our fragmented selves are seeking a place to tell their story. Triggers can come from anywhere. Some of us have very clear triggers, but some of us can be triggered by the most mundane or surprising things. When we are constantly triggered into trauma responses, inner peace becomes impossible. Relational harmony evades us.

We become hypervigilant of our own existence.

'What will trigger me today?'

'Who do I need to avoid today?'

'Will I be able to contain myself today?'

'How can I prepare myself for the potential distress I may feel today?'

The amount of energy that goes into self-management is exhausting, and depletes our capacity for aliveness and connection. Again, the shame creeps in.

'Why am I like this? Why do I need so much in order to cope?'

For some of us, fear creeps in: 'Will I be able to cope? I can't cope!'

It is usually our shame and fear that send us seeking medical care.

'Something is wrong with me and I can't function normally in the world. I am scared and I need help to feel better.'

> To stand up and ask for help is a huge step towards healing that takes an incredible amount of courage.

Unfortunately, there are millions of people speaking up every day, who are being unintentionally plunged back into a state of suppression. In the mainstream medical and mental health paradigm, fragmentation is often diagnosed as a disorder. The most common diagnoses include:

- Borderline Personality Disorder
- Bipolar Disorder
- Dissociative Identity Disorder
- Further along the severity spectrum, is Schizophrenia.

It is my strong belief that all of these diagnoses are manifestations of fragmentation in different expression and severity. And that the mainstream path to treatment, while well-meaning, often makes it worse, affirming our fragments' belief that they are not welcome in the world. It's as if the system tells them, 'Shhhh, be quiet! Get back in your box!'

What if we are not crazy? What if we do not need to quiet the voices, but listen to them? What if there were a different path to dealing with our mental health crisis? What if we do not need to medicate and still the body's requests for discharge, but welcome their unbridled expression?

There is another way . . . I've lived it.

My own healing process became the foundation for the way I work with clients today. I apply the same approach for clients across the fragmentation from mild inner conflict, all the way through to schizophrenia and spiritual emergency. The deepest fragmentation does not scare me because I have survived and integrated my own. Therefore, I can hold space for it. I believe this is my greatest gift— to sit peacefully with another's entangled pain and to welcome its expression for transformation. To me, there is incredible beauty in this process.

The approach is at once simple but complex.

We tune in. We increase safety through connection and belonging. We untangle the complex and often blended fragments. We let the body tell its story.

The non-linear, relational and expressive process invites coherence and integration. And over time, we find resolution and equilibrium.

It is always 'we'. The client is never alone in their process. Belonging to a shared experience is essential.

Personal Share

Through years in traditional therapy, the main thing I learned was how to create another layer of pretense. I learned what to say to get the therapist's approval and gold star of improvement. I learned what not to share that would lead to judgements being scribbled on their notepad, or in worse cases, being 'punished' with more medication. I learned to manipulate my way into receiving the 'you are socially acceptable' award. I learned to further disconnect from myself, ignore the signs and symptoms of threat that were screaming to be heard and to stuff my overwhelming emotions deep down into the pit of my stomach. It was the only way I knew how to get out of the system that was telling me something was wrong with me and showing me a non-negotiable roadmap to societal inclusion—take your meds and train your brain to be happy (or at least functional). I did what I was told, I behaved how I thought I was meant to, and I was downgraded from 'crazy' to one of the depressed and anxious masses, popping valiums once in a while to numb myself. This was as 'normal' as I was going to get.

I know that my therapists were well-meaning. And many of them were beautiful humans who were helping me the best way they knew how. And they did help me. I had a safe place to go to each week, where I was not totally alone with the nameless trauma swirling inside me. And the meds kept me from being overwhelmed by my underlying sense of threat.

I was coping with support. But I was not healing.

The main problem was that the therapists didn't truly know how to listen or respond to my trauma, and therefore, they could not create a safe place for my healing. The other problem was the rigid 'application' of psychology frameworks that did not allow for my own complex self-inquiry. In the rigidity, attunement was impossible. And without attunement, there was never any hope of healing.

Exploring somatics allowed me to tune into the unspoken story of the body. And leaning into truly safe relationships allowed me to de-armour and begin to get to know, accept and welcome my beautiful, complex, messy self.

It took me twenty years to figure out what I needed to heal: Safety. Belonging. Expression and sharing.

Twenty years of life lost to my trauma—this loss is a trauma in itself that I have taken time again and again to grieve over. My lost life, and the lost lives of millions of trauma survivors is what ignites my desire to contribute to a different approach to healing. Had we received trauma-informed care as young children, our lives would have taken a different turn.

Now working in the field, I see many clients who have a similar experience with mental healthcare. They have been in traditional talk therapy for years. They have made sense of their past and understood the links. But they don't feel any different. They are still simulating an acceptable reality through their external shell, and their inner world remains vastly different.

Salvation comes through answering the question, 'Why am I like this?' Through acknowledging the nervous system, the somatic experience and the role of relationships with poignancy and precision. The moment we truly make sense to ourselves, shame dissolves. The moment a safe other joins us in our process, healing becomes dynamic and we can discover who we truly are.

Invitation to Self-inquiry

- What do you understand about your external shell? What qualities have your developed in order to survive and belong?
- What parts of yourself do you hide in order to succeed in the modern world?
- Based on your understanding of trauma-born fragmentation, which of the fragments are playing out their paradoxes in your life? Do you seek to prove or disprove these paradoxes?
- If you have any common triggers, can you link them to a fragment?
- Now ask yourself: How can I start to care for my fragmented selves in a new way?

Somatic Healing Practice

Honouring the Healing Pendulum

Move onto your hands and knees. Allow yourself to settle in this position. Start to sway from side to side, left to right. Notice if the movements feel fluid or rigid. See if you can soften into them and slowly expand them so you are moving as far to the left and right as feels comfortable. You may play with the speed or your swaying. Notice if you are able to access the sway through your entire spine from the sacrum all the way to the top of your neck. Once you've reached your maximum range and optimum speed, stay in the practice for a while. Notice when it feels like the body wants to start slowing down or decreasing the range of the swaying. Allow yourself to naturally find stillness and centre in your own time. You may like to follow up the practice by spending some time in the 'Softening the Somatic Shell' practice at the end of Part III Chapter 3, or simply laying on your stomach for a while.

Affirm to Yourself

'I allow my healing pendulum to swing. I welcome my authentic process towards equilibrium.'

Trauma-informed Note:

If this exercises feels confronting in any way, you may like to opt for 'Softening the Somatic Shell' practice at the end of Part III Chapter 3, or the 'Invitation to Peace and Harmony' at the end of Part III Chapter 2. Your pendulum will swing when it is safe enough. Listen to what is true for you.

Part IV

The Unified Emotions of Trauma

In the face of oppression, we turn our emotions inwards to our beautiful bodies, or project them upon those who will not harm us.

While honouring the uniqueness of our trauma story, we can also acknowledge that there is a unified central experience in the face of trauma or oppression. The reasons we fragment and the emotions we experience are shared.

Understanding the unified emotions of trauma increases our own self-awareness, and builds a pathway to empathy and compassion for others. It is incredibly comforting to know that our trauma is not ours alone. We have survived together, and we are healing together. There is magic in unity.

1

The Trauma Triangle

When we are oppressed, it is natural to feel a) powerlessness, b) grief, and c) anger. When there is no safe place to express these emotions, we suppress them. While they remain suppressed, these emotions still rule the way we experience and relate in the world. I call this triad 'the trauma triangle'.

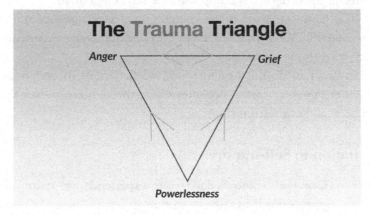

Image 4.1.1. The Trauma Triangle

Understanding that much of our dissonance and dysfunction in the world derives from these suppressed emotions can help us to tune in and inquire more deeply about our experience.

These emotions may rise to the surface when triggered by circumstance or relationships, or they may also simply sit beneath the surface, tinting our experience with their energy. Sometimes, they are buried beneath layers of fear or shame, and the only way to access them is through increasing our internal sense of safety and belonging. We can't start to heal our trauma triangle if we continue to pretend that all is well.

'I'm fine.'

'I'm okay.'

'I'm good.'

These are all common expressions of the survivor. We tell ourselves that to cope is to be fine. We tell ourselves that anything less than immediate danger is manageable and digestible. The thing is, we don't really digest the trauma. It lies dormant or mildly active inside us. The powerlessness. The grief. The anger. In order to truly metabolize our oppression, we need to own it. To feel it. To speak it. To free it. As we hold ourselves compassionately through this process, we learn that we are safe enough to start exploring our trauma in the care of our compassionate selves. All of it.

The trauma triangle is the central common experience of the oppressed self. While there are many other emotions and experiences to explore, this is a good place to start.

In order to do this healing work, we first need to understand how these three emotions decontextualize through our personality, our body and our relationships.

Invitation to Self-inquiry

- Have you acknowledged your experience of trauma or oppression? What is your story?
- Who were your oppressors/abusers?
- Can you connect to the concept of the trauma triangle? In what ways?
- Now ask yourself: Am I ready to start exploring my suppressed emotions as part of my healing?

Somatic Healing Practice

Self-acknowledgement

Find a comfortable seat. Wrap your arms around yourself as if you were hugging yourself. Tilt your chin towards your chest and close your eyes. Allow your breath to deepen a little. Acknowledge that you have survived trauma or oppression. You may feel like you wish to gently rock back and forth. If it feels safe, allow it.

Affirm to Yourself

'I acknowledge what my body has survived. That experience is over now. I welcome my healing.'

Trauma-informed Note:

If this is your first time acknowledging your survivor story, this may illicit many emotions or trigger memories. It is important to stay present in the body, in the physical space you are in. Open your eyes and look around the room to orient yourself. Rub your palms together and take a sip of water. Let yourself know 'I am safe in the here and now'. If you find you need more support to settle, move into the 'Inviting Safety' practice at the end of Part I Chapter 2.

2

Powerlessness

Powerlessness—or disempowerment—underpins the experience of our trauma. Ultimately, we are powerless to our abuser or experience of oppression. We are unable to a) set a boundary and stop the abuse, b) exit the abuse scenario, c) change the relational dynamic or the abuse story. The experience varies from feeling stuck and unable to create change, through to the hellish state of imprisonment.

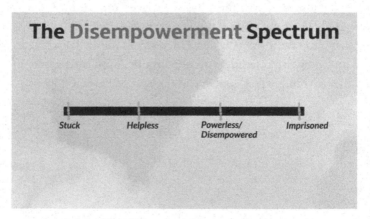

4.2.1. The Disempowerment Spectrum

I. Psychology and Organizing Principles

'I can't. I am trapped. I have no control over my experience.' Powerlessness is a direct response to feeling disempowered and disabled, or unable to change or transform our experience.

II. Neurophysiology

Powerlessness often triggers a freeze/shut-down response in the nervous system. When there is no hope of escape, we become a 'deer in the headlights'[19] and freeze until the danger passes.

III. Somatic Presentation

Somatically, powerlessness presents itself as physical weakness, often in the limbs. Other signs may include decrease in breath capacity, a forward curling of shoulders and spine, numbness and water retention. There may be links to chronic fatigue, fibromyalgia, thyroid or other auto-immune issues.

Location: Most commonly experienced in the skeleton and muscles, but cellular in nature.

Sensations: Limp, sluggish, still, saggy, weak, transparent or invisible, heavy, chained-up.

Colours: Grey or colourless.

The remedy to powerlessness is choice and expression. Every time we choose to express a feeling, set a boundary or ask for help, we are empowering ourselves, one expression at a time. Power naturally emerges from processing our trauma. To heal is to be empowered.

IV. Relating from Powerlessness

The way we adapt to an innate sense of powerlessness will depend on a number of factors.

---

[19] To know more about the 'Deer in the headlights' behaviour, see Sara Streeter's summary, '"Deer In The Headlights": PTSD In Wild Animals', Faunalytics, 11 October 2019. Available at: https://faunalytics.org/deer-in-the-headlights-ptsd-in-wild-animals/. Accessed April 2022.

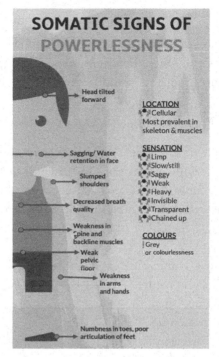

Image 4.2.2. Somatic Signs of Powerlessness

However, at the core, we will walk through life with an external locus of control.[20] That is, we believe our circumstances are finite/fixed and that we do not have the power to transform or change things. We may often have an experience of being stuck, but may accept that it is our lot. In relationships, powerlessness shows up as either as victimhood (proving our powerlessness) or power and domination (an attempt to disprove it).

a) *Victimhood—Proving Disempowerment*

   When we move into victimhood, we often hold a level of bitterness/resentment about our situation that

---

[20] 'Locus of control', Psychology Today, available at: https://www.psychologytoday.com/us/basics/locus-control. Accessed April 2022.

is triggered in many circumstances and relationship dynamics where we are not fulfilled/self-actualized. In this scenario, there is often a pattern of making others into the perpetrators: 'everyone is out to get me/everyone is mean or bad or deficient', or our experience may be that 'the world is not on our side'. When we exist in victimhood, we bury our grief and anger deep down and keep playing out our experience of disempowerment again and again.

    The common feeling that will be expressed would be 'I can't'.

b)   *Power and Domination—Disproving Disempowerment*

When we move into power and domination, we are unconsciously looking for a way to assert the power that we never could within the oppressive experience. This will often come in the form of structuring our lives in a way that we have the 'upper hand' in relationship dynamics. In more extreme versions, we may become manipulative, disrespectful or even abusive in order to cultivate or maintain a sense of power. Ultimately, we feel a sense of power due to the other's lack of power. Others may see us as low in empathy, controlling, bitter or angry. Underneath our anger is suppressed grief. Our psyche tells us that aggression would be more useful than grief to remedy our disempowerment.

Personal Share

In the thick of my illness, I was completely disempowered. Both my left and right foot would keep freezing. So there would be periods where I could not walk. Over time, the powerlessness moved to my hands. There were some years where I had braces on both wrists. My right hand lost all power and was in a hard brace. I could not hold my babies. I could not even hold a cup of tea. I worked with neurologists, physiotherapists and acupuncturists to try and stimulate the nervous system and build strength. But nothing helped.

The very physical experience of disempowerment was terrifying and kept perpetuating the feeling of powerlessness within. When the doctors would tell me I would have to live like that forever, and they couldn't help me, the powerlessness blended with hopelessness. So I stopped bothering to look for ways out of it.

One day, I discovered the power of water. I noticed, while in the bath, that my feet and hands would relax, and that my hands had a lot more mobility in the water. Intuitively, I ended up taking a large crystal that was sitting on the side of the bath and rubbing it on the soles of my feet. Slowly, my toes started to relax and unfurl and as they did, I began to weep. My tears held the deep sense of disempowerment and threads of grief and anger at my experience. For the first time, I was feeling the presence of my trauma triangle. It was like I was touching this energetic framework that had been living inside me. During that first bath, I wept for about an hour as I kept working the crystal into my feet. I started wiggling my toes, flexing my feet in ways that I never had before. And then I started to massage my hands. Stretching my fingers and rolling my wrists in the water. It was like they were receiving new life. The power and freedom to exist and express.

Once I learned this secret, I started working on my hands and feet daily in the water. As I worked, I would weep and acknowledge my trauma triangle. This process unlocked the healing power of my hands. Today, every time someone comes to me for touch therapy, I take a moment of deep gratitude for these hands that were once bound in braces, that now help so many others to feel safe and find their own power.

Loss of Self

Powerlessness breeds loss of self. One manifestation of this is giving up on ourselves. The other is furiously trying to find a way to express or assert ourselves. When we are powerless, we are a) not able to find and follow our own impulses, and b) not able to create and maintain our own boundaries. This ultimately leaves us unexpressed and unalive, or messy and uncontained, or some strange mix of both. The only way to heal 'loss of self' is to become empowered and contained. Unfortunately, one of the biggest problems in our world today is that often, our attempts to 'find ourselves' and become empowered result in the disempowerment or harm of others. If we have no self or 'centre' from which to exist, having boundaries

Image 4.2.3. Centre vs. No Centre

is impossible. When we don't have boundaries, we will never be able to respect ourselves or anyone else.

The Veil between the Abused and the Abuser

Sadly, our world is rife with abuse. It is intergenerational and systemic. Abuse occurs when boundaries are violated and harm is experienced.

If I were to categorize the abuser through the lens of trauma, I would suggest that the abuser is reacting to a sense of extreme powerlessness and loss of self, and seeks to find a sense of empowerment in ways that harm others.

The oppressed becomes the oppressor. The abused becomes the abuser. Trauma begets trauma. The cycle continues.

There is a thin veil between a traumatized self wildly trying to reclaim a sense of safety and power, and a traumatized self that harms another in the process. We call the latter the abuser.

An abuser disregards another person's right to safety, sovereignty, respect and choice. Abuse exists on a scale from lack of empathy, through to heinous acts of violation. Most of us who have been traumatized, have done things that we are not proud of, that go against the moral code of our conscious healing self, or have come at the expense of another. We've either done it out of lack of awareness or an instinct for survival.

This is our reaction to powerlessness. At our core, we are not so different.

Accountability: Recreating our Boundary

As an oppressed or traumatized individual (regardless of how we have acted out in the past), the moment we turn inwards to self-inquire and engage in our healing work, we break the cycle of relational harm. We come back to ourselves in an attempt to stop our trauma from spreading like wildfire. We create a boundary around ourselves that says, 'I exist here and I am accountable for the way I express myself in this world.'

The moment any of us turn inward to reflect, take accountability and start our healing journey, we are no longer the same uncontained human. We are no longer a victim. We are no longer an abuser. We are a human seeking refuge in our own care. Rooted in our centre, contained within our boundary. We are empowered. This is the remedy to powerlessness.

Our collective attempt to find and take accountability for ourselves, is what will end the cycle of abuse. Boundary work will save us all.

An aside: if like me, you have experienced abuse, it can be incredibly confusing to, all of a sudden, understand our abuser as a human, and perhaps even sense connection through the shared experience of powerlessness.

Part of our healing is to connect to our anger at our abusers. So, to empathize with them can feel like we are stripping them of responsibility and denying ourselves our rage. In this moment, it is important that we remember our ability to be complex—to hold both experiences at once. We can have our rage. We *must* have our rage. At the same time, we can allow monsters to become a little bit more human. The alchemy of anger and compassion invites the transition towards power and peace. In the end, that's exactly what we seek—to no longer feel oppressed or in pain.

Rather than seek forgiveness, let's find understanding. What we can see may no longer creep up on us and harm us.

The more truth we can hold, the more empowered we become.

Personal Share

There have been many perpetrators in my life. From my parents, to doctors, rapists, healers and boyfriends.

I have processed my rage at each of them. My grief, too. And I learned to set boundaries and protect myself so that no one could hurt me ever again. And I have learned to soften the walls of my heart, despite the incredible fear of more harm. To remain open to give and receive love. To welcome beauty and joy into my life. It's a delicate dance, to both self-protect and remain vulnerable; a life's work, perhaps. But the most profound healing came from understanding that these humans were all traumatized themselves. No, it didn't justify their actions. Not one bit. The harm they caused me was unacceptable and always will be. But these humans were incapable of loving me well, as they will ever remain. This learning allowed me to turn my attention to where it belongs. To my healing. My continued reclamation of peace and power. To those who can and do love me well. This knowledge allowed me to truly let go. I wouldn't call this forgiveness. I call this freedom.

Invitation to Self-inquiry

- Can you identify a sense of powerlessness inside you?
- How does it show up somatically?
- How does it show up relationally? Are you proving or disproving your powerlessness?
- Can you find links between your sense of powerlessness and the rest of the trauma triangle (grief and anger)?
- Do you feel that you experience loss of self/lack of personal boundary? What tells you this?
- Now ask yourself: How can I start to shift into my power?

Somatic Healing Practice

Welcoming Healing Power

Return to the 'Igniting Life Force and Will' practice at the end of Part I Chapter 2.

As you move through the practice, breathing into your navel, allow the sense of power to fill up your entire body. Acknowledge that your life force or will is your innate power. After some time, bring your arms to your sides and let the power extend into your hands and fingers, feet and toes. Open and close your palms. Curl and splay your toes. You may find that your spine naturally wants to articulate as part of the process. If it feels safe, allow it.

Affirm to Yourself

'My life force is my power. My healing is my power.'

Trauma-informed Note:

Connecting to a sense of power after feeling inherently disempowered can bring up feelings of anger or confusion. In the body, this may present itself as all of a sudden, feeling tension or clamping down, or a sense of overwhelm, rushing or buzzing energy. If this arises, notice the experience and see if it's safe to allow your body to find a natural response. Alternatively, you can either move to 'Inviting Safety' practice at the end of Part I Chapter 2, or lie down, or the 'Invitation to Peace and Harmony' practice at the end of Part III Chapter 2. You may also like to journal about your experience to invite further integration.

3

Anger

The abused or oppressed will always hold an element of suppressed anger, until healing takes place. We should be angry. Our right to sovereignty has been violated. However, during the experience of our abuse or oppression, it was likely unsafe to express our anger—either at all, or in its entirety. Anger's expression may have incited either further harm, or abandonment. We learned that in order to survive, or to belong, we needed to swallow it down.

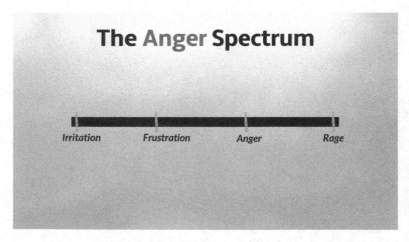

Image 4.3.1. The Anger Spectrum

I. Psychology and Organizing Principles of Anger

'I am harmed (by you, by the world, by myself).' This is how healthy anger should be interpreted. However, in the case of abuse and any form of oppression, one's relationship to anger becomes mis-calibrated.

When a child has witnessed 'aggressive anger', they will automatically: a) mark all anger as harmful, or b) mark aggression as healthy and normal. This causes us to disallow the emotion in its healthiest form. Healthy anger can be a very helpful emotion for letting us know that:

a) A boundary has been breached and then invite us to recreate a new or stronger boundary.
b) An agreement has not been upheld and then invite us to re-negotiate an agreement.

As a humanity, our mis-calibrated relationship to anger has produced a collective struggle with boundary-setting and conflict resolution, which are essential for harmonic and peaceful relationships. Anger shows up in forms ranging from irritation, through to rage. We will only express it at the level that it is safe to, so even if we hold suppressed rage, we may only admit mild levels of irritation until we can longer suppress it.

II. Neurophysiology

Suppressed anger exists as a co-activation mechanism in the nervous system. Either there will be two concurrent threat responses: fight/flight *and* freeze/shut down, or there will be one threat response as the baseline and a flicking into the alternate response when anger is triggered.

III. Somatic Presentation

The most common somatic signs of anger include: tightness in the forehead, jaw and neck, as well as stomach/gut issues.

Tension can also be stored in the pelvis, hips and lower back. There may also be narrowing of the eyes and pursed lips, as well as lots of heat present in the body.

Anger is a very physical emotion and when suppressed, can feel like a wild animal trapped inside us, trying to find a way out. This in itself is terrifying and causes us to clamp down and bury it deeper.

Location: Commonly stored in the abdomen/gut, head and neck.
Sensations: Hot/fiery, swirling, bubbling, bursting (from the inside out), choking, stabbing, throbbing.
Direction: Upwards.
Colours: Red, orange, grey, brown, black.

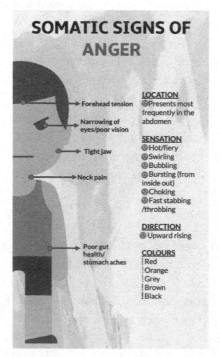

Image 4.3.2. Somatic Signs of Anger

IV. Relating from Anger

When we relate from anger, we relate in ways that disempower ourselves or others. We relate in ways where peace is impossible. The way anger shows up in our relationships will depend on the kind of miscalibration we have. The two main categories include:

a) *All Anger Is Bad:* 'Anger is wrong and it incites harm' (dissociation) or 'There is no anger/I am not angry' (dis-identification).

The way anger is suppressed or mal-expressed will depend not only on our experience of oppression, but on our familial, cultural and religious views around anger. For example, if we are brought up in a culture where anger is considered 'bad', it is more likely that we will dis-identify from it completely.

When we dis-identify from our anger, we become experts at suppressing it and even convincing ourselves that it doesn't exist. But our own anger is often enraged by our continued attempts to disown it, and eventually it finds its way to the surface. This often shows up as angry outbursts, that pierce a seemingly peaceful personality. If we have been expertly suppressing our anger for years, this comes as a rude shock, both to ourselves and to others close to us. The arrival of our expressed anger often followers a turning point in our life that may have acted as a trigger. Trigger events may include: childbirth, loss of a loved one, career change, international move, abusive relationship or difficult break-up.

Because these outbursts seem to come out of nowhere and go against who we think we are (and who we wish to be), they can often cause confusion, shame and relationship dysfunction.

b) *Aggressive Anger Is Normal:* 'It is okay for me to hurt you, and/or for you to hurt me.' Here, aggression becomes a 'normal' way to express in the world. It is okay to yell, to shame, and in some cases, to cause physical harm. Boundaries do not exist and therefore, neither self-respect nor respect for others is possible. When this mis-calibration occurs, the ability to relate in the world is severely compromised, because basic human rights to sovereignty are discarded and empathy becomes non-existent. The word 'harm' loses all meaning; it becomes an accepted part of relating.

The unconscious belief that aggressive anger is normal can lie inside not only those causing harm, but those being harmed; the victim as well as the perpetrator.

'The ignorant perpetrator' will walk around causing harm with either no knowledge of the havoc they wreak, or with some knowledge but complete lack of self-awareness as to why.

Where there is no empathy, there is also no self-awareness.

'The quiet victim' will identify their experience of harm as normal and acceptable, making excuses for the abuser.

As a therapist, I have met countless clients who have justified the actions of their abuser. I have witnessed friends doing the same. I have done it too. When we have learned that aggression is normal, we simply accept it, and our anger ceases to exist until we do the healing work to tap into it and let it roar.

The Poison Cocktail: Anger + Powerlessness

Our collective mis-calibrated relationship to anger, paired with our sense of powerlessness, is the cause of aggression, our continued oppression and polarity. It is the cocktail that poisons the well of humanity.

A big part of recovering from abuse and oppression is processing our suppressed anger and recalibrating our relationship to it. It is only once we have made friends with our own anger that we can start to set healthy boundaries, that serve to reinstate our sense of safety, peace and power. For 'do no harm'[21] to become our embodied philosophy, we have to claim our anger and transform it. Peace and power replace anger as our driving force.

The Relationship between Anger and Grief

Where there is anger, there is often grief. And where there is grief, there is often anger. This blending is what can make it harder to name and process our emotions. When suppressed anger and grief often tangle together, and are experienced as one painful entity, it becomes too much to bear.

We become angry because we have been disempowered and violated. We are grieving because we have lost the right to sovereignty, respect and care. 'It's not fair' is the common sentiment that goes with this emotional blend.

Being able to untangle the two emotions can make healing more accessible to our psyches. Slowly and gently, we can start to explore the unfairness of it all—the anger and the grief.

Personal Share

'It's not fair!'

I used to think so regularly during the days of my illness. 'It's not fair that I am sick and other people are well. It's not fair that I am in pain and immobile.' I wouldn't have been able to name anger or grief at that time. I just knew that it wasn't fair, but I needed to suck it up and get on with it. I needed to smile, be a 'good' sick person, a loving mother and wife, and do my best. And so I did.

---

[21] For more on 'First, do no harm', see Thomas Morris, 'Do no harm', Thomas Morris, 19 August 2019, available at: http://www.thomas-morris.uk/do-no-harm/#:~:text=This%20new%20awareness%20of%20just%20how%20dangerous%20medical,who%20claimed%20%28mistakenly%29%20to%20be%20quoting%20Thomas%20Sydenham. Accessed April 2022.

But I was angry.

I was angry at the way my life had unfolded. At the abuse that I had endured. I was angry at my body for being unwell. I was angry at other people for having happy, successful lives.

I was angry.

But I didn't dare allow my anger. I don't think I even knew it was there. It was so much a part of me, and my relationship to it was so mis-calibrated, that it didn't have a name. And I was so focused on being the best person I could be, which didn't leave room for any anger!

But it had to go somewhere. So it got stored up in my body. My gut was on fire with anger. I had candida, ulcers and constipation. I literally could not digest my anger. My head was exploding with anger—migraines and the most awful jaw pain. Some days, I would lay in a dark room, blinded by it. Some days, I could not open my mouth to talk, paralyzed by it.

Paired with my incredible sense of fear, it travelled into my hips and pelvis. The pain was excruciating.

Paired with grief, it travelled up to my lungs, producing fluid around my left lung and making it hard for me to breathe.

My entire torso was rife with anger. And my nervous system was coated with it.

Over time, the anger permeated my thoughts and actions. My empathy became lower and lower. I didn't care what other people were thinking or feeling. I just knew that I was in pain and unhappy, and my need to make myself feel a little better was more important than anything else at all.

My anger paired with utter powerlessness, led me to do some questionable things. I wouldn't say I was an abuser, but I definitely started to engage in subtle manipulation in some of my relationships. I don't think I even knew I was doing it. I don't think I was conscious of much at all. I was consumed by the pain of my life.

When I started to process my anger, it came as a shock to me. It was like a wild animal that had been unleashed and needed to

escape my human form. I had already been processing my trauma
for some time, so while I found it overwhelming, I had enough trust
in my process that I could let it out. I would get down on all fours
and breathe into my belly. My chest. And let it move. I let it move up
through my throat and expel through the most profound screams.
I would let it hiss, growl and bellow. The release that came through
my jaw was incredible. I would let it move through my hands into my
fists and pummel the floor. And I would let it move through my legs
and out the soles of my feet as I kicked the air.

So much aggression had been stored up. After each release,
my breath would become fuller, like space had opened up inside
me—space where I was free from all that old anger. And then
I would cry. Grief that I had been holding onto for so long. Grief
that it had even been able to lodge itself there in the first place.
And then another wave of anger would come. I worked like that
for some months. Grief and anger. Anger and grief. Letting it all
move through me. As I did, many of my symptoms of illness started
to disappear. My headaches and jaw pain vanished. My digestion
settled. The bruising on my legs started to heal. I'd been full of anger.
And I should have been angry, based on everything that had happened
to me. So much abuse. So much oppression.

As I held myself with deep compassion through my process,
I noticed that I seemed to have space to connect to the world in a
new way. I noticed that my judgmental nature continued to diminish,
and my empathy levels started rising. I learned that my judgements
were a byproduct of my anger and that my lack of empathy had
come from a lack of understanding. The more I understood myself,
the more my heart could return to its natural state of beauty. And the
more compassionate I was with my own wounded heart, the more
compassionate I could be with others.

Anger has been an emotion that I have continued to work with
in more recent years. My process became smoother, cleaner and
swifter. Rather than an animalistic process, I learned to channel and
master my anger. I developed a process where I would use tools

like punching bags and sandbags to help me discharge the very physical experience of anger. I would imbue them with the energy of whatever was triggering my anger. Then I would call on peace and power in my body and allow it to unleash itself. I would either punch, kick or throw the object. Instead of aggression, I would release pure power. It felt different . . . like ultra-clean energy leaving my body (as opposed to murky, aggressive energy, like in my earlier processing). The process has led to an increase in my flexibility, agility and my threshold for stress. What used to send me into overwhelm, now doesn't. It used to be that the moment someone showed any sense of anger or aggression, I would be triggered into a fear response. Now I can sit calmly with another person's anger with no need to retreat or retaliate. Transforming my anger has given me the greatest power of all: peace.

Invitation to Self-inquiry

- What is your relationship to anger?
- How does anger show up in your life?
- When you feel anger, does it show up in your body? How?
- Are you able to set boundaries and ask for others to keep their agreements? If not, why not?
- Are you able to respect other people's boundaries and respect agreements? If not, why not?
- Now ask yourself: How can I begin to recalibrate my relationship to anger?

Somatic Healing Practice

Reconnecting to Anger

- *Anger in the Upper Torso—Releasing through the Arms*
  Find a wall for your practice and stand at an arm's length away from it. Stretch your arms out and place your palms on the wall, lightly. Allow your eyes to close. Breathe into your upper torso. See if you are able to connect to a sense of

anger here. Use your breath to help you. Inhale to connect, exhale to allow it to move, live and express. Stay with this for some time. If you can feel a palpable sense of anger, take a deeper breath into it and as you exhale, send it down through the arms and press it through your hands into the wall. You may find that you naturally want to make noise, and if so, welcome it. Once you feel a sense of release, relax your arms. You may notice that they are shaking a little. Remove them from the wall and gently rub them or hug yourself (whichever feels best). You may like to repeat this process a number of times, until you feel a sense of space or feel like you have reached a natural end to the practice.

- *Anger in the Lower Torso—Releasing through the Legs*
  Find a wall for your practice and lie down with your feet against the wall. Breathe into your lower torso. See if you are able to connect to a sense of anger here. Use your breath to help you. Inhale to connect, exhale to allow it to move, live and express. Stay with this for some time. If you can feel a palpable sense of anger, take a deeper breath into it and as you exhale, send it down through the legs and press it through your feet into the wall. You may find that you naturally want to make noise, and if so, welcome it. Once you feel a sense of release, relax your legs and bring your knees in and hug them to your chest. You may like to repeat this process a number of times, until you feel a sense of space or feel like you have reached a natural end to the practice.

Affirm to Yourself

'I welcome my anger in ways that does not harm myself or others. I release it from my body.'

Trauma-informed Note:

Reconnecting to anger can be a highly charged process. The intention of this practice is to provide a gentle pathway to reconnection and ensure you feel safe 'dipping' into the experience. You may connect more with either a) or b), so work with the one that feels most resonant. If it feels like you have touched an internal store of anger that needs greater attention, you may want to seek professional support from a somatic therapist to do so. As you self-direct your healing process, it is important to gauge where your safety levels lie, practice within them, and ask for help when it is needed. Anger is one of the most difficult emotions to process due to the aggression that builds up when it is stored. Please practice safely.

4

Grief

Our grief tells the story of our loss and of our desire. The oppressed and traumatized self has so much to grieve. The lack of freedom. The lack of choice. The lack of care and support. When we don't understand that these things are worthy of grief, we can't welcome it. When grief lives without a name and without access to our tears, it becomes a grey haze in the air around us. We breathe it in each day, coating our heart and lungs with its pollution. It is only when we give grief a name and allow our conscious tears to flow, that the sky turns blue again and we can transcend the arc of grief from loss to desire.

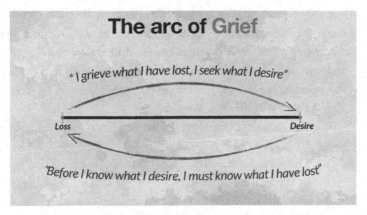

Image 4.4.1. The Arc of Grief

Grief exists as an arc between loss and desire. Once we connect to the arc towards desire, grief becomes more graceful. The experience of loss shows us what we truly value, and what we want to create in our life. When we allow desire to emerge, impulse and life force start to express themselves. When we welcome it, our grief allows us to transform again and again. Grief is part of our intrinsic human experience, and when viewed as such, can lead us to exist in a continuous evolutionary state that takes us towards self-actualization and true intimacy within ourselves and our relationships.

I. Psychology and Organizing Principles of Grief

'Something has been taken from me, and I feel the hole that is inside me—either presently or preemptively'. When we experience grief, we most commonly connect to a sense of loss. It may be that we have lost something in the present; that we are processing loss from the past; or that we are anticipating future loss. Whether past, present or future loss, the experience of grief lives firmly in the present.

Threads of Grief

Our suppressed grief has many threads to it. It shows itself in layers, and will emerge over time. Each time we unlock a piece of our story that shows us loss or unfulfilled desire, a thread of grief will unfurl. When it comes to trauma-related grief, some of the common threads of grief may include:
a) The harm that has been caused.
b) The absence of love and care, or betrayal of an attachment figure.
c) The sense of un-belonging that has been carried inside us for so long.
d) The various effects of the trauma on our lives.
e) The years that have been lost to dissociation and trauma.
f) The 'alternate reality' that did not eventuate due to abuse or oppression.

As threads of grief begin their journey of expression, it can be incredibly helpful to understand which thread we are processing. This helps us find coherence and move towards integration. When grief integrates, we move through the arc from loss to desire and can begin a journey of fulfillment. 'Now that I know what I desire so deeply, I will take steps to create it.'

II. Neurophysiology

In its suppressed state, grief exists as a parasympathetic activation in the nervous system. It may metabolize enough for us to sit quietly without it having too much of an impact. However, if there is too much grief to metabolize, it may take us into states of freeze or shut down.

III. Somatic Signs of Grief

Grief can be a full-body experience, however, it is often rooted and most present at the upper chest and heart. We may experience intercostal bracing, tight neck and shoulders, shortness of breath or lung concerns, strange rashes, downcast eyes or eyes that are desperately seeking connection. Our spine may also be slumped or fragile. Grief most commonly wants to express from the chest up through the mouth. It can feel like thick grey, brown or black smog that wants to dissolve into the ether. When expressed, it is common to start coughing it out like smoke.

Grief vs. Sadness

We tend to mislabel grief as sadness. Grief seeks resolution through generative movement, either in letting go (loss) or creation (desire).
Sadness is a byproduct of our discontent. Just as its polar, happiness, is a byproduct of our content.

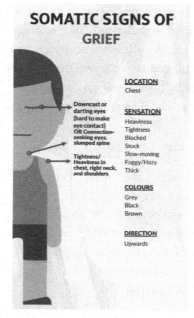

4.4.2. Somatic Signs of Grief

Sadness and happiness are both somewhat peaceful and still states. They do not seek resolution or transformation in the way grief does.

Grief is a cyclical storm that keeps us eternally transforming—hiding inside our cocoon and emerging as a beautiful butterfly, again and again.

Understanding the requirement for movement in transforming grief helps us process and integrate the entire arc, rather than just the loss. When we look only at the loss, integration is not available, because we are sitting with a hole or space inside ourselves that cannot transform. It is a bit like zooming into a map where we cannot see the destination, so we keep circling around the same neighbourhood, again and again. Once given access to a greater view of the map, we can start to move towards new fertile lands.

IV   Relating from Grief

When grief lives inside us, it will manifest in our response to the people around us and the world at large. We will either be consumed and flooded by our grief, or we will disallow and deny it completely.

a)   *Flooded by Grief*

When grief consumes us, the world becomes a very emotional place to live in. Our grief will be reflected back to us in the faces of our loved ones, the beauty of the sky, the sea, the birds and the trees. A touching movie. The sweetness of a baby. We are flooded with our own grief. We will respond to our flooding in one of two ways:

• *Entrapment*

After years of holding our grief inside, it becomes stuck and trapped. It may feel like we want to let it out, but we simply can't. Tears are not accessible. This can feel like we have heavy weight in our chest, or a suit of armour on that we can't take off. And the more we struggle with it, the heavier and tighter it becomes. When this happens to us, we may appear to the world as unfeeling, lacking empathy and softness. When in fact, the opposite is true. We are feeling everything, but our feelings are being held hostage inside us.

• *Pouring out*

Our grief appears to be never-ending. We cry at the drop of a hat. Endless tears that don't make sense. We will confuse ourselves and others, with the intensity of our experience. This kind of flooding often leads to labels of 'over-emotional' or 'highly sensitive' or a diagnosis of depression. We want to make the tears stop. And everyone else wants to make our tears stop. We live in a world where grief is not welcome—we simply don't know how to handle it. There are two things that can help this kind of grief: a) welcoming it, b) making sense of its origins and processing it one thread at a time.

b)   *Denying Grief*

To deny our grief, we pack it away so tightly that we cannot feel it. We wrap layer and layer of protection around it, so nothing will trigger it. We become strong, brittle and braced. We may have done such a good job of this that our other emotions may also be dulled. We may present ourselves as stoic and steadfast. Accepting and un-emotional. While this means we can move through life without being rocked too easily, it also means we move through life without experiencing deep states of feeling. Joy often eludes us. Ecstasy is impossible. Just as we do not feel loss, we do not feel desire.

While we may be 'safe' from our grief, we block the beauty of other feelings out—the very things that make us human. When we cannot feel, true human connection becomes impossible. Life is full of misconnections. In the end, this kind of grief shows itself as a kind of emptiness and loneliness. We might feel it behind our eyes. Like we are not quite there. Or an occasional pang in the prison of the heart space, or a twinge in the pit of the gut. Our close others may sometimes wonder why we don't emote in the same ways as them. We may be labelled as cold and unfeeling, which might make us feel somewhat alien, because we don't know any other way.

> In order to start healing, we need time to thaw. All those
> layers of protection need time to be unwrapped—
> layers of fear and shame that have been protecting
> us for so long. And sometimes, before we can even
> touch our grief, we need to process our anger against
> those who asked us to hide our grief in the first place.

Of all our emotions, grief is by far the most epic because it is
so layered and nuanced and needs an unending amount of self-
compassion. Grief is part of our life (trauma or no trauma). And
when we have denied it (perhaps for a lifetime), we need to welcome
it back into our experience. Grief needs time. Grief needs space.
Grief wants to belong to us. The moment it belongs, it softens.
Grief is gentle when it is no longer being told to hide.

Grief and Gratitude

Once we embark on our healing journey, it is common to start
feeling grateful for our healing. For our ability to breathe new life
into our chest. To see with expanded vision. To access beauty, play
and joy. To feel true empathy and compassion. Each time we taste
the sweetness of our gratitude, we invite ourselves to grieve again.
All the years where these experiences did not live and breathe inside
us. Understanding this relationship is important for our continued
processing. It will be our tendency to want to stay only in the
experience of gratitude. We have had enough grief. Enough pain
for a lifetime. But the point of healing is to feel it all. Once we get
to this stage, our grief will be diluted in its potency; palatable or
even sweet. Our gratitude-related grief may simply be a gentle flow
of tears, or it may be a slide down to a deeper layer of our story
asking for our attention. Our gratitude is an incredible resource that
increases our capacity to continue exploring our story. Each time we
feel its wonder, we can ask ourselves, 'Is there any grief here, too?'
and welcome it with as much warmth.

Personal Share

I had packed my grief away so tightly that I didn't know it was there. Well, part of me didn't. There was a part of me that kept wanting to touch it. To feel it. To let it flow. To drown and disappear into it. That feeling that I would drown and disappear into it triggered such intense fear inside me. There was no space for my grief. I was spending so much energy surviving and coping. I worried that if I let myself soften, even for a moment, I would shatter. That I wouldn't be able to keep going. That I'd die inside my grief. Looking back, I know that I was trying to keep myself safe because I wanted to be here. To have this life. Though at the time, I couldn't connect to that. I just knew that softening my strong external shell was not an option. So I buried my grief deeper and deeper inside me. I smiled. Fought the good fight. I lived in a constant state of disconnection from myself and everyone else. Sometimes, in the quiet of my bedroom, after a round of medical treatment or a bout of severe pain, I would feel my grief rise and choke up my throat. A tear or two would permeate the medicated glaze of my eyes. And then I would dissociate. It was the only way to protect myself. I would fly up to the ceiling and watch myself, zoned out in a fetal position in my bed, staring into space for hours, until sleep would come or an alarm would go off. I managed my grief by leaving my body.

I wasn't able to connect to my own grief until I started to thaw out my terrified body. Until I stopped turning lasers of anger and hate towards myself. Only then could I start to slowly grieve. In order to thaw out my body, I needed to be held. I let myself be gently massaged and to receive craniosacral therapy. This turned down the level of threat inside me. I started to feel my body. To come home to it. Only for moments, to start with. I began to connect to sensations. Movement. Tingling. Whooshing. Heat. Cool. Pain. And then I would leave again. But it was a start. It was as if I was dipping the toes of my consciousness in, testing the waters; 'Is it safe to be here?' Yes, yes, yes, yes . . . No. I was intuitively learning to discern, to associate, and to find my capacity for feeling. Sometimes, after a bodywork session, I would come home to the sanctuary of my bedroom and weep. I didn't call it grief. I called it sadness. I didn't make sense of it or connect it to any origin. I just let it flow briefly. And then I would sleep.

Most of the bodyworkers I chose to work with were very gentle. I never felt a sense of violation. However, one day, I tried a new bodyworker. A man (usually I preferred to work with women). His touch was initially gentle, but after a time, he came to work on my stomach. He did not ask for permission. He worked into the fascia and all of a sudden, it felt like he was plunging his hands into my guts. Of course he wasn't . . . but it felt like he was. The experience of violation was incredibly severe and it felt like I was being at once cut with a knife and my lungs wanted to explode. But I braced and quietened it all. The amount of energy it took not to show the level of pain I was experiencing was huge. Looking back, I know that I held such a deep sense of shame around my emotions that I was primed to hide them. But I also know that he was not a safe person to share these experiences with, so I was rightly protecting myself.

After the session, I ran into the street and bawled my eyes out on the side of the road. I started having flashbacks of being abused as a child. I felt confused and unstable. After about thirty minutes, I told myself, 'Natalia, pull yourself together and get home'. So I did. I hailed a taxi and cried the whole way home, as quietly as I could. When I got home, I locked myself in my room and continued. I lay on my side and held my stomach and howled and howled. After a couple of hours, a little voice told me, 'Natalia, this is your grief. You need to grieve now. All of it'. And so I did. I spent two weeks crying about my childhood abuse. And I let it go. But that was only the beginning.

My grief has emerged in layers through my healing journey and it still continues today, though not with that level of violence. It is contained, gentle and welcome.

I have grieved all that I have lost and all that I have yearned for. And I have taken time to honour the incredible desire I have for a different life. A better life. I have channeled that desire to build it, step by step. The more I grieve, the more grateful I become. And the more grateful I become, the more gently the grief flows. Sometimes I think I am done. That I have arrived at the sweet spot in life. And then I realize, I will never be done grieving. So much of my life was lost. There was so much pain and violation. And while I have so much to be grateful for, and the beauty of my life continues to unfold, that part of my life that was black, horrid and stolen by my trauma, will always exist in retrospect, in my archives. So I take those moments when I am reminded of those times and honour the presence of my grief. I thank it for reminding me how grateful I am. It often pops up in my most tender moments—the vulnerable expression of my children, the arms of a lover, amidst the wonder of my own breath. I have so much to be grateful for. And I have so much to grieve. And I welcome it all, in peace.

Invitation to Self-inquiry

• What is your relationship to grief? Are you aware of it? Do you welcome it or suppress it?
• Can you connect to the threads of grief? Which ones resonate?
• Are you able to traverse the spectrum of grief, from loss to desire? What do you desire?
• Now ask yourself: How can I begin to welcome my grieving process?

Somatic Healing Practice

Welcoming Grief

Find a couple of pillows and get comfortable lying down with them beneath your head. It helps to have the chest and head slightly elevated for this practice. Bring your hands to your heart space and settle into the position. Bring your breath and attention to your heart space. Notice if you can connect to any grief here. Use your breath to help you. As you inhale, connect, as you exhale, let it move and release through your breath. You may like to try inhaling through your nose and exhaling through an open mouth, and increasing the length of the breath. You may also like to move your mouth around to make different shapes as you exhale. You may find that sounds want to emerge, tears arise or you begin to cough. How can you safely welcome your grief into expression?

Affirm to Yourself

'I welcome my grief to live, breathe and leave me. I set it free.'

Trauma-informed Note:

If you have been suppressing a lot of grief, you may feel the impulse to cry for a long time. If this feels safe, welcome it, and move into the 'Inviting Safety' practice at the end of Part I Chapter 2 as you welcome it. If you experience a lot of coughing, soothe yourself with a warm cup of tea with honey. Remember, grief processes in layers, so please go gently. You can come back to it again and again, as it arises.

5

The Cage of Rage and Self-loathing

The biggest block to our own healing is the cage of rage and self-loathing that we build around ourselves. This is more than shame. This is more than anger. The is more than self-sabotage. This is the turning inwards of all the shame, anger and sometimes hatred, that has been directed towards us.

Because our psyche learns through experience and repetition, the more we are shamed and angered at, the more our psyche learns, 'I am shameful' and 'I am hateful'.

Our self-loathing exists on a spectrum from minimization to vile self-hatred. The more we loathe ourselves, the less we can respect ourselves. When we live inside the cage, self-love is impossible.

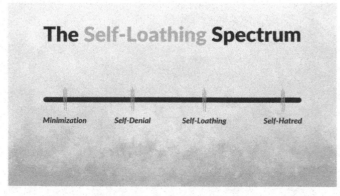

Image 4.5.1. The Self-loathing Spectrum

Loathing trumps appreciation. When we loathe ourselves, even just a little bit, it's hard to recognize our own goodness. To acknowledge our beauty, our kindness, our success or our progress. All the empathy and compassion that we so freely share with others, is not available to turn inwards to ourselves. There is no room for it. We are not worthy of it. This self-imposed cage keeps us separate and alone. It perpetuates our lack of belonging. And the cruel voice that develops inside us reinforces all the shaming and anger-fuelled words that created our self-loathing in the first place.

The external experiences of abuse or oppression are 'acted in' and become part of who we are. We become our own abuser.

The Inherited Voice

When we internalize the shame, anger or hate that has been bestowed upon us, it becomes a very strong part of our psyche. Often, there is a clear voice (or voices) that regularly enters our mindspace to tell us how terrible we are. The voice is so controlling that it often sits in our psychological driver's seat. It berates us. It makes sure that we question our worth, desires, achievements and actions. And should we dare to move towards any state of freedom or joy, it becomes louder, more demanding and tries and put us back in our cage.

We never talk about 'the inherited voice'. We dare not let anyone know that we have a mean bitch living inside our head. People might think we are crazy! We might be given a mental health diagnosis. We might be medicated. We might be shamed and ostracized. So most of us keep quiet.

This is one of the biggest issues with the mental health paradigm today. There is no welcome space for the fragmented or traumatized psyche to express itself without some kind of social condemnation. No matter how much we say, 'its okay to not be okay and it's okay to have a diagnosis, and its okay to take medication', we are missing the point. We don't want the labels and the medications. We want to find a way back to ourselves, rather than get trapped in another system that tells us we are damaged goods.

So those of us who are adamantly against labels and medications stay as far away from the mental health system as possible. We either keep quiet, or we find an alternate route to care. We respond to 'the inherited voice' in one of two ways:

a) Comply with its wishes, which often leads to self-depriving or destructive behaviour.

b) Battle with it; we might feel constantly exhausted trying to talk ourselves into healthy decisions that are not a product of our inner mean bitch.

Either way, 'the inherited voice' wins. We are either a slave to it, or at war with it. We may spend a lot of time trying to quieten it or grieving its presence, or feeling totally insane.

But the more we comply or battle, the stronger it becomes.

'The inherited voice' is not a fragment that has split off from ourselves in order to protect us through and beyond our trauma. We have inherited this voice, this part, from those who have harmed or oppressed us. It is not ours. It never was. This is our inter-generational trauma.

Unlike working with our fragmented selves, healing does not come from being compassionate with 'the inherited voice' and giving it a safe space to express and meet its needs. Healing comes from sending it out of our psyche and reclaiming our own spirit as sovereign. This process not only breaks us free, but it ends the cycle of intergenerational trauma and creates a new blueprint for our children, and their children to come.

A Note on Inter-Generational Healing in the 2020s

I firmly believe that we are a transformative generation, and it is our work healing our trauma that will pave the way for a better world to emerge over the next few generations. Our children will not end up in therapy or buried under endless self-help books. They will feel safer to exist from a place of authenticity and peace. And they will go on to birth the next generation (our grandchildren), who will build a world we cannot yet imagine, because we have never known it. It won't be about hustle. It will be about sustainability, inclusion, belonging and collaboration. These are all the buzzwords we speak of, but do not embody. We are simply laying the groundwork. It is imperative that we continue. It is our generation's collective goal to heal.

Externalizing 'The Inherited Voice'

In order to begin externalizing 'the inherited voice', we have to start to recognize what it sounds like and the kinds of things it encourages us to do.

'The inherited voice' will always seek to disempower us. Because when we are weak and small, we will never try to escape. 'The inherited voice' will tell us how unworthy we are. That we are incapable. It will encourage us to self-abandon, self-sabotage and self-harm. And sometimes, it will do it in such sneaky ways that we will believe it is helping us.

'The inherited voice' often presents itself like a narcissist. Either it overtly disempowers us, or it is clever and covert in its actions, making us believe that it is here to help us. Our job in healing is to get to know its words and patterns so well that we can no longer be outsmarted.

Some of the things it may do include:

- Push us beyond our limits to exhaustion.
- Instruct us to say 'yes' when really we mean 'no'.
- Encourage us to deny ourselves anything—food, connection, emotions, experiences; anything we desire.
- Shame us for our words or actions.
- Knock us down when we are feeling good.
- Kick us when we are already down.
- Encourage us to express when we are reactive and unable to find clarity.

Once we truly understand it, we can muster up all our strength and cast it out. Again. And again. And again.

Our strength to heal this aspect of our trauma comes from our continued processing—the transformation of powerlessness to empowerment, the re-calibration of our anger and the access to our own desire through the arc of grief.

Once we have taken all our fragments by the hand, let them share their stories, and welcome all our emotions, we will have an internal army of peaceful warriors on our side. Internal unity strengthens us to say 'no' to what is not ours.

Mean bitch be gone.

The process of externalizing 'the inherited voice' takes time, repetition and compassion. It will often trigger more layers of emotions to process, that connect all the way back to our root traumas. And we will need to grieve that it has taken hold of us for so long. Until one day… it becomes a faint whisper, an echo from the past, powerless to the truth of who we are: Liberated.

The cage will finally disappear and we will be able to step out into the sunlight.

> When there is no more cage of rage and self-loathing, self-love becomes a real option, not some phrase we've read in a self-help book.

The Rise of Alternative Healthcare and the Self-Help Empire

Many people with unresolved trauma recognize that they need support. They also recognize that what they need will not come in the form of prescriptions, pills and labels. We might not be able to articulate what's wrong, but our intuition tells us that we need both awareness and safe humans to help us. And our traumatized inner child is often hoping that some book or article or person is going to arrive and magically resolve all our problems.

For many of us, the healer becomes an authority—yet another external voice to listen to instead of our own. When we become transfixed with an external voice, we are unable to break out of our cage, because even with all the healing work we do, we stay disempowered.

Herein lies the conundrum of the alternative healthcare scene.

Many alternative health practitioners hold beautiful spaces for their traumatized clients. They take time to listen and explore our story. If they use touch, they hold us lovingly. They help us feel safe, seen and heard. Which is exactly what we need. There is some incredible work going on in the offices of osteopaths, the home clinics of hypnotherapists, and the healing spaces of energy masters.

However, in many cases, the healing only ever reaches the stage of nervous system regulation and emotional release. It is very rare that integrated transformation is achieved. It is very rare that clients walk away empowered to start building a life beyond their trauma. Instead, they become stuck in a well-meaning but potentially harmful power dynamic.

The two problems at play in this realm of healthcare are:

• **Nervous System Regulation Is Only One Part of Trauma-recovery**

  To be able to enter a session with a practitioner of any kind and feel a little safer, is a blessing. But it is not a cure. As our nervous system starts to regulate, we are primed for deeper healing processes. However, if no one guides us towards them, we will often root ourselves in a paradigm where as long as our nervous system can feel safe, we are healed. This is untrue, and may be evident in our continued coping mechanisms and relationship dysfunction. In fact, nervous system regulation—whether it's through alternative healthcare, or our own self-care (e.g. meditation)—becomes another coping mechanism. It is only one piece of a very complex healing puzzle.

- **The Healer Becomes the Attachment Figure**
  For many of us traumatized humans, to find someone we truly feel safe with, who we can soften with and tell our stories to, is the most beautiful experience. Our traumatized selves can finally be nurtured in a way they have been craving. The dynamic is ripe for transference. Our wounded parts want to turn our healer into the person (or people) that didn't give us the love we needed or deserved. When this happens, one of two dangerous scenarios may play out:

  a) *We Disempower Ourselves Further*
  It is very common for us to put our healer on a pedestal. To ask them to tell us what is wrong, to make it all better, to become the parent we never had. When someone becomes our healer, we give away our power again. We don't ignite our own impulses, agency, curiosity, discernment or sense-making abilities (which are essential to our transformation). Instead, we metaphorically (or actually) lie down and let someone else make us feel better. Many of us may stay in relationships with therapists or healers for years. It becomes an essential part of our routine to go to the one who makes us feel better. Again and again and again. This attachment stunts our own healing and growth. We learn: 'I feel better when I connect to this human. I need this other person to feel safe in the world.'

  b) *We Get Caught in a Harmful Power Dynamic*
  The practitioner–client relationship inherently holds a power dynamic. The client is seeking care from a place of disempowerment, and the practitioner holds the power to ignite change. Unfortunately, there are many practitioners who are unaware of the importance of this dynamic, or who use the dynamic

to further oppress the client (either unintentionally or intentionally). Unintentional harm comes from lack of clear boundaries, that have the client believe that the practitioner is more special to them than is true. In this case, we project and transfer all our attachment wounds into the dynamic. This may manifest as feeling abandoned or rejected by the practitioner, or find ourselves dreaming of when we will next see them, or wondering what they are like outside of the treatment room.

They become part of our trauma-fuelled fantasy. When we enter the state of projection[22] and transference,[23] we have no idea we are in it, or that our traumatized inner child is in the driver's seat. This can lead to intense feelings of confusion and shame, traumatizing us further. Intentional harm comes from the abuse of power. Sadly, there is abuse going on in therapy and healing rooms all over the world. It ranges from psychological manipulation through to sexual abuse.

A Note on Alternative Health Practitioners

I firmly believe that most practitioners are well-meaning and believe they are providing excellent care. Many are. But many are also completely unaware of attachment and the implications of transference in a trauma client. They are unaware that their role may actually stifle their client's innate healing properties. They are also unaware that their own attachment and trauma wounds are likely tainting the relationship. Many practitioners or healers derive some part of their self-worth from being the one who heals, from the

---

[22] 'Projection', Psychology Today, available at: https://www.psychologytoday.com/us/basics/projection. Accessed April 2022.

[23] 'Transference', Psychology Today, available at: https://www.psychologytoday.com/us/basics/transference. Accessed April 2022.

length of their client list, or the praise and testimonials they receive. The moment their clients become the source of their self-esteem, power dynamics become funky. The client may be seeking attunement and healing. But in this case, so is the practitioner. This is known as 'wounded healer syndrome'.[24] It can be incredibly harmful to the client and a trap that keeps many practitioners stuck and unable to advance in their own healing journey.

The conundrum is this:

- The mainstream mental healthcare system has a big hole in it, partly due to lack of awareness and partly due to lack of resources. So no matter how much it regulates itself, people are going to seek out alternative routes to healing, where they can be seen, heard and held.
- The alternative healthcare system (and the thousands of modalities that exist within it) does not typically educate on trauma-informed care.

The solution is two-fold:

a) *Inclusivity*
   Re-calibrate the mainstream mental health system to recognize and include alternative solutions. The holes in the system can be so beautifully filled with existing resources. We need to welcome healers, rather than condemn them.

b) *Awareness and Shared Vision*
   Educate all healthcare providers on trauma-informed care. If we create a healthcare ecosystem that operates with a shared vision for healing, we can work together, unified

---

[24] 'The Wounded Healer', Academy of Indian Philosophy, 1 March 2018, available at: https://academyofindianphilosophy.com/the-wounded-healer/. Accessed April 2022.

in our intent not to re-traumatize.[25] Different healthcare providers can work together, each doing their own part towards a shared vision.

This is a mammoth job. But it is one of my greatest wishes to be a small part of this healthcare revolution. I've made a start by creating a range of trauma-informed trainings to educate practitioners and also empower the general public to be more aware of their own experience of trauma. There is a long road to go, and before we take that road, we need to build it.

Together, we can dismantle the cage of trauma that so many of us live in, and create a net of care that will hold us as we travel down the path of healing.

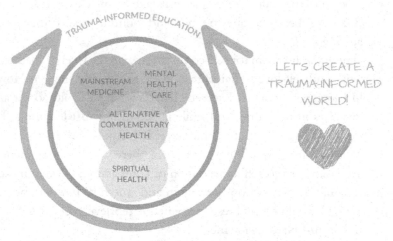

Image 4.5.2. Trauma-informed World

Personal Share

The mean bitch that lived inside my head was a beast. She berated me daily. She encouraged me to starve myself. She encouraged me

[25] For more on re-traumatization, see 'PTSD Retraumatization', BrightQuest Treatment Centers, available at: https://www.brightquest.com/post-traumatic-stress-disorder/retraumatization/. Accessed April 2022.

to work myself to the bone till I fell sick, and more. She did not let me rest. She did not let me care for myself. She told me I was weak, pathetic, unlovable, fat, ugly, useless. She told me to kill myself many times. She told me I would amount to nothing and it wasn't worth trying. When I would try to improve myself, she told me it was useless. She told me I did not belong, that I was a waste of space and that I should have never been born.

For over thirty years, I lived with her inside my head, torturing me.

During the height of her cruelty, I became anorexic. I would slap my head with my hands. I would deny myself warmth when I was cold. I would deny myself connection and care, even when I was desperate for it. She told me I deserved it all. And that withstanding this suffering and aloneness was the only way I could even begin to make up for the great mistake of my existence.

I swung between obeying her and fighting her. Either was exhausting.

There was no room for self-compassion with the level of loathing present. And self-love? That phrase made me quietly snigger! How could I love myself when I secretly hated myself? I could go for all the spa days in the world, and smile in the mirror just like the self-help books told me to, but I could never love myself. All I saw was a vile human staring back at me. Of course, there were brief moments when I connected to self-appreciation or compassion, but that mean bitch would quickly swoop her way in and smash it. It would be so quick that I would forget these moments of reprieve ever existed.

It was just black inside me.

I remember that when I did a six-week CBT course, they spoke about the inner critic. The voice inside our head that is mean-spirited. It made sense that this was her. But there were some problems with this framework. The basic parts of the model didn't touch the complexity of my fragmented psyche. It asked me to polarize into good and bad. It was a formula to perfect, rather than a process to embody. The bigger issue was that my inner mean bitch was smarter than the therapist. She directed me to say all the things I needed to prove to the therapist that I understood the concept and had mastered my inner critic. A therapy gold star! Inside, that mean bitch was laughing her head off. 'Stupid therapist!' So I left that course with the therapist's approval but an even more powerful bitch inside my head. Great.

Still black. But pretending to be pink or blue or whatever colour showed I was fine and dandy.

I only really came to understand where this voice came from when I started healing my trauma and getting to know my fragmented selves. All of them seemed to respond to my self-compassion.

Except this voice. In fact, she was trying to block my access to the fragments.

Once the others started to become strong enough, I had enough internal unity to see the bitch for what she was. An amalgamation of my maternal and paternal trauma. A part of me that had formed as a result of the way I had been treated.

The endless shaming, taunting and name-calling of my mother. The repeated physical abuse and psychological manipulation of my father. Those forces had fused to become part of me.

When I first realized who she was and how she had become a part of me, I felt disgust rise in my throat. I ended up purging for a couple of days. Of course I was disgusted. The way I had been treated was disgusting. And the imprint it had left on my psyche, my body and my spirit was, in essence, a tragedy.

When I allowed myself to acknowledge the tragedy of my experience, I wept. I let the grief flow. And I raged. I pummelled my fists and kicked the air (familiar with this process by now). I was processing at a new layer.

And when I was done, I took a breath into a new space inside me. A sense of resolve and strength that I hadn't felt before. I was not going to let that voice control me anymore. And in that moment, she lost all her power.

She tried for some time, heckling, bellowing and raging. She became her most manipulative and cunning, trying to find a loophole to regain control. But I could see her every time. And the moment I spotted her, she would deflate, powerless before my gaze.

She still rears up from time to time, often after periods of silence, when I believe she has left for good. Sometimes I wonder if she will ever really leave. I'm not sure she will. But she can no longer disrupt my peace. Instead, each time she opens her mouth, I'm reminded how far I have come, and my gratitude silences her with grace.

Invitation to Self-inquiry

- Can you find yourself on the spectrum of self-loathing? Where do you sit?
- Do you resonate with 'the inherited voice'? Whose voice do you believe you have internalized?
- When does 'the inherited voice' show up? What kinds of things does it encourage you to do?
- Does 'the inherited voice' ever pose as well-meaning? Can you decipher its manipulation tactics?
- Now ask yourself: How can I start to externalize 'the inherited voice'?

Somatic Healing Practice

Washing Away What Is Not Yours

For this practice, you can either run a bath or prepare for a warm shower. Immerse yourself in the water. Be aware of it on your skin. Allow it to wash away what is not yours. To enhance the practice, you may like to try working with your breath, inhaling for two counts and exhaling for four counts. It may feel like you are gently pushing the exhale out of your nostrils. After a few rounds, you many notice the impulse to take a big inhale, so allow it. Then allow your breathing to return to its natural state. You may also feel an impulse to cry or shake. Notice if it is safe to do so. If not, you can cross your arms in front of your chest in a protective position, lengthen your inhale and orient to the room around you, coming out of the practice.

Affirm to Yourself

'I cleanse myself of what does not belong to me. If it is not mine, I let it go in peace.'

Trauma-informed Note:

If you hold intergenerational trauma or have a very strong 'inherited voice', two things may occur: a) You may connect to the presence or energy of your lineage. If you are visual, you may see a line of ancestors in your mind's eye. You may, all of a sudden, sense clarity about the nature of your intergenerational trauma. b) 'The inherited voice' may rear its head and try and block your process. If this happens, notice if you are able to catch it. This may feel confronting and invite another layer of emotional processing that requires your attention first. If you have any kind of experience during the practice in the water, be sure to dry off and stay warm after. Spending some time curled up in bed or under a blanket in a peaceful space will assist with integration. You may also like to journal.

6

The Wound of Separation

The wound of separation lies at the core of our traumatized self. Imagine a little baby, left alone, unclothed on the median strip in the middle of New York City.

That's how the wound of separation feels. Petrifying. Confusing. Engulfing.

As a child, when our basic human needs for safety, connection and care go unmet, they stay unmet. But we can't stay on that metaphorical median strip. That reality is not sustainable. We would perish there. So we find a way to survive. Our little nervous system adapts. We shut down our emotions. We learn to relate in ways that are acceptable, minimize our experience of harm or provide us with crumbs of false-love.

Every adaptation we make, everything we do, is a function of trying not to feel the horror of being on that median strip. We are a myriad of coping mechanisms, distractions, band-aids and fallacies. These make us feel a little safer, a little more acceptable, a little more powerful, a little more lovable. And a little less alone and scared.

We spend our whole lives trying to escape the pain of being alone on that median strip. But as with all healing, feeling is required for transformation. It is not until we have enough capacity to feel the intensity of this wound that it will start to show up on our radar.

As we continue on our healing journey, our capacity to feel fear, powerlessness, anger and grief increases. We learn that it is safe to sit with ourselves. We also discard layer upon layer of shame and replace it with self-compassion. Through the process, we also start taking more space to do our healing work. To feel our feelings and to step away from people and places that no longer serve us. It is often these people and places that are plugging the wound of separation; covering it over so that we don't feel it. While we are buried in someone else's dysfunction, or focusing our energy on anything external, we will not be able to feel the crux of our trauma. And our exceedingly clever psyche has structured it this way. We are unconsciously protecting ourselves against an unliveable experience.

The thing is, it may have been unliveable for our baby selves, but it is not unliveable for our adult conscious healing self. Not at all. The wound of separation must be healed in order to reclaim our place in the world—to mark ourselves safe and allow ourselves to belong here.

Defensive Accommodations

Defensive accommodations are the actions we take in order to increase our sense of safety. I first read about this term in the book *Nurturing Resilience* by Kathy Kain and Stephen Terrell.[26] However, the term 'accommodation', as it pertains to psychology, was introduced by Jean Piaget[27] in the 1930s.

We all have coping mechanisms, or accommodations. These are attempts to self-soothe and self-regulate. The way we know if they are healthy or defensive, depends on the answer to this question:

---

[26] Kathy L. Kain, Stephen J. Terrell, *Nurturing Resilience: Helping Clients Move Forward from Developmental Trauma—An Integrative Somatic Approach* (Berkeley: North Atlantic Books, 2018).

[27] For more on Jean Piaget, see Alexander Burgemeester, 'What is the Difference Between Assimilation and Accommodation?', available at: https://www.psychologized.org/what-is-the-difference-between-assimilation-and-accommodation/. Accessed April 2022.

'If I take this person, activity or experience away, am I able to remain safe and stable in my experience?'

If the answer is 'yes', then we are merely making healthy choices.

If the answer is 'no', then we have been avoiding what's true—that we can't cope at all.

Defensive accommodations fall into three categories:

a) **Unconscious**
We have no idea that we are attempting to avoid our authentic experience.

b) **Conscious**
We know that we are self-soothing (or self-sabotaging), but we do it anyway. We sense that we do not have the capacity to cope without it at this time.

c) **Emergency**
Our level of distress is so high that we feel like if we do not perform this action, we may be a risk to ourselves or someone else. There is a felt sense of no choice. It's no longer an accommodation, it's a necessity. This is a very dangerous state to be in, and sadly, so many exist here for prolonged periods, or even choose to end their lives because it is not a sustainable way to live.

Many defensive accommodations can exist in both the conscious and unconscious categories. These may include:

- Binge-eating/self-starving
- Binge drinking or drug use
- Over-exercising
- Overworking
- Over-socializing
- Engaging in unhealthy/harmful/abusive relationships
- Excessive meditation

However, emergency accommodations exist in their own category and include experiences such as:

- Self-harm, e.g. cutting
- Self-medicating (prescription)
- Abuse of others (either verbal or physical)

A Note on Self-Harm and Suicide

I have worked with many self-harming and suicidal clients. I have also lived in these states myself for prolonged periods. The common experience, without fail, is the emergent need to feel something— anything other than what is being experienced. For some of us, it is blinding rage. For some of us, it is the deepest grief. For many of us, it is this unnameable experience of being totally unsafe, alone and terrified—that we simply cannot exist here. In my experience, as both a survivor and a therapist, the only way these feelings will truly subside (rather than continuing to be masked and dealt with), is to go to this very existential core—the wound of separation—and heal it.

Personal Share

The first time I felt the wound of separation was three years into my healing journey. I had long recovered from my physical illness and was already working in the field, supporting other trauma survivors.

All seemed well in my world. I was a successful therapist and clinic director. In general, I thought I was at peace, but I was fooling myself. Yes, I had done so much healing work. I had processed fear, shame, powerlessness, anger and grief. My empathy levels and intuition were at the highest they'd ever been and I was loving myself well, engaging in self-care daily.

But I was burying myself in my work. And in a toxic relationship.

I believed that all the healing work I had done was essential for me to move onto the next phase in my journey. But I wasn't quite ready, so I found a way to block my progress, diverting my attention elsewhere. External toxicity is much easier to handle than the wound of separation.

It was not until I had the courage to leave the toxic relationship and take a break from work to heal, that the wound came up for healing. I had all the self-care tools I needed in order to love myself through it. And I had a few good people I could call on to support me in my darkest moments. I will be forever grateful to these humans who hung out on the other end of the phone, came to hug me while I wept and made cups of tea to soothe my hoarse throat.

In the space of my aloneness, I let my anxiety rise. I did not try to settle or distract from it. It rose into fear, then terror. My eyes were wide and my body taut. I felt disoriented and wild, afraid that I would die alone, lying on the floor of my bedroom. The cries and the screams that I let my body expel were unlike anything I've ever heard. They shattered some kind of trauma matrix inside me. They held it all. The utter confusion of being alone and scared in this world.

I felt like that terrified baby alone on the median strip.

I had flashback after flashback. Lying alone in my cot crying. Lying alone in my cot listening to my mother screaming or sobbing somewhere nearby.

Flash forward to being kicked out of home at eighteen, sleeping in some scuzzy share-house with creeps.

Flash forward to lying on the cold asphalt after being raped.

Flash forward to tracing my veins with a safety pin. Then a knife. Slapping myself in the head. Repeat. Repeat. Repeat.

Flash forward again to huddling up in the hospital all alone, in pain, terrified, no one to care for me.

So much aloneness. So much fear. The thread was crystal clear.

After the series of flashbacks, I found myself present, shivering and moaning on the floor. My hands clenching the edge of the rug. I pulled my weighted blanket over my head and let myself know 'Natalia, it's over. You are safe now. Look where you are. You are safe.'

With this affirmation and the comfort of the blanket, I let my body shake and twitch, till it all left me. And after a time, I knew that it was true. I was safe here in this world, with my aloneness.

I breathed into the new truth and let it permeate my cells, to become the new template of my existence. And so it was. After that process, I started to feel more to be able to sit in stillness (without the cloak of meditation). In silence. In my own company. And it felt safe. It even felt good.

I noticed more freedom in my body and took it as a cue to move to the next level of my journey with my physical body. I joined a dance class. I engaged a personal trainer. I was not only safe to exist, but I was safe to start being curious, and to open myself up to joy.

This wound needed to process in a few layers, as I integrated a new part of myself—the vibrant, playful lioness. It was proven to me again, that healing is so non-linear.

I had been so used to seeking toxicity in order not to feel, that I wandered back to toxic waters again, not long after. Another man, this time in the form of a great love, but clearly a deeply traumatized soul. That part of me that wanted union, connection, care . . . to be held . . . the part of me that didn't want to be alone . . . it begged me to soothe it in the arms of another. So I listened to it. And I abandoned the parts of myself that knew he was not safe. I put myself in harm's way so as not to feel that same wretched wound.

And again, I fooled myself thinking I had reached the next level in my journey. And perhaps I had. The joy that I experienced in that relationship had been completely unknown to me. It opened me up to understand what I want, and also more clearly define what I don't want. When he broke my heart, it was the first time I felt the heartache of a grown adult woman, not the distress of a young child. The difference was incredibly palpable. As I gently put the pieces of my heart back together, I knew that I would never be a traumatized child again. That I was safe here, even in the midst of such deep relational pain.

My heartache showed me that I had healed.

Invitation to Self-inquiry

- What kind of accommodations do you have in place? Are they healthy or are they defensive? What happens when you take them away?
- Can you resonate with the 'baby on the median strip'? When have you felt that way and what did you do to either self-soothe or avoid it?
- Do you recognize the wound of separation in anyone close to you?
- Now ask yourself: How can I approach a state where I am safe in my solitude?

Somatic Healing Practice

Deactivating Defenses

To prepare for this practice, choose one defensive accommodation that feels safe enough not to engage with, for a whole day. You may notice discomfort or distress rising through the day. Notice how that materializes. When you are ready, find a safe place to lie down on your side, wrapped up in a blanket. Create a safe cocoon for yourself. You may find that your body wants to twitch or shake or move around. You may feel like crying. Or have some memories show up. If it feels safe enough, stay with this process and open your eyes to look around the physical space you are in and be aware of the blanket cocooning you. Stay here until you feel a sense of release or increased safety. It may be anywhere from a few minutes to an hour.

Affirm to Yourself

'I am safe in my solitude in the here and now. I invite past versions of myself to join me here. That old fear can leave my body peacefully.'

Trauma-informed Note:

This practice can feel quite activating, so before embarking on it, ensure that you have integrated your work processing the trauma triangle first, if possible. It is also helpful to work in small segments, so you may wish to try working with one defensive accommodation over three to five sessions of the practice. You can then repeat the process as you begin to remove more coping mechanisms from your life. It may also be supportive to assign a trusted friend as a 'trauma-healing support buddy' that you can reach out to if you become overwhelmed in the experience of processing solitude and have the desire to re-engage with the defensive accommodation.

Part V

The Point of Freedom

Illumination empowers us to become our own creators.

Once we've pulled back the curtain to glimpse into a different reality . . .

Once we've bought the unconscious self into conscious awareness . . .

Once we've rescued our fragmented selves from the dark corners of our psyche and gathered them into our compassionate care . . .

There is no going back.

We have reached 'The point of freedom'.
We have everything we need to become our own creator.
'The point of freedom' demands that we become accountable, for every choice we make.
Illumination is eternal.
Freedom is recreated again and again, one conscious choice at a time.

When we reach this point in our journey, we can consciously pause in the beauty of it. The lightness. The space. The power. This is the point of departure for a new way of living and relating. And even if we are triggered back into old habits, once we have arrived at this place, we will always be able to find a way back to it, again and again. It is sacred and it is ours. There's nothing to process here. This is a time for deep integration and honouring how far we have come.

Part VI

Embodiment—The Laws of Peace and Power

The laws of peace and power protect us from oppression and harm; and ensure that we do not instigate it for others. To heal, is to embody them.

1. Reclaiming Sovereignty
2. Capacity and Personal Sustainability
3. Complete Accountability
4. Receptivity
5. Purity of Power
6. Reverence

Illumination brings possibility. Hope. Compassion. Choice. Agency. We have the opportunity to create a new blueprint for the way we live and relate in the world. This is when our real work begins. When we are safe enough. Aware enough. Empowered enough. Like any masterpiece, creating ourselves takes time, patience, and attention. This is embodiment.

Our choices are like brushstrokes.

We are living art.

If we find we don't like the way we are progressing, we can change direction, course-correct, or paint over our human canvas and begin again.

Knowing this, we need no longer be afraid.

Illumination is eternal and no one can ever take it from us.

Instead of searching for healing, we can embody it, and share it.

The laws of peace and power protect us all from oppression or harm.

Embodiment is how we heal ourselves and each other.

1

Reclaiming Sovereignty

To be sovereign is to be free from oppression.

When we are sovereign, we have the basic rights to freedom, choice and expression.

Sovereignty is a state to be treasured, protected and maintained. Without sovereignty, we are not our own. We are at the mercy of another. A person. A family. A community. A culture. A system.

In the modern day world, many of us do not have access to total sovereignty. This is because the relationships and systems that we exist within, often ask us to deny our sovereignty. Safety, belonging, sharing and expression come at a cost.

The cost of our sovereignty.

In order to exist peacefully within the dynamics, we have to shape-shift and in some ways, self-deny or self-abandon.

The moment we lose sovereignty; we will never truly be able to access a state of 'well-being'.

Our eternal quest for well-being is the search for total sovereignty. We need to name it because naming it is the real game changer. We can stop fumbling around in the dark and reaching for props and pills to simulate the experience we desire—sovereignty.

Much of our distress and displacement comes from a desire for sovereignty that is not available to us within certain dynamics or systems.

Somatic Signs of Sovereignty

When we lack sovereignty, we may feel:

- Weight bearing down on us
- Being squashed or compressed
- Binding around the chest
- A helmet on the head, placing pressure on the skull and/or jaw
- Tightness in the hips
- Tension in our neck, back and the backs of the legs (fascial backline)
- Pain in the feet, issues with walking
- An invisible fog around us

When we start to gain a sense of sovereignty, we may feel:

- Increase of space inside the chest
- Release of tension in the head/jaw
- Increased flexibility of the hips and legs
- Ease in the feet and our gait
- Clearer vision

Sovereignty and Systems

While we seek sovereignty, we also need and want relationships and systems. As humans, we are fundamentally dynamic and responsive. We are not meant to exist alone. Relationships and systems provide foundation, structure and support—all of which we need in order to develop and thrive.

When we feel oppressed, our two impulses contradict each other.

'I want to live within the dynamic' *but* 'I want to be free from the dynamic.'

'I want to belong.' *but* 'I want to individuate.'

Oppression disorganizes our psyche. Our confusion tends to take us towards polarity. There's no space for grey. In polarity,

Image 6.1.1. Somatic Signs of Lack of Sovereignty

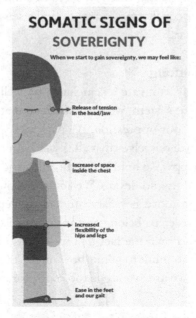

Image 6.1.2. Somatic Signs of Sovereignty

either we are sovereign and free or we are oppressed and trapped. Polarization causes us to respond to our desire for sovereignty in one of the two ways:

- **Suffering**
  While we exist in the dynamic or system, we suffer due to the experience of our oppression. We cannot be happy here, but here is where we are. We place belonging and support above freedom and authenticity.
- **Self-exclusion**
  We choose to claim our perceived sovereignty and exit the oppressive dynamic. We forgo belonging and support, so as to access freedom and authenticity. But we will continue to whiff the stale stench of exclusion. It can never truly be denied, no matter how hard we try.

In our modern world, in order to escape the unbearable unfairness of this polarity, many of us have adopted a third way of responding to our conflicting desires to find a sense of peace within oppressive dynamics.

- **Shape-shifting**
  In order to cultivate a semblance of well-being within the dynamic or system, we shape-shift so that we don't feel the weight of our oppression. We pack away parts of ourselves to convince ourselves that all is well with the world and that we are happy. We hold in our thoughts and feelings. We deny our impulses and desires. We adulterate ourselves. We might be getting more familiar with the concept that we shape-shift in order to belong and maintain relationships, but we do need to own the fact that we are also fooling ourselves, because we think to admit how unjust the world may be or unhappy we are, would be too much for us to bear.

This third way of being is the most dangerous, because it takes us the furthest away from our authenticity. We forget who we are and what we truly want.

In recent generations, we have become a pack of shape shifters, and most of us don't even know it! This is our mass collective trauma response.

The Dynamics of Sovereignty

In each of these three responses to oppression, we are disempowered. We either suffer, self-exclude or shape-shift. In order to remedy this, we need to cultivate an experience of sovereignty that is not only sustainable, but collaborative and dynamic.

Our sovereignty exists in the mastery of dynamics. Responsiveness is the key to our individual and collective freedom. Finding our sovereignty is a process of learning to respond—to dance with the world around us. But before we can dance, we need to learn the steps. We need to practice. Make mistakes. We need to slowly build our repertoire of moves that allow to exist both individually and together.

Through responsiveness, we end polarity. It's no longer about oppression versus freedom, it's about learning to live well in the here and now. We embrace the grey—the subtlety and nuance of what it's like to be in a constant, dynamic relationship with ourselves, each other, and the world at large.

Sovereignty is a continued practice of learning how to relate in the world, with peace and power.

The Truth about Abuse

The truth is that when we are living in a truly oppressive or abusive dynamic, we will not be able to access total sovereignty. No matter how much we try, we will not be able to feel a sense of well-being.

As a survivor and a therapist, I know—too well—that when we are living within the clutches of a harmful person or system, and we

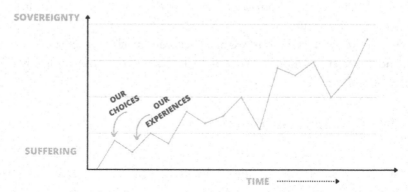

Image 6.1.3. The Path of Healing

really do not have the resources to leave, we will continue to cycle through painful experiences again and again. In most cases, no one can save us or extricate us from the situation. And the insistence of others to 'just leave' when we really do not feel able to do so, can trigger a further sense of powerlessness and even hopelessness.

So while we may not be able to access total sovereignty, we can start to slowly understand our experience and cultivate practices that increase our sense of safety and empowerment.

The fundamental laws of peace and power remain the same, and we can exercise them in the ways that are available to us. Sometimes, our commitment to our inner work translates into such a sense of peace and power that we can either change the system from the inside out, or at some point, peacefully walk away and build a completely new one from the ground up.

Personal Share

It took me nearly forty years to find total sovereignty. It's as if my life was an existential game of snakes and ladders. The extra-hard, advanced 'you're lucky to get out alive because these snakes are poisonous and will kill you' version. In my version of the game,

I'd have to find the materials and tools to build a ladder, haul myself up, rung by rung, and claim a little bit of freedom . . . then some snake in disguise would bite me and send me spiralling down into another oppressive experience. Sometimes, I would wallow in it. Sometimes I wouldn't even know that it had happened.

I'd find myself in some shitty oppressive situation without the slightest idea that I was oppressed at all—it was just my life. Until the light bulb of awareness let me know that something wasn't okay. That I was oppressed . . . again. But sure enough, my will to create something better would drive me to hunt for new materials and tools, build another bloody ladder and get out. Each time I would go on the hunt for new materials and tools, I would learn something. My awareness would increase and I would find a way to get out of the hole. The hole of my family. The hole of my mental health misdiagnosis. The hole of my physical illness. The hole of my spiritual bypass. The hole of a psychologically abusive relationship.

The constant search for well-being was futile until I understood that it depended entirely on my experience of sovereignty. That they were one and the same.

My first epiphany about the importance of responsiveness was during a mentorship with a Qi Gong master in Bali. During my time with her, I learned how to respond to the elements. We worked mainly with the earth and water. I learned how to feel them and embody them. I learned that energy work was a way of life, not a practice. I learned how to cultivate my *qi* (energy) and how to quieten it. And I learned that through mastering my own energy and presence, I could positively impact the people around me.

Learning the art of Qi Gong was a turning point for me, where I felt empowered to respond to myself, other people and the world in a new way. I felt beautiful, powerful and divinely protected. But I was not divinely protected at all. What energy work did not teach me was to understand and master my own energy and remain sovereign. Nor did it teach me about spiritual bypassing, wounded healer syndrome and the traumatized child inside me that was desperate for belonging, love and care.

Energy work is incredibly powerful, but when it is played with, without the knowledge of protection, dynamism, projection and transference, it can be harmful. It can leave us open to harm, and it can also harm others. While energy work led me to become a shiny, bright being and a sought-after therapist and 'healer', it left me uncontained and unprotected in the world. Initially, I did not know what was mine and what was not. Lack of clear boundaries led me into some unpleasant interactions, feeling depleted and eventually surprised to find myself in a very psychologically harmful relationship. For some time, I was sure I would never leave. My traumatized mind convinced me that I needed to stay there. That the pain was going to teach me and make me stronger; that there was some spiritual lesson to learn there, or karma to be paid.

It was being in this dynamic that led me to learn about triggers, transference, projection and trauma bonds. Again, the questions 'Why am I like this?' and 'What's wrong with me?' prompted my search for more answers. As always, once I understood the 'why', I could find the necessary materials and tools, build the ladder and get out.

Firstly, I built my capacity for activation. I learned to become strong in the face of rage. I learned not to react. Initially, the fits of anger would send me into deep states of fear and powerlessness. But over time, I cultivated enough resilience to remain relatively unaffected in the face of threat. During this time, I was working with a personal trainer. The very physical experience of lifting weights to strengthen my physical body and developing my agility through boxing, transferred into my emotional state. I felt like I was in training, becoming a peaceful warrior.

Next, I learned how to maintain my own sense of reality—not to have it distorted or denied. 'I understand your experience. I have a different reality', came out of my mouth frequently. It always fell on deaf ears, but it ensured I remained psychologically sovereign. I also learned how to set a boundary and follow through with consequence. 'If you raise your voice again, I am going to leave.' And I would actually leave, to claim my spatial sovereignty.

I cultivated my inner peace and power over a year. As I claimed my sovereignty, I became stronger. Eventually, I found the resolve to leave. Because I knew I was energetically strong enough to deal with the consequences. And there were many. And I was strong enough.

After a life of climbing out of holes, I finally breathed into my total sovereignty.

Healthy. Fit. Balanced. Self-aware. Self-caring. Self-sustaining.

Peaceful. Powerful.

Free.

And I vowed never to lose it again.

Invitation to Self-inquiry

- Do you experience sovereignty or oppression? In what areas of your life are you sovereign? Where are you oppressed? What are the people, experiences or systems that oppress you?
- Do you tend towards: a) suffering, b) self-exclusion, or c) shape-shifting?
- Do you believe that you are primarily responsive or reactive?
- If you are in an abusive or oppressive dynamic, do you have the strength to walk away? If not, in what ways can you start to cultivate your peace and power each day?
- Now ask yourself: In what ways can I cultivate my sense of sovereignty—big or small?

Somatic Healing Practice

Somatic Sovereignty

On a yoga mat, go onto your hands and knees. Become aware of the length of your spine. Start by tilting your head and neck up and down, like you are nodding 'yes'. Then from side to side, like you are saying 'no'. Sense the freedom and movement in the back of your neck. Next, do the 'cat–cow' yoga pose. If you are not familiar with this pose, you move your spine between arching it like a cat, and moving into a concave position, which is known as cow. Find your comfortable limit with this movement and sense the freedom available in the spine all the way from the top of the neck down to the sacrum and hips.

Next, see if you can start to move your spine from side to side and engage the movement of your hips, neck and head. Allow your movement to be led by the spine and non-directed, aware of the articulation of your vertebrae. Let your body lead. Allow your movements to expand and change as much as you like, all the while connecting to the sense of freedom in the body. If you feel to move into other spontaneous movements, stretches or expressions, go for it!

Affirm to Yourself

'I am sovereign. I choose movement and freedom.'

Trauma-informed Note:

If you are not used to somatic movement practice, or have been feeling a deep sense of oppression in your life, this practice may trigger a sense of shame or fear. Either one may make you feel like you cannot proceed with the practice. Take a moment to question if that is true for you. If you feel safe to continue, please do. If you feel unsafe, to do so, come out of the practice or move to the 'Inviting Safety' practice at the end of Part I Chapter 2. You may like to journal about your experience.

2

Capacity and Personal Sustainability

We all have a certain amount of capacity for aliveness. Our capacity is constantly changing. Within a day, it can increase or decrease by quite a lot. Learning to understand and respect our capacity will ensure that we stay connected to our innate ability to rejuvenate, repair and heal. Our bodies are incredibly wise and have a profound ability to recover from just about anything. When we exist beyond our capacity, we enter overwhelm and there will be clear signs of this. The initial signs are fatigue, stress and heightened emotion. Over time, these can develop into mental and physical health concerns and relationship dysfunction.

Most of us live outside our capacity and as a result, are constantly seeking an increased sense of well-being. Until we create a life where we can honour our capacity, to primarily live within it, and return to it swiftly when we exceed it, we will be seeking an impossible cure.

The remedy to our dysregulation is personal sustainability. Personal sustainability is the result of receptivity and responsiveness.

Our ability to tune in and respond to our signals of overwhelm is the key to our re-calibration.

When we have exceeded our capacity, we need to find a way to move the needle. We can look to our core needs for safety, belonging and expression/sharing, in order to assess what we need to do to get back within our capacity. Some of the ways in which we can access these resources include:

- **Safety:** Rest, space and down regulation, e.g. through meditation, mindfulness, yoga, massage/gentle bodywork, listening to calming music.
- **Belonging:** Spending time with people where we feel safe, seen, heard and welcome—this can be social or within a therapeutic context.
- **Expression/Sharing:** Releasing energy or emotion through words, tears, art, movement—all expression provides release. When we share these experiences with another person or group, the reparative effect multiplies, because we access a sense of belonging.

The things we need to help us return to our capacity will be different. In order to self-care appropriately, we need to explore what works for us. Over time, we can build a toolkit that we can select from with great intention.

We can start with the question: 'What will help me increase my capacity for aliveness right now?' Initially, we may find it hard or even impossible to find the answer, but as we build our toolkit and practice working with it, it becomes easier to meet ourselves in the most nurturing ways.

In order to maintain our capacity for aliveness and become personally sustainable, self-care needs to become a way of life, rather than a reaction to our dysregulation. Building a life where capacity is king and protected above all, requires us to go back to the topic of 'reclaiming sovereignty'. Do we have the power and freedom we need to live a life where we can put our well-being first?

Cultivating Capacity

Our capacity expands and strengthens through honouring it. That is, when we exist within it, our baseline energy will amplify, as will our ability to recover and heal.

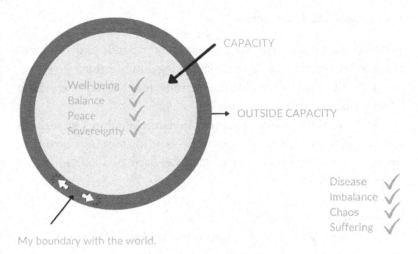

CAPACITY

Well-being ✓
Balance ✓
Peace ✓
Sovereignty ✓

OUTSIDE CAPACITY

Disease ✓
Imbalance ✓
Chaos ✓
Suffering ✓

My boundary with the world.

Image 6.2.1. Capacity

Our capacity contracts and weakens when we live beyond it. That is, when we exist beyond our capacity, our baseline energy shrinks and our ability to recover and heal decreases. This means that the longer we have lived beyond our capacity, or the further we have travelled away from it, the more time we need to a) return to it, and b) re-expand it.

As long as we are living and breathing, we have a capacity for aliveness. Even if we are overwhelmed, burnt out, sick or struggling with our mental health, we have a capacity for aliveness. This means we can return to it and start to slowly expand it.

In order to understand the reasons we exist beyond our capacity, and how we got so far away from it, we need to have looked into our 'why' (which is the focus of the first four parts of this book). Once we understand, we can start to find a way back to ourselves. Our aliveness. Our breath.

The quest to cultivate and maintain our capacity requires us to choose it. Over and over again. It requires us to find our own boundary for aliveness and respect it.

Expansion and Contraction

Just like our breath, our capacity naturally expands and contracts. It is not fixed and finite, but moving, living and breathing.

To live in a state of well-being, we must learn to move with both our expansions and contractions.

Most of us tend to move against our natural rhythm. Our inability to respond to ourselves causes us to become a) stuck in contraction, or b) lost in expansion, or c) flicking between two extreme states again and again.

a) *Stuck in Contraction*
Here, we are oppressed and suffering. We feel trapped and cannot move. Either we fight against the contraction and become more contracted in the process, or we resign ourselves to this being the only reality and root ourselves here; oppressing ourselves further.

Contraction is the cocoon of transformation. Once we welcome our contraction as a time for restoration, reflection and repair, everything changes. Contraction is a place for our own learning and development. If we remain curious about what is available to us during this time, without forcing our way out, we will feel the inevitable movement of growth that will naturally take us into our next expansion. The point is, we have to allow this natural process to unfold.

b) *Lost in Expansion*
Here, we are ungrounded and without foundation. It is more difficult to be discerning or consistent because we are riding a wave of never-ending energy, but unable to truly harness and master it. When we are lost in expansion, integration can't happen. Initially, we may think all is well and feel wonderful, then all of a sudden, we might find ourselves feeling overwhelmed or lost or in a place that we hadn't intended (a job, a relationship, lacking health).

The main reason we become lost in expansion is because we are running from something that we don't want to feel. It may be that our foundations are not ideal . . . or that we have no foundation at all. When we do not have a safe ground beneath our feet, it can feel like we want to fly up into the sky. It may seem that learning to fly is easier than learning to walk. Inevitably, if we want to sustain our flight, we need to learn to walk first. We also need to stay firmly on the ground and build the rocket ship that will support an extended journey, and plan a route to wherever it is we want to go.

Healing asks us to come down to the ground and explore the truth of our reality. We may find there is chaos to clear up, or that we have been teetering on a tightrope above a blackhole. Whatever we find, our job is to lay fresh soil beneath our feet, regroup, rest and begin again. When there is nothing to run from, we can walk slowly and sustainably with the clearest intention.

c) *Flicking between Contraction and Expansion*
When we have not yet learned to follow our rhythm and master our energy, we may find ourselves flicking between extreme states of a) and b). Here, we feel like we are yo-yoing, unstable and erratic; flicking between feeling like we are making amazing strides and like we are a hopeless wreck. This is the essential experience of what we call 'mania'. The distress and anxiety that comes with these highs and lows takes us into deeper extremes. If we can honour the pendulum and start by gracefully finding our limits (as opposed to raging against them), we will often find that the intensity decreases over time.

If we have been either a) stuck in contraction or b) lost in expansion, we may find that when we begin to unstick ourselves, that our pendulum starts to swing wildly. This can cause huge amounts of distress, because we are worried that we will never find the ground beneath our feet. A period of rebalancing and recalibration is needed. We are simply learning to find our centre. Ground. Equilibrium. Peace. Harmony. This will only emerge through time, space and under the guidance of our own self-compassion.

Our pendulum swings so that we can find our true capacity. The experience of swinging is what builds resilience. We learn: 'I am safe, even in the midst of my own intensity (the highs and the lows)'.

Capacity and resilience are born simply through the act of living with self-compassion, and letting go of judgement; letting our pendulum swing.

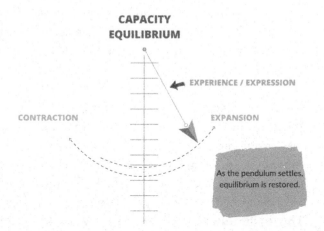

Image 6.2.2. Pendulum: Finding Capacity and Equilibrium

Fear of Going Backwards

As we begin our healing journey, we may find that we want to cling to the new state. We are so grateful to have escaped the place we were trapped or lost in. And we never ever want to go back. 'I don't want to go back to how it was before.' This fear causes us to fight our natural rhythm, again.

The fear of going backwards is a common immobilizer on our healing journey that can loop us back into our dysfunction. We need to remind ourselves that illumination is eternal. There's no going back. And we need to welcome the swing of the pendulum and the non-linear nature of our healing journey. It takes time to build the foundations of peace and power.

When we own this fear, we can swiftly transform it into courageous intention: 'I will never go back to how it was before . . . and so I will continue to listen to myself, remain compassionate and trust my healing process.'

The only thing that stops our healing is our inability to listen and respond. Once we understand the nature of our capacity and can welcome our personal rhythm, we can always return to it, again and again. No matter how far we stray, we have a map to get back home.

Personal Share

The first time I truly learned about the concept of capacity was during the process of learning to walk again. I'd been having intermittent problems with my feet for nearly a decade. I had recurring nerve damage and inflammation, which would mean that both my feet would intermittently drop and I'd be unable to lift them. So in order to walk, I had to lift my leg from my hip. Either I could do it slightly and drag my foot on the floor, or I could lift my hip really high and let my foot follow and flop to the ground. There were times when I tried wearing a brace, but I found it more cumbersome than helpful, so I ended up freestyling most of the time.

It just became another thing I had to tolerate and make the best of. I didn't have control of when my feet would be working or not, so there was this constant feeling of powerlessness and destabilization. Sometimes I could walk. Sometimes I couldn't. Over time, I developed incredible pain in my hips and back. It became very severe. Knowing what I do now about the interconnectivity of the body, of course altering the way I walked caused contraction in my hips and spine, which triggered pain. Though I believe my pain was largely due to trapped emotions relating to abuse. I've shared in an earlier part of this book how I ended up in hospital for two months and in rehab for three. It was in those three months attending rehab when I learned about capacity.

I was an out-patient. So each day, I would be collected from my curbside and get dropped off at the rehab centre. It was about ten steps from my bedroom to the curbside. And about five from the curbside of the rehab centre to their reception. Fifteen steps in all.

Those fifteen steps were hell. By the time I had taken ten steps to the car, I had already triggered a pain response. And I had to take a fast-acting opioid in the car, and brace myself for the three hours of rehab ahead.

The rehab plan consisted of hydrotherapy, physiotherapy and counselling. I was always exhausted before I got into the hydrotherapy pool. When I made my way into the water, the pain was less. And movement was more fluid. But it was still painful. It exhausted me. I was holding back tears and my cheeks were burning with shame during every session.

After the hydrotherapy pool, I would sit on a chair in the shower, talking myself into not passing out. To the physio's dismay, I wasn't able to do any of the active exercises. There was no power in my legs or core. All I could do was lie on the table and let him mobilize my feet, while I faded into a cloud of pain and exhaustion.

Next would be the counsellor. I have no idea what happened in those sessions. I was completely dissociated from the first two hours. Then they would give me some cheap tea with lots of sugar, so I'd have enough energy to walk the five steps to the car. And the ten steps from my curbside into my bedroom. Each time, I would pop another painkiller, sometimes a valium as well, and will myself to sleep, where I would be free from pain.

I asked the rehab therapists if I could do less. They told me it was the head doctor's call. I told the head doctor that it was making my pain worse. He told me I had to build resilience and that was the only way to recover and get strong. So I obeyed.

Every day, it would be the same. The lack of progress made me feel hopeless and broken.

After three months, the rehab doctor suggested I continue to attend for another three months because I was not responding as quickly as they would have liked. But I begged my doctor not to send me. So I was released.

I knew there had to be a different way. I'm not sure how I knew. But I just knew. So I decided to track how many steps I could take before I had a rush of pain. I practised walking up and down my long hallway. The first day, it was six steps. On the seventh step, wooooosh! A surge of pain went through my hips and up my back. So I took a painkiller and went to bed for the day.

The next day, I tried walking only five steps and then leaned against the cold wall. No pain. I stayed leaning there for a few minutes. Still no pain. I stepped forward again—five more steps. Then the sixth step. And again, there was a whoosh of pain. Again, I took a painkiller and went to bed.

But it got me thinking. I clearly had a threshold. A window where there was no pain. If I exceeded it, pain came. If I stayed within it, I was pain-free. So I started to experiment. Explore. If I took a break and rested before I reached my capacity for pain-free movement, it would increase. I learned that by existing within my capacity, it would naturally expand. So I worked with this concept. And I started to see improvement. Daily. Quickly. Very soon, I was walking with ease around the house. Some days, I had to push beyond my capacity. In order to spend time with my children, or go to the doctor, or spend time with a visitor. I knew these things would take me out of the sweet spot and trigger pain. And they always did. But I also learned that I could recoup by making sure I rested after the pain spiked.

Once I was walking around with ease, I started to apply the concept to my overall energy; to my life. I learned to listen to the signs that were telling me I was approaching my threshold for pain-free existence and to respect it. I learned that less is more. Rest is essential and that self-care was the only way I was going to approach a greater state of well-being.

I had so much guilt and shame rise within as I started to look after myself. The mean bitch inside my head would tell me I was selfish and undeserving. But I ignored that bitch. My well-being was more important than anything anyone could tell me (even a powerful voice inside my own head).

The moment I started to understand and honour my capacity, I became more vital. Stronger. More emotionally balanced. My capacity for aliveness grew over time.

Years later, as I moved into the role of a clinic director and managing a team, I started existing beyond my capacity again and went into burnout. But I knew the early warning signs and immediately took time off to rest and re-calibrate.

These days, self-care is a fundamental part of my life. I work less, I look after myself more.

There are many people I know who don't understand how I can engage in so much self-care. I do it all. Exercise, meditation, therapy, massage, yoga, laying by my pool . . . to name just a few. Sometimes I feel their incredulous judgement, as they look at me from inside their burnt-out bodies, with frazzled eyes. And I just smile. Self-care is the reason I am alive today. It's the reason I can be a calm and connected mother, an attentive therapist, a kickass CEO, and remain compassionate in the face of ugliness.

There are times where I push beyond my limits. Maybe I have a deadline or a goal to reach, or want to do something extra for my kids or help a friend in need or just go and blow off steam. But the moment I step outside my capacity, I know it. And I will make a point to find a way back in ASAP.

Whenever I push myself too hard and notice those warning signs, I remember what it's like not to be able to walk, or to be laying in a hospital bed. I will never let myself go anywhere near that again. My health and well-being is a sacred gift to be treasured, always. I am grateful for every breath.

Invitation to Self-inquiry

- Am I living within my capacity or beyond it?
- What are the things that nourish me/increase my capacity? How can I build my self-care toolkit with intention?
- What are the experiences/relationships/dynamics that take me beyond my capacity? How can I start to shift these? Which of these can I easily let go of? Which of these need my time and attention to facilitate change?
- Am I following my personal rhythm or fighting against it? Am I currently a) stuck in contraction, b) lost in expansion, or c) flicking between states? What can I do to invite my healing process to unfold?
- Am I afraid of going back to a 'bad' place? How is this showing up and what can I do to connect to my courageous intention for my healing?
- Now ask yourself: How can I structure my life in a way that allows me to honour my capacity?

Somatic Healing Practice

Expansion and Contraction

Find a comfortable place either laying down on your back or sitting with your back straight. Place one hand on your chest and the other on your abdomen. Take a moment to settle. Tune in to your breath. The inhale and the exhale. As you inhale, connect to the expansion it brings in your body. As you exhale, connect to the contraction it brings in your body. Without trying to alter your breath in any way, find your inhale (expansion) and exhale (contraction). This is your capacity for aliveness. Right here in your breath. If it feels comfortable to do so, gently increase the length of your inhale (expansion) and exhale (contractions). Notice your innate ability to increase your limits little by little, simply with your intention.

Do this six times, just to the level that feels comfortable and safe. Then let go of intention and notice what arises, as you breathe naturally.

Affirm to Yourself

'I honour my breath. My life force. My aliveness.'

Trauma-informed Note:

If this is the first time you have connected your breath to the concept of your aliveness/capacity, it may feel overwhelming. In this case, do not try to increase your inhale or exhale, simply stay with what is natural and available. If you still feel overwhelmed, you can turn over and lay on your stomach and be present with the ground while your system settles. Let the floor support you. The intention of the practice is to listen to your capacity—make this your priority, rather than completing the practice.

3

Complete Accountability

If we desire peace and power, we must take complete accountability for our lives. We are responsible for it all. Every choice. Every reaction. Every word. Every breath. They are all brushstrokes that create the artwork of the Self, and they also contribute to the collective masterpiece that is our world. Our accountability will not only protect us, but it will protect others from us. In order to become accountable, we have to feel empowered, rather than disempowered. The moment we are oppressed, we are in some way disempowered. As a result, others become accountable for our experience. A partner. A parent. A friend. A boss. A doctor. A community. A system.

When we are not truly accountable, we are living in victimhood.

'It's not my fault.'

'They made me.'

'I'm not allowed. It's against the rules.'

'I don't want to let him down.'

If that person, people or system diminishes our sense of agency in the world, we lose both peace and power. Our ability to be accountable is a direct reflection of our ability to connect to impulse (desire) and agency (choice).

Because powerlessness is a fundamental experience of trauma (and much of our modern world existence), it is hard for many of us to take complete accountability for our lives. We simply can't.

There are people, experiences or systems stopping us. And sometimes, even when nothing is actually stopping us, we stop ourselves, because our experience of powerlessness is more than just in the present, it's existential. Felt. Somatic.

'I can't.' 'I'm just like this.' 'This is how it is.' 'I can't change it.'

'I can't leave the relationship. Quit the job. Earn the money. Take the holiday. Follow my dream. Say no to the barrage of requests coming my way. Put my health first.'

Our powerlessness, paired with our fear and shame, traps us. Every time we say we can't, we are expressing from a state of trauma and entrapment. We disconnect from the universal truth that we are in a constant state of change.

To reconnect to our innate power to change, we need to step into accountability.

Accountability begins with sheer will.

Will stokes our desire; ignites our impulse. Impulse says 'I want that and I'm going to try and claim it'. When impulse is followed, it ignites agency—an act of free will. A choice.

Agency says 'I choose this. I reach for it. I create it.' When we are able to connect to both impulse and agency, we can stand up and begin to take accountability for our lives. Accountability integrates slowly. Over time. We need enough internal safety and strength to navigate through the journey. And we need to work through the layers of shame and fear that tell us that our impulses are wrong, or that our agency will incite some form of harm or exclusion.

If our power has been diminished over time, it can feel like the responsibility is all too much; that we will be crushed under the weight of it, or suffocated by the perceived noose around our neck.

Accountability is scary. Foreign.

When we have lived through oppression, there has always been someone else holding the ropes of that noose. To take it into our own hands feels inconceivable. But once it's in our hands, we can slowly untie it, and breathe the air fully into our lungs—be free.

Ironically, our inability to be accountable keeps us trapped in our state of oppression.

The Overwhelm of Power

When we start working on our accountability, we can become overwhelmed by the immensity of the power that we hold. It's as if we were little kids who had been asked to drive our parent's car. And if we have lived through trauma, that really is the case. Many of our fragmented selves are young in age. They emerged during the time of trauma, and got stuck there. They never had a chance to grow up. So when all of a sudden, we ask them to hold our hands and step forward into a new life, they feel overwhelmed. Either terrified of the unknown. Or incredibly awkward and inept.

Feeling incapable, slow, clunky or having no idea how to handle something at all, is a common experience when we are trying to step into a more accountable way of living and relating. And these feelings often trigger further states of fear and shame, that can then send us into feelings of intense frustration and anger, or fling us back into our existential powerlessness. When we don't catch this phase for what it is, one of the two things happen: a) our frustration and anger leak onto those who do not deserve it; b) we give up. We give back the power to wherever it came from and choose a life less accountable. We find some cage to crawl back into.

In order to move through this stage and claim the life we want, we need to understand what's going on and hold ourselves with compassion. We have to allow our traumatized child and all our fragmented selves to grow up under the guidance of our conscious healing self. There will be missteps. Difficulty. Perhaps anxiety and frustration. We will have to learn to look after ourselves through all of it and keep going.

Just like a child learning to ride a bike, we will get the hang of it. With practice and guidance. And one day, we will get in the driver's seat of the big, shiny car, and learn to drive that, too.

And when we do, the world is ours.

When we become accountable, our innate power no longer overwhelms us and we can start harnessing it in the ways that best serve us.

Re-parenting

In order to help ourselves become accountable, we need to engage in the process of re-parenting. Our conscious healing self needs to take on the role of a parent, custodian, shepherd, leader and guide. We have to be our own cheerleader, our own coach, our own disciplinarian and our own source of infinite nurture and care. We have to help ourselves grow into the kind of adult we dream of being.

As any parent knows, this takes inordinate amounts of patience and will often come with frustration, missteps and exhaustion. Parenting is tiring but rewarding! If we consider all our fragmented selves, we are the parent of many siblings trying to figure out how to get along and find their own unique expressions. It's big work!

This conscious re-patterning starts by replacing the seed of our existence.

The trauma self originates from fear and aloneness (or exclusion). The healing self originates from safety and belonging. If we can start to find ways to help ourselves (all of ourselves) feel a little bit safer, and welcome all our emotions, experiences and dysfunction into our own care, we will find the path to incredible transformation. We will bloom within the garden of our own self-compassion and invite a more integrated and authentic way of living and relating, that will continue to change over time.

As we embark on the epic journey of re-parenting, it will be normal to feel periods of deep fatigue. Our nervous system and psyche are working overtime, having old experiences and impulses, witnessing and catching these impulses, setting boundaries and recalibrating, and finding new pathways for expressing and relating. It's like our existential ecosystem is working triple-time; weeding, sewing, planting, pruning and watering the healing self.

The amount of energy re-parenting takes makes us humble. The grit. The vulnerability. The insane amounts of courage. We will forever recognize them in ourselves and each other. A new kind of empathy is born in the process.

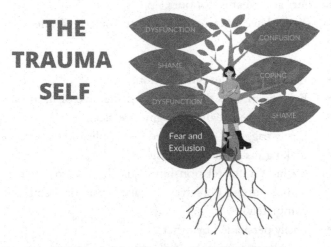

Image 6.3.1. The Traumatized Self

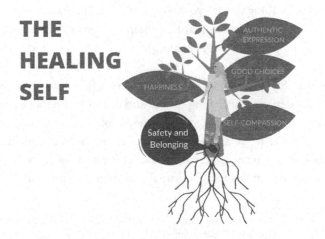

Image 6.3.2. The Healing Self

Containment

As we continue on our healing journey, we develop containment. Once we have a centre and a boundary with the world, we can better contain our experiences. This allows us to differentiate. We learn what is ours and what is not ours.

When we have little to no capacity for containment, we may find ourselves:

- Unable to master our emotions.
- Relating in ways that are rude, dismissive or harmful.
- Speaking before our thoughts are clear.
- Easily triggered or offended by people and experiences.
- Making rash, reactive decisions.
- Rushing into relationships quickly before trust is built (either putting ourselves in harm's way or losing ourselves completely).
- Easily persuaded by others.
- Unable to practise self-discipline (e.g. anytime we try out a new self-care regime—diet, exercise, meditation, staying single—we can't stick with it).
- Doing things that we know are harmful to ourselves or others, but not being able to help ourselves (like dating the wrong person, lying, cheating).

The inability to contain our experiences often leads to feeling energetically depleted or feeling erratic and unstable, unable to move with power and purpose, and often has harmful effects on the people around us. It is as if we are leaking murky energy into the world.

Containment is a practice to be cultivated over time. My interpretation originates from spiritual and tantric philosophy.[28]

---

[28] Tantra https://somananda.org/tantra/#:~:text=In%20this%20sense%2C%20 Tantra%20means%20the%20liberation%20of,form%20the%20basis%20of%20 all%20authentic%20yogic%20practices.

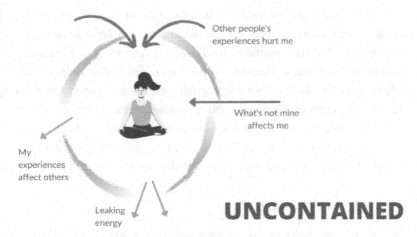

Image 6.3.3. Uncontained

Containment says: 'I can sense my impulse and experience within me; and I choose not to express it beyond me.'

As we sit with our experience, we remain independent in it. In this way, it does not affect the world around us. 'I am in peace as I sit with myself. I have the power to transform my feeling state, simply through my independent experience.'

In essence, this is the art of meditation.

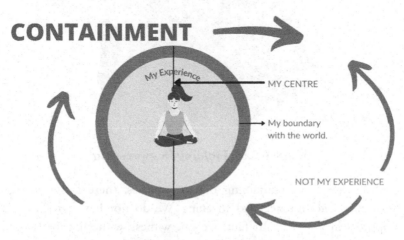

Image 6.3.4. Containment

When we have unresolved trauma and suppressed emotions, containment is impossible. This is because we are holding onto old experiences that are harmful to us. There is no room for us to practice containing new ones. Many of us have also never been shown what containment looks like. Our role models have either shown us how to suppress or explode. Before we can increase our ability to contain, we often first need to empty out the old emotional energy and come into contact with people who can show us what embodied containment looks and feels like. As always, we learn through lived experiences.

Holding vs Containing

When we are holding or suppressing our experiences, there is tension, charge and oftentimes minimization or denial at play. It drains us of energy and causes us to fragment and separate our internal experience from our external one. We lose authenticity and harm ourselves in the process.

Image 6.3.5. Holding/Suppressing

When we are containing our experiences, there is sensation, movement, acceptance and meaning. We do not have to alter or suppress in any way. In fact, we can witness without expression. There is no loss of authenticity or sense of harm in this process.

Containing
Experience

Image 6.3.6. Containing Experience

Authenticity and the Expression Trap

If we have been shape-shifting and quietening ourselves for most of our lives, the moment we find our voice, we want to let it bellow into the world: 'This is who I am! I will not stay quiet anymore! I am going to be my authentic self!'

It is true that opening our voice is a huge part of the healing journey. However, if we stop here, our uncontained voice may end up wreaking havoc around us, expressing from our unresolved wounds. We may think we are free once we are no longer afraid to speak up. But if our voice oppresses, minimizes or disregards another, we are not free at all, and neither are those around us.

Once we have freed our voice, the next step is to learn to contain and master it. If we do not continue, we are stuck in the trap of our perceived authenticity.

In order to master our voice, we need to master our nervous system. When we feel any sense of urgency that we must express in a certain way, it comes from unresolved charge in the nervous system—a sense of internal threat and the continued quest for safety.

The nervous system says: 'If I don't express this, I will feel discomfort, or perhaps explode. I need to express to regain a sense of safety.'

This is often very true. But the continued search for internal peace and relational harmony asks us to acknowledge this and continue to soothe and heal in safe places, rather than litter the world with our unconscious expression.

> When our voice is truly free, we will find peace both in silence and expression.
> In mastery, there is no need, only infinite choice.

Containment and Expression

Learning to contain will alter the way we express in the world. Containment affords us the opportunity to find clarity before expression. We can discern what is true for us, and also how our words will ripple out into the world.

When our expression is peaceful, clear and intentional, it holds incredible power. We can be sure that we are speaking with intention to share in ways that empower ourselves and others.

This is the place from which 'do no harm' can truly be embodied.

Containment first ends the war inside us. Next, it promotes peace around us. Our commitment to our own containment will change the world.

Trigger Management and De-activation

Our ability to contain opens the doorway to managing and de-activating our triggers.

When we are triggered, an external stimulus hits an 'emotional nerve' that causes us to express reactively. Reactions rarely lead us to where we want to be, which is fundamentally in a place of internal peace and relational harmony. Instead, they leave us feeling distressed and often create relational dissonance.

Triggers are generally a response to feeling either a) violated; b) neglected, or c) misunderstood.

Our reactions will vary depending on the state of our nervous system and the unique way our trauma has decontextualized inside us. Our reactions are often the inaugural domino in a chain of reactions that take us further and further away from where we want to be. They take us away from peace and towards war.

Containment provides the internal space we need to shift gears from reactivity into responsiveness.

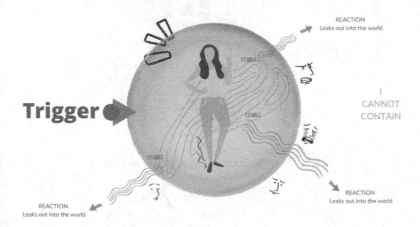

Image 6.3.7. Trigger Reaction

When we respond rather than react, we can start to create distance between our experience and our expression. The domino effect comes to an end in that moment. We claim the power to redirect the narrative towards our best intentions.

Internalizing Reactions

Many of us start working with our triggers before we have developed enough capacity for containment. We know that we don't want to keep reacting all over the place, so we learn to turn the reactive experience inwards, instead of directing it outwards. We don't want to be the person creating a problem. Our intention is pure! However, when we internalize our reaction, it takes a huge toll on the nervous system and again, we fragment and lose authenticity. When we continue to 'hold our tongue' as a means of managing triggers, it rarely works. The suppressed emotion and charge often build up inside us until we finally either a) explode (often after the proverbial 'straw that broke the camel's back'); or b) self-harm as a means of altering our feeling state.

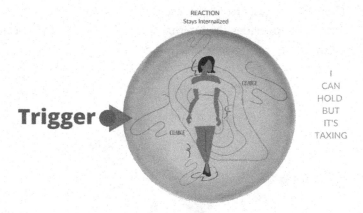

6.3.8. Internalizing Trigger Reaction

6.3.9. Fragmentation and Loss of Authenticity

Releasing Charge

The next step on the journey of trigger-mastery is to learn how to release charge safely. When we are triggered, we can learn how to temporarily hold the reaction and find safe ways to release the charge outside of the triggering dynamic. This may look like finding a safe place to cry or rant, journalling, pounding a pillow or a punching bag or going for a swim. Expression paired with intention will allow the charge to release from our system.

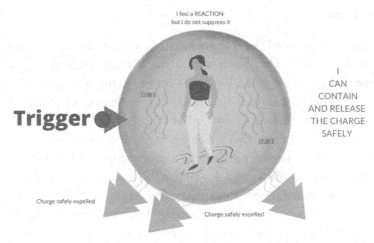

Image 6.3.10. Trigger Containment and Release

Redirection

As we develop deep intimacy with our fragmented selves and recognize the felt experience of our triggers, we become better able to redirect triggers. This manifests as feeling a much milder trigger experience, paired with a prompt recognition of the fragment who is present and experiencing. The awareness ignites a deep sense of compassion and letting go. The trigger is redirected back outside of us. The time to recalibrate is minimal.

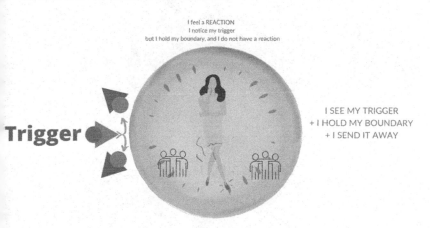

Image 6.3.11. Trigger Redirection

Deactivation

In order to completely deactivate a trauma trigger, we need to go and heal the root of it. When our trauma is triggered, one of our fragmented selves is saying, 'Is it my turn to tell my story yet?' The only way to heal is to give it a chance. When we listen, our fragment will tell us what it's feeling, why, what it never received during the original experience, and what it needs now in order to feel safe, seen and heard. When we provide a safe space for expression and release, we find resolution and integration. When the trauma is resolved and the fragment is integrated, there is nothing left to be triggered. It's deactivated. It may take multiple attempts to deactivate a trigger, particularly in cases where trauma has been acute, chronic, or stored for decades. But it is possible. For most trauma survivors, there are multiple triggers for each of the fragmented selves that we need to spend time working with. Each time we deactivate a trigger, our psyche frees up and our nervous system moves closer to safety—our capacity for aliveness increases, as does our ability to contain our

I HEAL MY TRAUMA
+ THE TRIGGER
NO LONGER EXISTS

Image 6.3.12. Healed Trigger

experiences. We can spiral deeper not only into our healing, but into the beauty of life—we enter post-traumatic growth.[29]

Present Trigger vs. Trauma Trigger

Trigger work becomes confusing when we are trying to heal our trauma, but are engaged in disrespectful or harmful dynamics in the present. Here, we have to learn to differentiate between our unhealed trauma and justified reactions in the present. There are three different experiences that may arise:

a) **Trauma Response:** The person who triggers us is not doing anything disrespectful or harmful, but our trauma is being triggered. In this case, our reaction is entirely a trauma response and we are transferring an old experience onto the other person.

Trauma Response

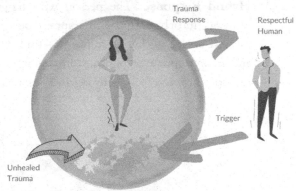

Image 6.3.13. Trauma Response

---

[29] Lorna Collier, 'Growth after trauma: Why are some people more resilient than others—and can it be taught?', *American Psychological Association*, Vol. 47, No. 10, November 2016, p. 48. Available at: https://www.apa.org/monitor/2016/11/growth-trauma. Accessed April 2022.

b) **Appropriate Response to Disrespect:** The person who triggers us is doing something harmful, but our trauma is not being triggered. In this case, our reaction is an entirely appropriate response to the present experience.

Appropriate Response (to disrespect)

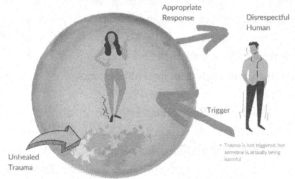

Image 6.3.14. Appropriate Response to Disrespect

c) **Hybrid Response:** The person who triggers us is being disrespectful or harmful *and* our trauma is being triggered. In this case, we are having hybrid response—both a trauma response and an appropriate response expressed in one overwhelming reaction. This can feel confusing and destabilizing.

Hybrid Response

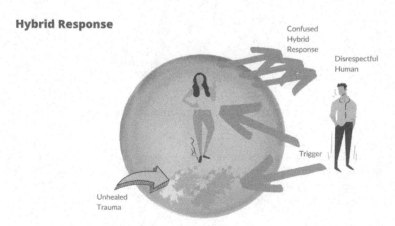

Image 6.3.15. Hybrid Response

The more we learn about our trauma and fragmented selves, the better we can understand how we are experiencing in present dynamics. This points us towards the places that need more healing and allows us to begin to discern which relationships are nourishing our growth or impeding it. Many of us with unresolved trauma find ourselves in relationships that do not truly serve us... because we are repeating past harmful dynamics or following an unhealthy map for love. As we heal, we learn that we are worthy of so much more. Once we have enough capacity to start to master our own experience, we can look towards setting the boundaries we need for relational restructuring.... The final piece of the accountability puzzle.

Boundaries

Boundaries are expressions of limits that establish our sovereignty and increase our sense of balance and peace. When they are respected, we experience harmony. When maintained, they are the infrastructure of personal and relational sustainability.

Unfortunately, many of us do not know how to set, maintain or respect boundaries—our own or each other's. This may be because:

a) Most of us have not been educated about boundaries and respectful relating.

b) Boundaries can only originate from clarity and peace, and most of us are distressed and/or confused at some level.

c) The relationships or systems that we live within, do not care about our boundaries and often squash our attempts to set and maintain them.

d) We do not possess the perceptive powers to understand non-verbal boundaries, therefore, we are incapable of respecting them.

e) We cannot contain our emotions and impulses, so we are incapable of sustained respect.

f) We are afraid that setting a boundary will cause either harm or exclusion (rejection or abandonment).

A boundary is a line in the sand that says: 'Here. Here is my limit. Please respect it.' There are many different kinds of boundaries:

- Physical
- Emotional
- Spiritual
- Spatial

The way we truly know when a boundary is being breached, is through a felt, somatic experience that says: 'No, this isn't okay for me'. This clear 'no' may be in response to our own experience, or a dynamic experience with a person or group. In addition to feeling our own 'no', boundaries require us to be able to feel and respond to another person's 'no'.

'No' is often a silent expression, that only our nervous system can truly 'hear'. In order to master the art of boundaries, we need to learn to listen with more than our ears. When we are tuned into our felt sense, we will find that boundaries are presenting to us all day long. They let us know when we need food, rest, expression, connection. They let us know who we want to let in and who we want to keep out. They are gentle warnings guiding us to maintain a sense of safety and equilibrium.

Our inability to listen and respond to boundaries is the single greatest cause of discontent, disease and disrespect.

Fluidity

Boundaries are dynamic. They exist between a layer of our experience and something or someone else.

Therefore, boundaries are also unique in every dynamic. That is, the boundaries that we set in one relationship or system will be different from the boundaries we set in another. They are responsive, rather than fixed.

Because we are in constant change, so too, are our boundaries. They are fluid and responsive to the complex experiences between us and the world around us. Unfortunately, many of us think we are setting boundaries, when we are actually setting defenses.

Defenses—Rigidity and Rules

Fluidity is something we lose when we are in the face of threat (present or perceived). Our quest for safety means that rigidity is essential. We have to defend and protect; fluidity would leave us susceptible to surprise attack. So we develop rigid defenses to keep ourselves safe.

The ability to discern and differentiate is also lost in the face of threat. We do not have the processing capacity to develop different boundary systems that are continuously recalibrating. So we take a 'rule of thumb' approach. 'These are my boundaries and I will not change them under any circumstance.'

We call these boundaries, but they are actually defenses. Boundaries are responsive and fluid. They welcome communication and collective evolution. 'Let's listen to and respect each other and see how we can dance in the world.'

Defenses are non-responsive and rigid. They keep us safe in our fortress; alone. 'You better listen to me, but I have no interest in listening to you. It's my way or the highway.'

Boundary Work as Essential to Healing Trauma

Most of us have no idea how to do the whole boundary thing.

Our unresolved trauma often has us engaging with a complete lack of boundaries in some areas and iron-thick defenses in other areas. We are either totally unprotected, or locked inside our fortress. Without healthy, fluid, malleable boundary-setting skills, we simply will not be able to relate in the world. Not in ways that bring us peace, power and the intimacy we seek.

Boundaries are the key to safe, vulnerable, authentic connection; and underneath it all, that's the essence of what we are searching for our entire lives (trauma or no trauma).

When we start to work with boundaries, it will trigger all of our fragmented selves in one way or another. Every emotion we have been running from will show itself. Our nervous system will enter overwhelm. And we will feel confused, and perhaps ashamed. All the things we have been trying to hard not to feel, we will feel with incredible intensity. This is why our journey with boundaries occurs slowly over time, as we develop awareness about our why, and cultivate our capacity to contain and transform these experiences.

Some of the reactions we may have to our boundary setting process include:

Boundary	Reaction
When we express a limit, need or desire	Fear of being shamed, harmed or excluded (rejected or abandoned)
When we try to stay away from unhealthy people, work less, rest more, reduce social media	The wound of aloneness
When we try not to rush into a relationship too quickly	The craving for connection and the grief of not having it
When we claim our truth and do not let someone minimize or gaslight us	Fear of being shamed, harmed or excluded (rejected or abandoned)
When we respect someone else's limit, need or desire (when we usually don't)	The wound of aloneness
When we allow someone else to claim their truth and do not minimize or gaslight them	The wound of aloneness

As we step into the gift of our sovereignty, we will see and feel it all. Through this embodied illumination, we can truly begin to heal. We can maintain our newfound peace, and we can ignite the same within those around us. This is the art of intimacy. Boundaries are also the gateway to play and joy. Once we trust our ability to relate and respond safely, we no longer need to live in a state of hypervigilance, waiting to be harmed or excluded. Many of us who grew up in trauma or oppression never got to play. It wasn't safe or welcome. As we continue our healing work and learn the art of boundaries and find safety in fluidity, we can become curious explorers and revel in the magic of play and delight. Little by little, we can open ourselves to joy.

When we can be accountable for all of it—our choices (actions and words), containment, triggers, boundaries, delight and joy—we can have anything we desire.

Personal Share

I've been learning how to be accountable for years now. The more I heal my trauma, the safer I feel inside myself. And the more capacity I've had to start mastering my expression in the world. And creating the life I want and deserve. I'm still going!

For most of my life, I had no sense of sovereignty. My experience of safety and belonging was dependent on my oppressors. And affectively, I became my own oppressor. I was so used to my well-being being outside of my control, that I just left it there. In powerlessness, we are accountable for nothing.

Every leap forward has been as the result of stepping up my accountability game. Even though I was terrified. Even though it triggered deeper layers of trauma for healing. Even though there was no ground to catch me. Even though taking responsibility for my life brought about difficult consequences.

The difficult consequences were all temporary.

- When I told the doctors I was not bipolar and detoxed off meds, I went into a suicidal state. But out the other end, I was free from medications and able to start working in a career I loved and get married to the (then) love of my life.

- When I decided to quit medical treatment and medication, my body entered a healing crisis for a couple of months. I was scared I would die several times. But it found homeostasis through time, space and care. I was healthy and well!
- When I left my marriage, I was alone in the world, a recovering co-dependent with no savings in a foreign country. But I figured out how to live alone, be independent, be a great single mama and cultivate a harmonious co-parenting relationship. I also got to figure out who I truly was as a sovereign woman.
- When I left an abusive relationship, later on, I was faced with aggression and manipulation that sent me into huge states of terror. But I learned how to walk away peacefully and protect myself. The level of power and peace that emerged afterwards was incredible.

I'm still stepping into my accountability and my power. I feel like I am a living Rubik's cube. I keep going back over the lessons I have learned. Clarifying them. Embodying them. Containing. Responding. Deactivating triggers. Setting boundaries.

My will has always been strong. It's following the impulse, where I trip up. Every time before a big leap, I feel wildly afraid. And I'm riddled with preemptive shame. 'Who am I to do this?' 'Who am I to desire this? 'I'm not like those other shiny, bright humans.' 'My expression or choice will lead to some awful disaster.'

But I catch myself.

I remember that I deserve my life. Happiness. Sovereignty. And that I actually already have them. I've earned them. I think having lived in oppression for most of my life, it has taken time to really believe that I am free; that I am not going to fall back into an old, dark dungeon. Sometimes the fear can be so strong that the world starts to morph around me and I think I am trapped again. I have to access my conscious healing self. Look around and remind myself of my freedom.

I slow down. Take a breath. Move my body.

I bring my fragmented selves close to my heart and shift into compassion.

I release what no longer serves me. I set intention. And I remind myself that this is my life. That I am safe. Empowered. And it is me who must sow the seeds of my future.

I am committed to becoming a peaceful warrior in the world. And it is my commitment, along with my compassion that allows me to continue to find my purest expression, where I have peace, purpose and eternal protection. Complete accountability.

Invitation to Self-inquiry

- How accountable are you for your life? In what areas are you taking responsibility and in what areas could you be more attentive?
- If you feel like someone or something else holds power over your experience, who are they and how can you take back your power?
- Do you feel and follow your impulses? Are you empowered, or are you holding back? Why? What happens when you think about following your impulse and finding agency?
- Can you contain your thoughts and emotions peacefully or do you tend to either hold or leak/explode? Why do you think this is occurring and what can you do to alter this, even if in a small way?
- How do you respond to triggers? What stage of the journey are you at?
- Are you able to sense when you are experiencing: a) a trauma response; b) a reasonable response; c) a hybrid response?
- Do you tend towards no boundaries, defenses posing as boundaries, or a mix of the two? Understanding what you do about your 'why', how can you start to shift this?
- Now ask yourself: How can I begin to be more accountable for my life?

Somatic Healing Practice

Sovereignty and Containment

Find a comfortable seated position. Take some breaths into your body. Become aware of your physical form. Not trying to alter anything. Just noticing you. Bring your awareness to your skin. Where you end and 'not you' begins. This is your physical boundary with the world. Bring your attention to 1 cm away from the skin. Your energy exists here, too. Using your sensing skills, find how far your energy extends beyond your body. It may be a centimeter or as much as a meter. Once you find your energetic boundary with the world, you may like to put an intentional ring around it. Perhaps give it a colour. Notice that this is you and your experience. And anything beyond it is not. Intend to protect your experience as solely your own.

Affirm to Yourself

'I claim my experience as my own, and I offer anything that is not mine, back to its origin. I protect my sovereignty and invite the sovereignty of others.'

4

Receptivity

Receptivity is the art of pairing perception and responsiveness. It is the essence of flow state.

Our ability to perceive enhances with the more healing work we do. We become safe enough to listen more deeply to ourselves and to each other. Our ability to respond (rather than react) also increases as we gain a greater sense of sovereignty.

When we feel truly safe inside ourselves, we can adopt receptivity as a way of being, and a place to return to, again and again. Here, we are both strong and soft. Masculine and feminine. We embrace ourselves and each other, in all of our imperfection, with no need to brace against expression of any kind.

Our receptivity is what keeps us mindful, present and evolutionary. It is also what allows others to feel truly safe, seen, heard and held in their entirety by us.

This is the greatest gift we can bestow upon ourselves and the world.

Perceptive Powers

Our ability to perceive is often dampened by the charge we hold in our nervous system and the noise of the world that leads us to bias, judgement and the loss of truth.

If we are dissociated, if we do not have a centre, or do not know how to contain and differentiate (to be sovereign), we will not be able to perceive with clarity. Our perceptions will be coloured by our own sense of threat or distorted by the views of others.

Our inability to perceive neutral truth leads us to exist merely as a reaction or a hologram. When we don't know any other way, it becomes our normal modus operandi.

In order to start cultivating our perceptive powers, we have to come home to our bodies, our nervous systems and all the things we have been running from. We have to feel them first and clear out our human container. As dynamic creatures, we learn about the people around us in the process. As we learn about ourselves, we learn about each other. As we empty out what has been colouring our view of the world, we can see others more clearly.

We can start to perceive the unique unconscious, the unspoken subtext, and the quiet whispers of our hearts that are all searching for the same thing.

Perceptive powers are the currency of healers, shamans, psychics and prophets, but really, they are accessible to us all.

Perception promotes embodied empathy.

Empathy

Empathy is the ability to perceive what is true for ourselves, and for another, then engage in a way that acknowledges both experiences. It requires us to expand our awareness to perceive in two places at once. When we are rooted at our centre and sovereign in our experience, only then can we truly empathize.

Empathy says: 'I understand your experience, and I understand my response to your experience. I honour you in a way that also honours me.'

In empathy, we meet each other without diminishing each other.

Empathy is the birthplace of attunement.

As we continue to attune to someone, we can shift into compassion and provide the most supportive care. In its most potent

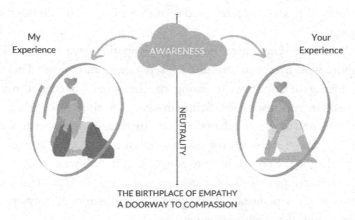

Image 6.4.1. Empathy

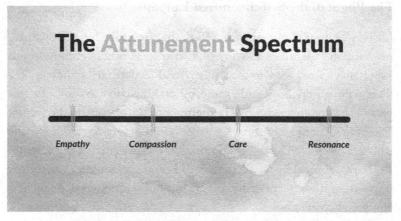

Image 6.4.2. The Attunement Spectrum

form, attunement shows up as pure resonance. When we resonate with someone, our silent presence becomes an incredible source of healing.

Empathy vs. Sympathy and Pity

Until we have found sovereignty, we tend to confuse empathy with sympathy or pity.

Sympathy says: 'I understand your experience, but I do not meet you in it.'

When we sympathize, rather than empathize, we are providing support with a certain amount of separation and space. There is no sharing of capacity, or easing of the other's burden through connection and resonance. Sympathy has a healthy place when we want to show care, in a relationally or situationally appropriate way.

Pity says: 'I am sorry for your pain, but I do judge it in one way or another, and I do not wish to resonate in it with you.'

When we pity, we look down on another. We repel and place ourselves on a pedestal. While perhaps unintentional, pity sparks more pain in those who receive it.

The Plight of the Self-diagnosed Empath

Misconceptions about empathy led to the rise of the term 'empath'.[30] An 'empath' identifies as someone who feels others emotions and experiences a negative impact. They tend to deny accountability for their own experiences and blame others' 'negative energy'. In this process, everyone becomes a perpetrator and they remain the victim. The term 'energy vampire'[31] was developed to describe someone who has 'negative energy' and impacts the experience of the empath.

Sadly, this popularized paradigm keeps many trauma survivors trapped in their experience of victimhood and co-dependency; completely powerless.

While 'empaths' have often lived through large amounts of trauma or oppression, it is the projection of the past trauma into the present that causes an eternal sense of harm to arise within.

---

[30] Leah Campbell, 'What Is an Empath and How Do You Know If You Are One?', Verywell Mind, 17 June 2021, available at: https://www.verywellmind.com/what-is-an-empath-and-how-do-you-know-if-you-are-one-5119883. Accessed April 2022.

[31] 'How to Recognize and Respond to Energy Vampires at Home, Work, and More', Healthline, available at: https://www.healthline.com/health/mental-health/energy-vampires#:~:text=Energy%20vampires%20are%20people%20who%20%E2%80%94%20sometimes%20intentionally,can%20be%20your%20spouse%20or%20your%20best%20friend. Accessed April 2022.

Our projections keep us living in a fantasy where vampires are out to get us, and we await a saviour who will never traverse the border into reality and save us.

The charge in the nervous system, the fragility of the heart, and the cries of the fragmented selves are in constant play.

The expressions of others may be mirroring old harmful dynamics, or triggering suppressed emotions that are simply waiting for a pathway to express. Sometimes, witnessing another's pain or dysfunction lifts our own into expression. If we do not have the ability to differentiate or the capacity to feel and contain, the only possible solution is to make someone or something else accountable for our experience.

In order for empaths to heal and release the 'self-diagnosed' label, there is a need to increase our sense of safety and sovereignty.

As we become more empowered, cultivate a centre, create boundaries and develop our perceptive powers, we learn that 'the whole world is not an asshole'. We learn that we are sovereign, with the power to deflect what is not ours, back to its source. As we do this, we step deeper into accountability—caring for our fragmented selves, deactivating our triggers and resolving our trauma.

Self-abandonment, Co-dependency and Trauma Bonds

When we do not exist in a state of receptivity, we will be unable to healthily respond to our own needs and the needs of others.

If we cannot perceive, we cannot respond.

Due to our tendency towards polarity and the inability to access embodied empathy, we tend to root at one end of the perception spectrum.

If we can only perceive ourselves, we can only respond to ourselves. We become selfish.

If we can only perceive others, we can only respond to others. We become self-abandoning.

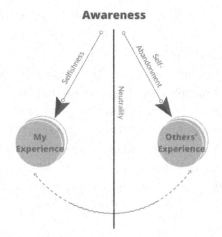

Image 6.4.3. Selfish vs. Self-abandonment

If we are fragmented (which most of us are), some of our fragments may root in each polarity. So we may be incredibly selfish in some areas, and incredibly self-abandoning in others.

These tendencies originate from survival responses. And so, in order to survive, we unconsciously seek relationships and dynamics that will facilitate us to stay where we are. They become our unassuming accomplices to remaining in our state of trauma.

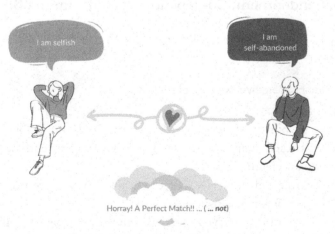

Image 6.4.4. Co-dependency

This is known as co-dependency. It is also the essence of all trauma bonds. In co-dependent relationships, the core experience is: 'I am only okay, if you are okay. If you are not okay, I am not okay.'

Both parties end up shape-shifting and self-abandoning in order to feel okay.

In the case of trauma bonds, the experience intensifies where either one or both parties are seeking soothing and healing in the arms of another. We become each other's band-aids, comforters, drug of choice . . . and eventually, the source of each other's discontent.

When we enter a relationship with the unconscious intention of healing our trauma, there will always be dysfunction to follow.

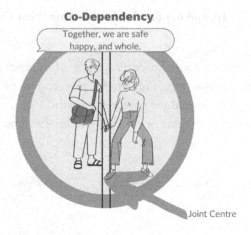

Image 6.4.5. Co-dependency Joint Centre

No one can heal us. This realization often plunges us into the depths of our grief, anger and the wound of separation. But it is from this process that we can redirect ourselves into the care of our own accountability and our desire for healthy love.

The moment we learn to perceive our own wounding (and each other's), everything changes. We can stop using the relationship to deny or soothe our pain, and start doing the work to heal—to claim sovereignty, which is essential for relationship harmony. When two

Image 6.4.6. Co-dependency Not Okay

(or more) adults choose to enter a state of receptivity, they enter a conscious relationship. This is the playground of alchemy and accelerates our potential for personal growth.

Receptivity underpins our capacity to love and be loved.

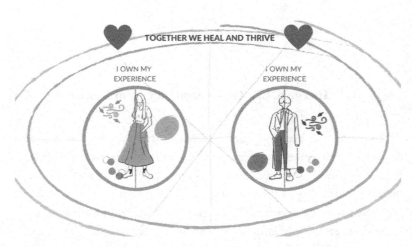

Image 6.4.7. Conscious Relationship

The Balance of Giving and Receiving

Receptivity allows us to learn to both give and receive. To step forward and to step back. To tend to others when our capacity allows, and to tend to ourselves when we need our own care. Boundaries emerge and evolve with ease and grace. Polarity disappears.

We embrace fluidity, flexibility and allow our energy to flow where it is needed, without selfishness or self-abandonment. We can stop clinging to fixed identities and ways of being and relating . . . and simply dance. Rather than cling to a love language, we speak many, and we can open ourselves to receive in multiple ways. We no longer need others to give or receive in a certain way; and so we are all free.

In receptivity, our hearts are open and take their place where they belong: centre-stage.

Love is no longer a mystery or something to seek and create. It is embodied.

Receptivity is the result of feeling truly welcome in the world. First, we must be safe. Empowered. Sovereign. When there is no threat of harm or exclusion, we may exist in our purest form: receptivity.

Personal Share

For most of my life, I had no experience of embodied empathy. I was stuck in my pain. There was no space for anything beyond that. So everything was either a cause or an effect of my pain. And my world needed to revolve around how I was feeling—which, most of the time, was like living death. But at the same time, I couldn't look after myself. I would self-abandon in order to keep the peace, gain approval, connection and belonging. So I was a mess of selfishness and self-abandonment. Because I had no context for anything beyond my very narrow perception of the world, this was just my reality. It was just normal. It was terrible. And I was accountable for nothing.

After my initial deep-healing process, my perception expanded. I understood that I was a product of my trauma, and I could all of a sudden understand how others were products of theirs. I started to understand our individual and collective 'why', and in the process, I started to be able to contain and differentiate my experience. But it was new, not yet integrated and certainly not mastered . . . Not by a long shot.

Because my healing caused me to energetically 'rip' open, my perception over-expanded. It was as if I could see everything. I felt like I could see other people's pasts and sometimes, their futures. They appeared like the feeling of wormholes opening behind and in front of them. Sometimes it felt like I could see multiple realities expanding in different directions. Choice A would lead to one reality, choice B to another and so on. It was like I was living in some constantly shifting energetic orb. People called me a healer and a shaman, and for a time, I accepted the title, but I soon realized it did not belong to me, and handed it back.

By this stage, I was integrated enough to understand that our dynamic nature meant that no one could predict the future, but we could tune into our preferred storyline and walk towards it. I also noticed that in order to stay firmly fixed on a storyline, we would have to encourage others to join us in our vision—either overtly or covertly. There is a fine line between manifestation and manipulation. And as I explored, I found myself becoming both the manipulated and the manipulator. While I felt like I was full of empathy and compassion, it came at a cost. I needed other people to express in a certain way in order to bestow my gifts upon them. Similarly, I needed to twist myself into a pretzel in order to remain in certain dynamics. This played out in both the personal and professional layers of life. I found myself in an abusive relationship and running a business where I felt constantly depleted and disrespected. It took me some years to make sense of it all and exit—to step towards my sovereignty.

I was becoming more receptive, more empathetic and more accountable for my life, bit by bit.

Mastery takes time and happens in layers. I was tuning in, becoming more and more receptive, but still, I found myself hiding in another relationship that was feeding my need to be loved and in a new business dynamic that was not much better than the last one. There was improvement. Less harm, but still betrayal and depletion. Clearly, I had more healing work to do.

I can own my end of it. I was using force. I had been hijacked by the parts of me that wanted to be loved and cared for. And those parts of me wanted things to be a way they were not. They let me ignore red flags, allow disrespectful behaviour and deplete myself— all in the name of safety and belonging. Ironically, the more I forced, the further away I travelled from my sovereignty.

As I started to let go of it all, I began to realize how wildly unsafe I felt. That while I had come a long way in my journey, I was still finding ways to hide. To shirk accountability. To deny deeper layers of pain and aloneness. And so, as is my style, I plunged myself into the wound. I felt it. I writhed in it. I made sense of it and I released it. I let it go. This time, when I let go, I felt an inordinate amount of peace. My awareness expanded again and I understood just how alone I'd felt my entire life. And I could respond to that. I could love myself with a little more fervour. This time, I had ground beneath my feet. A real sense of safety and sovereignty. All the work I had been doing for years had brought me here. I was independent. Successful. Sovereign. And no one could take that away for me.

The moment I realized this, I cried and cried. Now that the danger was gone, it was safe to dance with the world. My heart expanded in my chest, ready to give and receive in a new way.

Invitation to Self-inquiry

- Would you consider yourself as someone who is responsive and has empathy? How do you know?
- Do you identify as an empath or find that other people's expressions harm you?
- Do you identify as co-dependent? What tells you this?
- Are you able to both give and receive? And are you open to multiple love languages?

- Now ask yourself: What can I do to be a little more receptive to myself and the people around me?

Somatic Healing Practice

Expanding Awareness

Choose an object that will be your secondary point of awareness and put it in your line of sight. It may be a piece of art, a plant, a flickering candle or similar.

Find a comfortable seat. Allow your body to settle. Become aware of your breath as it rises and falls in your chest. Place your hands on your heart space and close your eyes. Connect within and bring your full awareness to your breath. Take time to notice how it feels, without needing to change it. When you are ready, stay present with your breath, and gently open your eyes to bring awareness to the object you chose. Notice if you are able to be aware of both your breath and the external object at the same time. How do you respond to this experience? Just notice.

Affirm to Yourself

'I have the capacity to hold my awareness in two places at once . . . within myself and beyond myself.'

Returning to Centre

For this practice, either choose to stand with your feet slightly apart or lie down on the floor on your back with your arms by your side. Take time to settle. Bring your awareness to the length of your spine. Trace your attention up and down, becoming aware of each vertebra. Now place your attention at your sacrum and as you inhale next, draw your attention and breathe all the way from the base of your spine to the top of your neck. As you exhale, follow your attention back down the spine to the sacrum. Inhale to travel up, exhale to travel down. As you continue the practice, you may play with elongating your breath, and articulating your spine intuitively. Let yourself know that this is your physical centre. Your spine. As you continue, notice how the practice cultivates both strength and fluidity.

Affirm to Yourself

'As I return to my physical centre, I welcome strength, fluidity and clarity.'

Trauma-informed Note:

If you are sensitive to energy, the second practice may cause a rush of energy to run through you. If this occurs, come out of the practice and lay on your stomach for a while till you settle. Take time to orient to the room, rub your hands together and take a sip of water.

You may like to pair this practice with 'Sovereignty and Containment' practice at the end of Part VI Chapter 3, if you are working on healing co-dependency.

5

Purity of Power

The distortion, misuse and abuse of power is a function of our personal and collective trauma. Our quest to heal our sense of existential powerlessness is at the root of it all.

As we become empowered and step into sovereignty, there is less and less need to force, wield or 'take' power. We learn that power is not something to be taken or harnessed for manipulation.

It exists in the stability of our centre, the strength and flexibility of our boundaries, and our abilities to perceive, empathize and place accountability in the hands of its rightful owners.

In its purest form, power is free from:

a) Force
b) Manipulation
c) Competition

No Force

When the assertion of our supposed power requires another to change, shape-shift or adapt, we are moving from a state of force. When our desired outcome diminishes the authenticity or freedom of others, we disempower ourselves and each other.

'I need you to behave or exist in a certain way, for me to achieve my goal.'

'Without your adherence to my rules, I can't exist or function the way I want to.'

'If you can't do as I say, I cannot be in a relationship with you.'

Do we choose the cage built from force, or the wilderness of exclusion? Either way, we become trapped and powerless. Or alone and limited. Nobody wins.

The cage often seems safer than the wilderness.

We build cages. We crawl into cages. Blindly.

Image 6.5.1. Cages

We co-create a state of eternal codependency with force.

Force is often mistaken for power.

We tell ourselves we are empowered and that we are empowering others, but often, we are trying to convince ourselves that that's the case.

The reason we use force is because some part of ourselves is desperately afraid. We are afraid that if we let go, we will end up in some vast wasteland of danger and aloneness.

If we tear down the cage, the ones we have been caging will run away. If we crawl out of the cage, we won't be able to survive alone in the big bad world.

So we simply stay put. Building or existing within dynamics that keep us 'safe', connected and at the mercy of their dysfunction.

We feel the force. The pressure. The weight of it.

We brace. Buck up. And keep going . . . until we can't anymore.

Force is the glue of our collective misery. When we let go of force, we will become unstuck. We may fall, and so may those who we have been 'sticking' to. And we may all feel the painful thud of it.

In the ruins of this old force lies our authenticity. Our freedom. And that's where power is born. Among the debris of past dysfunction. In our choice to find a new way of existing, relating and co-creating. In our accountability. In our receptivity to evolution.

Power says: 'I remain in a constant state of choice that honours my well-being and best intentions, and does not dishonour yours. I invite you to walk alongside me, but the choice remains yours. There is no force here.'

Agency and choice remain in the hands of the individual.

An Aside: Force, Fight and the Path of Healing

When force is part of our way of living and relating, it can seep into our attempts to heal, and stop the process in its tracks. We become so fixed on the outcome of our well-being, it becomes like trying to break through a brick wall. We push and push and push, and nothing much changes. In fact, we tire ourselves out in the process. This appears as being over-dedicated to the healing process. Engaging in every holistic practice under the sun and becoming rigid in our various well-being protocols. We build what we think is a healing bubble, but it's just another cage. Sometimes, it is in the letting go of outcome, of force, that we can step back and drop into the space or rest or emotional process that we really need to ignite the next phase of our healing journey. When we finally let go of force, we stop expelling energy and return to our centre. When we step back from the brick wall and stop forcing and fighting, our vision expands, and we may just notice a secret doorway to the next adventure, waiting for us to peacefully walk through.

No Manipulation

Our unconscious quest for safety and belonging tends to drive us towards manipulation. It may be overt or covert, gross or subtle, but many of us have learned that we have the power to get closer to what we want if we manipulate. Life becomes a game—for some of us, unconsciously, and for some of us, incredibly consciously.

Gross manipulation shows up as gaslighting. We deny each other's reality in order to maintain a sense of perceived relational well-being. We gaslight ourselves so we don't have to face the truth.

If a reality doesn't exist, we do not have to respond to it, nor are we accountable for it.

Minimization is a watered-down version of gaslighting. We may not deny a reality altogether, but we squash it, decrease its importance and impact and ignore at least part of the truth. We do this because we perhaps can't cope with something in its entirety. We can't deal with what someone else is telling us. Or we can't manage our own distress. Not completely.

Our capacity is limited, so we adjust our perceptions and expressions to allow us to keep coping, continuing to step forward. Minimization allows us to increase our stamina and stay the course . . . for a time.

There are two forms of subtler manipulation:

a) **Breadcrumbs**

Breadcrumbs are the promise of something more. 'Here is a taste of what's to come, if you shape-shift to my specifications.'
Breadcrumbs tug on the strings of the heart that craves intimacy and belonging. For those of us desperate to be loved and cared for, we will follow the trail thinking we are on the way to what we seek, then all of a sudden, realize we were lured into a cage; alone and unloved.

Those of us who dole out breadcrumbs, often have no idea that we are doing it due to an unconscious attempt to maintain some sort of connection, with no intention of truly nurturing it.

Breadcrumbs are not as overt as the popularized concept of love-bombing.[32] They are given in just the right dose and frequency, so as not to alert us to dissonance. It's only over time that we realize we are starving for more, not properly fed, or that we are unable to give someone the nourishment they need, feeling either barren or eaten alive.

b) **Word-craft**

Word-craft uses the nuance of words to distort meaning, reality or shift the sense of accountability from its true source. Word-craft is the weapon of the sales person. The subtlest change in phrasing, the switching out of a synonym, the ability to put words in the mouth of another. When we manipulate with words, we are attempting to wield power over another person's experience. The problem is that both parties are knocked off-centre by this, and equilibrium becomes impossible for everyone.

When we let go of manipulation, we say: 'I welcome your reality in its entirety, even if I do not like or agree with it. You are sovereign in your experience and so am I'.

When we are no longer seeking to manipulate each other, we can learn where the areas of authentic resonance and dissonance exist. We can choose to truly learn to get along. Or we can choose to leave.

---

[32] Suzanne Degges-White, 'Love Bombing: A Narcissist's Secret Weapon', Psychology Today, 13 April 2018. Available at: https://www.psychologytoday.com/us/blog/lifetime-connections/201804/love-bombing-narcissists-secret-weapon. Accessed April 2022.

No Competition

Competition says: 'My success is diminished by your success. Therefore, I need to be better than you in order to feel successful.'

The desire for success comes from the parts of us that feel unloved; that haven't been seen, heard and celebrated. We need love to survive, so when at our core, we feel unloved, competition emerges as a survival skill.

It's as if we are pigs in a trough, scrambling for the last scrap of food. Some of us will hurtle toward the scrum to win the food. We must eat, above all else. Some of us will stand back and let the others take it; we never had a chance anyway, and our potential feast may deprive others of the 'nourishment' they need. This manifestation is more common for those who grew up in circumstances where there was not enough to go around, or their 'nourishment' came at the expense of another.

Whether we are active or passive, competition can get ugly. There is nothing collaborative or peaceful about it. The winner is often never satisfied and the losers are starving and resentful.

The moment we enter competition, we lose sovereignty and enter co-dependency. Our sense of success or worth becomes dependent on another. When we let go of competition, we say: 'My success need not come at the expense of yours. Your success need not come at the expense of mine.'

When there is not enough food to go around, we must journey to other pastures, plant seeds and grow our own food. Our quest to thrive is the root of all evolution.

Shifting into a state of 'no competition' is part of the re-parenting process. When we come to know that we are made from love, there is no need to compete for it.

The Balance and Ownership of Power

Imbalance of power exists in most dynamics. It is incredibly rare that we are all equal. Our attempts to tell ourselves and each other that we are equal is a delusion that causes more suffering than good.

The Balance of Power

Image 6.5.2. The Balance of Power

The road to equilibrium comes from acknowledging imbalance, and harnessing the true dynamics for good. When power is owned and shared, we can use power to empower. When power is denied, those who hold it are unable to harness it for good. And those who exist in positions of less power, stay there, often travelling further into their powerlessness. If we truly want to share power and approach a state of harmony, those who hold power have to stand up and say, 'I acknowledge my place of privilege and power and I choose to harness it to help those who have less than I do.'

Bringing the uncomfortable truth into expression is the key to working with any dynamic to shift it.

Saviour Syndrome and Grieving the Loss of Power

Power is inherently internal and therefore, cannot be simply transferred or transplanted from one person or group to another.

When we try and bestow power on someone, it rarely sticks. This can be frustrating for both the giver and the receiver. 'Saviour syndrome' is an adaptation of the 'wounded healer' archetype. Here, those in power have a deep desire to remedy the imbalance of power in the world. And so they spend their time and energy trying to share theirs to those who are disempowered. When the imbalance of power is not rectified, they can experience feelings of frustration and depletion. 'I am trying so hard to do good in the world and empower others. Why is it not working?'

At the same time, the disempowered others are not able to truly shift into empowerment, so they experience their own sense of frustration and confusion—the supposed 'gifts' they have received are not integrating, and in fact, it seems like they have been drinking some kind of disempowering poison. Nobody wins.

In this paradigm, no one is truly empowered. The saviour is depleted and can never give enough, perhaps inadvertently becoming the oppressor. The oppressed are not freed from oppression.

Image 6.5.3. Trying to Share Power

Here, both parties have a desire for collective empowerment and collective sovereignty. However, the role of accountability has not been properly considered. The 'saviour' wants to take accountability for everyone else. And the oppressed has not cultivated the capacity to be truly accountable.

Together, we need to grieve the loss of power. Those of us who have adopted the role of saviours need to grieve the fact that 'I can't make it all better, no matter what I do'. And the oppressed need to grieve the fact that 'no one is coming to save me'. The experience may link back to trauma-fuelled family or cultural dynamics. Or it may simply be an existential experience.

It is only when we acknowledge the gross injustice in the world, and grieve it, that the balance of power can begin to be restored.

Power and Perception

Power is about the sharing of capacity. Before we can truly empower others, we need to understand our own. Our power and our ability to harness it for good, will increase in line with our ability to perceive. Perception is power in its purest form.

The more clearly we see ourselves and each other, not just at face value, but at the unconscious level, the more clarity we gain. When we understand the unconscious tendencies and organizing principles that drive us, we can engage in ways that honour our deepest fears and desires. We can maintain our own sense of safety and sovereignty, and engage in ways that support others to find theirs.

The concept of 'power to empower' asks us to share capacity, knowledge, skills and support to empower others to cultivate their own sense of power.

Power will only emerge through our own accountability and receptivity to holding it. It must be cultivated and held with great reverence.

Image 6.5.4. Power to Empower

Personal Share

I've crawled into cages and I've built cages. A lifetime of trying to figure out why I felt trapped or depleted.

I think I was born in a cage. Born into oppression. I learned that I was powerless, and that if I behaved in a certain way, I'd receive breadcrumbs of love. Oh how I craved those breadcrumbs! I strived to be the good girl. The achiever. The pleaser. I would twist myself in knots for approval. A kind word. A cuddle. And I would blame myself when I received anything else—whether it was silence, shame or harm. I was at fault.

I learned that I could use my actions and words to make it a little bit better. And I fooled myself into thinking that a different outcome was possible. That if I was good enough, smart enough, pretty enough, kind enough, that the love and belonging I craved would be mine. Of course, it never was. And the more I shape-shifted, the further away I travelled from myself and the more disconnected I became. Alone. Unloved. Wondering 'Why am I like this? Why can't I feel how I want to feel?' The existential question was far beyond my processing capacity. The pain of oppression and exclusion became a ravine in my heart, that I expertly avoided travelling too. I filled it with roses and covered it with soil and built a self on top of it. But it was still there. It was still the blueprint for my relationship with power . . . and love. You know, I truly believe now that they are one and the same. I kept looking for my power and my love outside of myself. And anytime someone showed me a breadcrumb, I would lap it up. And I would use my gift of word-craft to illicit more breadcrumbs. For a long time, that's the only way I knew how to relate, how to get scraps of love and power.

A few times, men promised to build me a beautiful castle to carry me into another reality. And I'd step into the castle and it would either morph into a prison, or vanish the moment I entered. I'd wonder 'Why is this happening again? How did I get blindsided like this?' It took me a long time to realize that if I truly wanted to stand in my power and live the life of my dreams, I needed to cultivate it myself. If I truly wanted the love I deserved, I needed to learn to spot the false princes and banish them from my sight. I needed to take the reins of my life, and travel away from the land of promises, to a new land where I could build my own castle.

But perhaps, I first needed to stay in an ordinary house. To be realistic. And so I learned to build. I crafted tools. I laid the foundation brick by brick. I toiled and sweated. I would get fatigued and want to give up. I'd grieve that no one was coming to save me. I writhed in the anger of betrayal. All those people who did not treat me with the respect and care that I deserved. And little by little, I let it go. And each time I let go, there was more space to become accountable for a little more power and a little more purpose. I kept my head down. And I worked. Every so often, I would take a break and survey my progress. And sure enough, there was progress. And one day, I had enough power that I no longer needed to wait for someone to save me. And I no longer craved those breadcrumbs of love, nor did I feel the need to use my voice to illicit them. Because I felt safe in myself. I truly loved myself. The moment I claimed my power, I claimed my worth.

After all I have been through, I hold it with the deepest reverence. And my full heart knows that to truly share—to emancipate the oppressed—the only thing I can do is share my map and toolkit. Rather than hold the power for others, I must teach them to find their own.

Invitation to Self-inquiry

- What is your relationship to power?
- Do you use force, manipulation or competition? In what ways? What would it be like to let go of them?
- Are you aware of the balance of power in your relationships? What are you aware of?
- Do you use power to empower? How do you know this?
- Now ask yourself: What steps can I take to aid purity of power?

Somatic Healing Practice

Balance of power

Stand with your feet flat on the floor. Close your eyes. Become aware of the soles of your feet on the ground. Can they soften and relax into the ground a little more than before? Notice the balance of weight through your feet. Are you resting more on the balls of the feet or the heels of the feet? Do you tend to place more weight on the inside or outside of your feet? Begin to play with the balance of weight. Rock forward, backward and side-to-side. See if you can allow your spine to be fluid and follow the movement of your feet and how that feels. Play with the boundary of your balance. How far in each direction can you lean before you lose balance? Does this change with time? Does it change if you engage more parts of your body in the process? Where do you feel the most secure and stable? Find the position and settle into it for a while before ending the practice.

Affirm to Yourself

'I choose where I place my attention and energy. My choice and my boundary are my power.'

Trauma-informed Note:

For those who are currently in oppressive dynamics, this exercise may illicit feelings of grief or anger. If this happens, take time to come out of the practice and be with your experience. For those who connect to an embodied sense of the balance of power for the first time, this may ignite a rush of awareness that presents as anxiety/ rushing energy. In this case, come out of the practice and lay on your stomach to connect to the ground. Once you are settled again, roll onto your back and orient to the physical space you are in to integrate before coming out of the practice.

6

Reverence

The final law of peace and power is reverence. In reverence, we offer sacred attention and care to all energy and awareness. Our own and each other's.

Rather than seek perfection, we strive for authenticity.

Rather than seek outcome, we orient to intention.

Rather than claim righteousness, we welcome all perspectives.

Rather than ask others to be anywhere they are not, we meet them where they are—even if that means to let them go.

Rather than hold the weight of the world, we simply hold our own. And stabilize within the temporary chaos that may bring.

We welcome a new kind of peace. A deeper sense of compassion.

Reverent with our life force. Our capacity. Our boundaries.

Reverent with our expression. Our words. Our actions.

Reverent with the ownership and responsibility of our power.

In reverence, we set each other free.

Image 6.6.1. Reverence

Final Thoughts

As I continued to answer the question 'why am I like this?', I made a little more sense to myself. And I could let go of the shame that was cloaking me; layers and layers of it. I could slowly come home to my beautiful body and rediscover every cell that belonged to me. I stopped adapting to the trauma of the past and evolving into the woman I wanted and deserved to become. Rather than a rolling reaction to threat, my life became a series of conscious, compassionate choices that embodied the laws of peace and power.

I found grace.

I am still a work in progress. Messy. Fallible. As capable of missteps as anyone. But I am present. Welcoming of myself in my entirety. Forgiving of my imperfection. Celebratory of the transformation I have undergone. Intentional with my presence in the world. Reverent of my life.

I know peace.

As you continue to find your own answers and illuminate your personal path to reclamation, I invite you to welcome those pockets of peace as they start to emerge. To orient to those people who welcome and hold you with compassion. To open your heart, your lungs and your throat, and share yourself in this world.

We belong here. Every one of us.